DECOLONIZING FEMINISMS

Piya Chatterjee, *Series Editor*

MAKING LIVABLE WORLDS

Afro–Puerto Rican Women Building

Environmental Justice

HILDA LLORÉNS

UNIVERSITY OF WASHINGTON PRESS
Seattle

Making Livable Worlds was supported by grants from the University of Rhode Island's Humanities Center and Division of Research and Economic Development.

Photographs are by the author.

UNIVERSITY OF WASHINGTON PRESS
uwapress.uw.edu

LIBRARY OF CONGRESS CATALOGING-IN-PUBLICATION DATA
Names: Lloréns, Hilda, author.
Title: Making livable worlds : Afro–Puerto Rican women building environmental justice / Hilda Lloréns.
Description: Seattle : University of Washington Press, 2021. | Series: Decolonizing feminisms | Includes bibliographical references and index.
Identifiers: LCCN 2021010742 (print) | LCCN 2021010743 (ebook) | ISBN 9780295749396 (hardcover) | ISBN 9780295749402 (paperback) | ISBN 9780295749419 (ebook)
Subjects: LCSH: Women—Puerto Rico—Social conditions. | African Americans—Puerto Rico. | Ecofeminism—Puerto Rico—History.
Classification: LCC HQ1522 .L56 2021 (print) | LCC HQ1522 (ebook) | DDC 305.4097295—dc23
LC record available at https://lccn.loc.gov/2021010742
LC ebook record available at https://lccn.loc.gov/2021010743

To my kinswomen—for their courage and perseverance

CONTENTS

ACKNOWLEDGMENTS

I am indebted to the generosity of the many people in the Puerto Rico archipelago, as well as in the continental United States, who offered me their time and stories; who opened the doors of their homes and communities; who took me on walks along the coast, in the mangroves, and in the forest; who introduced me to family and neighbors; and who, when I visited, offered me water, food, and fruits and vegetables to eat or to take with me. It was while doing the homework for this book that I truly met my kindred. These are people who care for the sea, the rivers, the plants, the soil and air, and the human and nonhuman animals that live here with us and fight every day to save their/our home from the destructive forces of the ecocidal present.

I am particularly grateful to have met, learned from, and collaborated with Ruth "Tata" Santiago, who has been a teacher-mentor and friend to me during the last five years. Her tireless environmental advocacy, activism, and deep reservoir of knowledge is simply astonishing. I am also indebted to Nelson Santos, Leticia Ramos, Roberto Thomas Jimenez, Hernaliz Vázquez, Ismenia Figueroa, Carmen de Jesús, Omar Alfonso, Victor Alvarado, Yaminette Rodriguez, Alberto Colón, and Mabette Colón, for sharing their stories and knowledge and for welcoming me into their lives time and again.

I am thankful to Larin McLaughlin, Neecole Bostick, and Beth Fuget at the University of Washington Press and the series editor, Piya Chatterjee, for their tireless editorial and administrative work to bring this book to fruition. I am indebted to the generosity of the anonymous book reviewers who thoughtfully engaged with early versions of the manuscript. Their suggestions greatly enriched this work.

I am thankful to my department chair, Dr. Kristine Bovy, as well as the dean of arts and sciences, Jeanette Riley, and the associate dean, Brian Krueger, for granting the course releases that allowed me the time to finish this book. I thank my colleagues in the Sociology and Anthropology Department, and particularly Rosaria Pisa, Christine Zozula, and Julie Keller, for their support and encouragement.

I am grateful to the University of Rhode Island's Humanities Center for awarding *Making Livable Worlds* a 2020–21 Subvention Grant. I was fortunate to have also been awarded a 2020–21 Project Completion Grant, from URI's Division of Research and Economic Development. I thank Dr. Evelyn Sterne and Dr. Peter J. Snyder for their assistance.

I am indebted to academic friends whose camaraderie and encouragement have sustained me along the way. For their unconditional *compañía*, I am grateful to Catalina de Onís, Maritza Stanchich, Samuel Martínez, Martha Elena Rojas, and Holly Dunsworth. For their support and words of encouragement over the years, I am thankful to Darien Davis, David Griffith, Aviva Chomsky, Manuel Valdés Pizzini, Zaire Dinzey Flores, Ana Yolanda Ramos Zayas, Zaira Rivera Casellas, Rosa Carrasquillo, Xavier Totti, Alejandro Torres Abreu, Miguel del Pozo, Ricardo Pérez, Don Walicek, Anne Valk, Arcadio Diaz Quiñones, Hector Cordero, Carlos Vargas Ramos, Isar Godreau, Mariluz Franco Ortiz, and Tracey Dalton.

I have presented parts of this work at several conferences, panels, and workshops. For the invitations to present it, I am thankful to Frances Negrón-Muntaner, Myriam J. A. Chancy, Shareen Hertel, Michael Rodríguez-Muñiz, Jorge L. Giovannetti, and Carmen Sara Maldonado Irizarry, as well as the Princeton Environmental Institute and the Program in Latin American Studies, the Latin American Studies Center at the University of Maryland, the University of Connecticut's 2018 Economic & Social Rights Group Workshop, the 2019 Energy and the Left Workshop at New York University, the Universitat Autònoma de Barcelona's 2019 Energy and Environmental Justice: A Multidisciplinary Workshop, Colectiva Feminista en Construcción's Summer 2020 Escuela Feminista Radical, and to Editora Educación Emergente.

For their friendship, warmth, and care, I am grateful to Neida Jimenez and David Sangurima and their children, Amaya and Amaru; Marty Rojas and Peter Asen and their children, Isabel and Ruben; Anne Wolfe and Adam Buck and their daughter, Zoe; Wanda Miglus; Julia LaChica; Rosalind Fielder; Concha Gomez; and Kirsten Ernst.

I am indebted to the support of my extended family, and particularly to Mitchell Lloréns, Rachel Lloréns, Lydia Ayala (RIP), Carlos Garcia-Goyco (RIP), Rina Biaggi, Nicole García, Carenín Garcia-Goyco, Karla Rios, Zulma Rios, Teresa DeJesus, Maria Correa, Sonia Rodriguez, and Evelyn Rodriguez.

My nuclear family, Carlos G. García-Quijano, Khalil G. García-Lloréns, Ana Hilda Colón, Isabel Quijano, and our dog companions, Amiga and Billie, are my life-support system. Their love, understanding, and affirmation are a great source of comfort. I am deeply grateful to Carlos

G. García-Quijano for his companionship, and for his rich ethnographic work, brilliant anthropological insight, sharp questions and challenges, and methodological advice, all of which has greatly enriched this/my work.

I am solely responsible for any errors contained in this book.

MAKING LIVABLE WORLDS

INTRODUCTION

Persevering through Life's Turbulent Ongoingness

THE AFRO–PUERTO RICAN WOMEN DOCUMENTED IN THIS BOOK are everyday builders, visionaries, believers, path breakers, and problem solvers who don't take no for an answer and who make a way out of no way. These are not women whose lives are regulated by despair. On the contrary, they are women whose kinship, community, and alliance-building practices illustrate that they understood long ago that the social world they inherited was a construction unequally stacked against them and thus they could set out to reconstruct it in ways that sustain their own, their family's, and their community's life and well-being. In this book I tell stories of perseverance, continuity, forging and maintaining good relations, and survival. The women documented here work to make good lives for their families and communities, often against all odds. Despite the social, economic, political, and environmental crises they might confront, shared here are the life herstories of socioecological justice-making, hope, affirmation, creativeness, joy, and everyday practices of worldmaking. Though feelings of loss, suffering, and sorrow are part and parcel of their/our lives, so are the everyday blessings and beauty that come with being alive: the birth of a child or a grandchild, the celebration of a loved one's fifteenth or eightieth birthday, the joys of high school and college graduations, time spent playing dominoes under the shadow of a mango tree on a balmy day, or coming together in community to discuss environmental injustice and to demand reparations from the local and federal governments and from the multinational companies causing harm. The following three vignettes document instances and practices of community-building, mutual support, solidarity, care, and self-sufficiency and offer a glimpse of the lives of some of the women who populate this book.

ANA HILDA, HARTFORD, CONNECTICUT, DECEMBER 1989

The strong smell of Puerto Rican food hit my nostrils as soon as I opened the heavy green metal door of our apartment building on Washington Street. The familiar narrow hallway was warm and toasty, and I was relieved to be out of the frigid cold. I had walked a block from the city bus stop on Park Street, the same stop where I caught the bus with my friends in the morning and where we got off each afternoon. I was a sophomore at Hartford Public High School. My aunt and cousins lived in a nearby apartment building, and my family was close. We spent a lot of time together, mainly at my mother's apartment, where my older brother and I also lived. As I climbed the three steps that led to our first-floor apartment I heard loud chatter coming from behind our door. This was not unusual. On most days there were family and/or friends visiting with my mother when I got home from school.

It was barely four in the afternoon, but winter's darkness had already started to descend upon the cold day. I opened the door that led directly to the kitchen in our bright, lively apartment, and I saw my mom standing over the stove. At the kitchen table, my aunt Teresa, my cousin Evelyn, and our neighbor Carmen were busy assembling, wrapping, and tying *pasteles*.[1] "*Bendición,*" I said to the women. "*Dios te bendiga,*" my mom and aunt answered as I walked past them toward my shared bedroom in the back of the apartment. I changed my school clothes and joined the women at the kitchen table. My job was to tie the *pasteles*, a job I had been doing since I was a little kid, when we made the *pasteles* across kitchen tables in the many houses we lived in on the island. Most of the three hundred pasteles had been preordered. As the youngest of the women assembled in my mom's kitchen, I integrated myself quietly into the assembly line. I was a welcomed laborer, but I was not expected to have much to say or contribute to grown women's conversation, so I mostly listened. They gossiped, laughed, and talked about men, neighbors, and sometimes their wayward children or a worrisome ache or pain, while the other women gave out advice and opinions or consented in agreement and support.

The assembly line would shift and change as the night went on, with my cousin and neighbor leaving, another neighbor stopping in, or my brother stepping in for a while to tie the pasteles when he got back from work. I would eventually tire and go to bed, but my mother and aunt would stay up late until they finished making the *pasteles*, storing them away, washing all the dishes, and cleaning the kitchen until it was spotless. My mother paid her helpers in *pasteles*, a bottle of *coquito*, and/or a plate of *arroz con dulce*. She herself would deliver the dozens and dozens of made-to-order *pasteles* to the apartments of her Puerto Rican clients. Whoever wanted to help with the delivery was always welcomed to go along for the ride. Most of the time two or three of us hopped in the car with my mom to make the deliveries. We liked to keep each other company so that we would not feel lonely in that dark, wintry northern city.

MILAGROS, NORTHEAST PUERTO RICO, DECEMBER 2017

The very first time I walked around the hidden-away northeastern seaside community where Milagros lived, I was stunned at both the tranquil beauty of the aquamarine Atlantic Sea, whose small waves gently broke on the sandy shore, and the visible destruction wrought by this same sea and the strong winds of Hurricanes Irma and María only a few months earlier. On that clear, sunny, balmy, and quintessentially postcard-like Caribbean day, I stood on the seashore and pointed my son in the direction of Vieques, a Puerto Rican offshore municipality visible across the ocean. The idyllic view was disrupted when I turned my back on the water to look at the destroyed houses and the debris scattered for all to see—furniture, plates, shoes, clothes, photographs, windows, and roof parts—a testament to the lives of the humans who dwelled there. The bodies of mangled palm trees and tattered mangroves framed the wrecked dwellings.

As I ventured deeper into the community with my son in tow, we saw a woman standing on top of the blue-tarped roof of a house. We stopped to observe her from a distance. She was fiddling with a television antenna, the kind of aluminum antenna that was common when I was a child in the 1970s and '80s in Puerto Rico but that is rare today. To warn her that we were approaching, I said playfully in her direction, "And people think that women don't climb on roofs to fix things. . . ." She looked at us and let out a laugh, simultaneously waving us in her direction. She climbed down a ladder that was affixed to the side of the house and greeted us. I introduced myself and told her that I was there to understand how people in her community were faring after the hurricanes. Seemingly eager to chat, she immediately invited us into the damaged house. She explained that she was on her roof trying to get a television signal, that in past days she had been able to get one but today it seemed she was out of luck. I told her that I noticed solar panels on her house's wooden roof, and responding to this, she showed me a solar battery storage system attached to her kitchen wall. She explained that a decade ago she had installed the panels and the battery herself. "This community is off the grid. We have no electricity here, and when I first moved here, I used candlelight to see and wood fire to cook, but then I decided to study to become an electrician, and that's when I installed my solar panels. I did it all myself."

Milagros, a single Black woman in her midfifties, then showed me a photo album of what her mint green wooden house, which she built herself little by little, looked like before the storm. She told me, "I built my piece of paradise here and then Irma and María came and nearly destroyed it. But I am still here building it again piece by piece, little by little. The storms do not scare me. This is my refuge, my happiness, and I plan on living here until my last day."

CONVIVENCIA AMBIENTAL PLANNING MEETING, SALINAS, PUERTO RICO, JULY 2018

Children and their parents, mainly mothers, began to trickle into the El Coquí community center on that warm July evening. Everyone began to set up the center's tables and chairs, and to open the windows before taking their seats. Tata passed around granola bars for whoever wanted one and bottled water was distributed by one of the mothers. Once seated, Tata explained that this year's theme was "To survive we have to cohabitate." She said, "The solidarity community members showed one another and the way we came together to help each other after the storm is a great lesson for how to survive calamity."

In its twelfth year in 2018, the camp was hosted annually by the community organization Diálogo Ambiental. Eleven families had gathered to plan the activities of the week-long camp for youths aged twelve to eighteen. This year the camp would be held at a rental beach house in a nearby neighborhood that Diálogo was able to afford as a result of the donations they received after the hurricane struck. The parents and children in attendance were elated that the camp would be held in such a nice house adjacent to one of the shallow Jobos Bay lagoons. Though these families lived and worked in this scenic and beautiful territory adjacent to the Caribbean Sea, they seldom had the opportunity to act like tourists in their own backyard.

This free camp was run entirely by volunteer community members and parents working as guides, instructors, chaperones, cooks, and helpers. At the meeting, one of the volunteer parents told the prospective campers and their families that they would each need to bring a tent, an air mattress, sheets, a pillow, a towel, one plate, a cup, and a set of utensils as well as hygiene products, adding, "If you do not have these things, let us know, and we will try and find these items for you. Also, if you have extras of these things, please bring them to share with others." Several parents volunteered to bring extra items to share. Another volunteer reminded everyone that there was a strict policy against junk food and told the parents that they were welcome to donate healthy foods, fruits, and bottled water. Yaminette, one of the camp's cofounders, who was in charge of the youths' nutrition for the week, explained that the kids would take turns preparing breakfast, lunch, and dinner under her supervision and that of adult volunteers, and that most of the food they would prepare would be donated by nearby farms and markets.

The camp focused on teaching youths, all of whom were low-income children who live in nearby communities in Salinas and Guayama, about the local ecosystem and its plants, animals, and waters, as well as about its health and the significance of protecting it. The week's activities included a guided kayak tour of the bay led by a local elder fisherman, a guided birding tour of the estuarine reserve, painting a mural under the tutelage of a local artist, listening to representatives from the local Sierra Club who would talk about how to spot and protect marine animals that live in the bay, and a guided walking tour of Aguirre to understand the history of the neighborhood, the sugar mill, and the estuary. In the evenings, local activists and cultural workers would give the campers chats about resilience and community solidarity.

When the planning meeting was adjourned, everyone began to fold and stack the chairs and tables and to close the windows. The solar-powered lights were switched off, and the community center was locked. It was dark, and the stars and moon were on full display on this clear and balmy Caribbean night. We paused outside the center briefly to say our goodbyes. Some families walked back home, while others got into cars and drove away. The promise of an exciting week at camp was still a few weeks away.

The stories, testimonies, knowledge, practices, and words of Ana Hilda, Milagros, Tata and the rest of the Convivencia Ambiental crew, and many others will figure prominently in the pages to come. The context of their experience spans a great deal of the often turbulent Puerto Rican economic and social experiment that began with European, and later American, colonial conquest and intensified with the mid-twentieth-century modernization project. But as recently as the early 2000s, we had no idea how turbulent and chaotic the intersection of late-stage capitalism and climate change was going to be. As this book documents, the economic decline that Puerto Rico had already been experiencing became catastrophic as a result of the 2008 global financial economic crisis, and set the stage for the devastating conditions wrought upon the archipelago by the 2017 hurricane season. In the face of calamity, Afro–Puerto Rican women on the archipelago and in the diaspora did what they had done for generations: they continued to work at making livable worlds.

FIVE YEARS IN PUERTO RICAN TIME

Since I began the homework for this book in the summer of 2015, Puerto Rico's archipelago has experienced a dizzying array of economic, climatic, environmental, political, geological, and viral calamities. Ordinary people have been steadily organizing, protesting, litigating, and speaking up against what look and sometimes feel like insurmountable odds. What follows in these chapters is an autotheoretical and engaged ethnographic reflection, as well as a critical description of what it means to be in a United States colonial archipelago of small islands living with, living through, and struggling against the powerful forces of the present. In our era, climate catastrophe is experienced in tandem with the decline of liberal democratic governance and its safety net programs. Liberal democratic governance has been upended by the neoliberal austerity agenda led mostly by men, mostly white, and hell-bent on making money via extraction, pollution, and contamination of everything they sell off—which is, well, everything: the sea, the coasts, the forests, the water, the sand, and the soil. This global neoliberal agenda has been carried out with the state-sanctioned anti-Indigenous and anti-Black terror and violence emblematic of European expansion and colonization of the Americas and the Global South.

Puerto Rico was a desperately impoverished archipelago under Spain's colonial rule. As a US colonial territory, it became a showcase of American democracy and modernization in the Caribbean. But the promises of modernization fell short. The US occupation brought to the archipelago its own set of economic, political, and environmental calamities. The "modernization" project began in the mid-twentieth century mainly in Puerto Rico, the large island. Then came the grand nation-building construction projects using borrowed money in the mid-1990s, the end of tax code Section 936 in 2006—which since 1976 had given US corporations tax exemptions on income originating in US territories—and the collapse of the world's financial markets in 2008. On June 29, 2015, Governor Alejandro Garcia Padilla declared that the archipelago's $72 billion debt was "not payable." That made for some spectacular global headlines.

It also paved the way for President Obama to sign into law PROMESA (the Puerto Rico Oversight, Management, and Economic Stability Act) on June 30, 2016. The act gave an appointed federal oversight board extensive control over the archipelago's budget and finances. Questions such as "Who accrued this 'debt' and therefore who should pay it?" remain unanswered. The Junta (as the board is locally known), supported by Judge Laura Taylor Swain's rulings, has refused to allow for the auditing of the debt despite long-standing demands from civil society groups.

On September 21, 2016, a fire at the Aguirre Power Plant Complex caused a blackout that left over 1.5 million households without electricity and hundreds of thousands without water for several days. This led to massive losses of frozen foods throughout the archipelago's markets, and chaos on the roads when traffic lights stopped working. Unbeknown to the population, this was a prelude to what would come exactly a year later. It was also an election year, and the New Progressive Party's candidate, Ricardo Roselló, son of previous governor Pedro Roselló, won the 2016 gubernatorial race, ending the Popular Democratic Party's stronghold.

Then on September 6, 2017, Hurricane Irma, Category 5, devastated the offshore municipalities of Vieques and Culebra, and several eastern municipalities of Puerto Rico (the large island), leaving around eighty thousand households without electricity. Two weeks later, on September 20, 2017, Hurricane María hit. It would become the tenth most intense Atlantic hurricane on record and the third deadliest.[2] It made landfall on the large island's east coast, ravaging everything in its path. Hurricanes Irma and María combined dealt a deathly blow to the island's fragile electrical grid. The archipelago experienced the longest blackout in US history and the second longest ever recorded globally (Santiago, de Onís, and Lloréns 2020).[3] In the eleven months it took to restore the electricity to the large island, hospitals, morgues, and funeral homes were overwhelmed with the rising number of deaths (Schwartz and Black 2017).

On September 21, 2017, President Trump declared the archipelago a Federal Disaster Zone, activating assistance from the Federal Emergency Management Agency.[4] On October 3, 2017, the US president threw paper towel rolls at a crowd gathered at a relief shelter during his visit to the island. "Puerto Rico has thrown our budget a little out of whack," he chided, and then he diminished the catastrophic conditions on the ground. The president's callousness was a painful reminder of the archipelago's second-class colonial status. During the visit, Governor Roselló appeared delighted to repeat the lie, upon President Trump's request, that the hurricane had caused only sixteen deaths.[5] Meanwhile, the country was in disarray. People were suffering without water or electricity. Their houses were torn to pieces, their roads were impassable, and bridges were broken. They were suffering mental anguish, trauma, and confusion, grieving incalculable losses.

Under Governor Roselló, the recovery was mired with governmental ineptitude, mismanagement of funds, and controversy over cases such as the nefarious Whitefish Energy contract to the tune of $300 million (Atiles Osoria 2020). During this time, the number of Puerto Ricans migrating to the continental US to find relief from the disaster rose into the hundreds of thousands (Meléndez and Hinojosa 2017; Hinojosa, Román, and Meléndez 2018).

Nearly a year after the storms, electricity was fully restored to Puerto Rico, but Vieques and Culebra depended on generators until January and March 2019, respectively. Then came two weeks of massive, multisectoral protests demanding the resignation of Governor Roselló. The protests began after the Center for Investigative Journalism released 889 pages of private phone chats between Governor Roselló and his closest male official and other aides on July 13, 2019. In the chats, they made misogynist jokes, made light of Hurricane María's dead, made fun of gay people, ridiculed a New Progressive Party (PNP in Spanish) supporter for his weight, joked about shooting San Juan's mayor, and displayed cruelty and disrespect toward his constituency (LeBrón 2019; Bonilla 2019; Phillips 2019; García-Quijano and Lloréns 2019). Governor Roselló's resignation became effective seventeen days later, on August 2, 2019, at which time attorney Pedro Pierluisi was hastily sworn in. As it turned out, the swearing-in was unconstitutional, and he was removed from office five days later, on August 7, 2019. That evening, Secretary of Justice Wanda Vazquez-Garced was sworn in as governor. She is the second woman to hold the office.

On December 28, 2019, residents of Puerto Rico's southwestern region began to feel tremors that have yet to subside. On January 6, 2020, as residents got ready to celebrate Three Kings Day, a popular Catholic holiday, the town of Guánica became the epicenter of a magnitude 5.8 earthquake. The next day, there were several more sizable disturbances, with tremors registering as high as 6.4. As Catalina de Onís and others explain,

"Aftershocks and new quakes have persisted, including a 5.9 temblor on January 11. In all, more than 1,000 rocked the southern area in just the first two weeks of January, with many reaching 4.5 or greater magnitude" (de Onís, Lloréns, and Santiago 2020).

It is clear that the effects of catastrophic climate change, which often imperil small island nations first, combined with neoliberal austerity measures, are putting people's lives in the archipelago at great risk. Problems with the very basics of survival—such as food, clean water, electricity, decent public health, housing, and education—coupled with continued environmental degradation, land dispossession, gentrification, and increasingly callous federal economic policies make the possibility of having prosperous, healthy lives untenable for most people in the archipelago. Some scholars have argued that Puerto Rico is experiencing an accelerated version of the state-sponsored population expulsion that began with the 1948 industrialization process (Negrón-Muntaner 2018; Morales 2019d). But I contend that in the neoliberal era, the logic of "letting them die"—Black and Indigenous people, the poorest, the old, and those who are too sick—has supplanted the earlier "expulsion" model.

The COVID-19 pandemic has complicated Puerto Rico's already dire situation. In March 2020 the local government was lauded for being among the first US jurisdictions to impose a curfew and declare a state of emergency. But in haste, the government, as if replaying the Whitefish scandal, entered into a $38 million contract for one million antibody tests with Apex General Contracts, a local construction company with no experience selling medical supplies. (It has since been canceled [Ayala and Mazzei 2020; Hernández Cabiya 2020].) By early June the governor began reopening the economy even as the pandemic remained uncontained and cases continued to rise steadily.[6] It is unlikely that Puerto Rico's defunded public health-care system will be able to effectively contain a raging pandemic. Vieques has no working hospital, and Culebra has only a small first aid clinic. To be treated for serious conditions, people in these offshore municipalities must travel to Puerto Rico, but the public ferry service to get there is famously unreliable. In May 2020, amid the pandemic, a severe drought began and water rationing went into effect (Dolce 2020). On July 30, 2020, Tropical Storm Isaias caused widespread flooding and landslides and left thousands without power and water for several days. As of this writing, Puerto Rico is still recovering from it (Coto 2020).

ONTOLOGICAL TURBULENCE

The events confronted by the people in the archipelago in the last five years illustrate that we live within a turbulent ongoingness. Instability manifests in all areas of our human lives. In fact, turbulence is central to our ontological reality (Gergen 1991). Living unfolds with/in ontological dynamism, within the taken-for-granted knowledge that instability, uncertainty, unpredictability, and change are core features of life. With the world "still-in-the-making" around us, we are continually *coming into being in relation* to external as well as internal inputs (Shotter 2012, 140). Accelerating climate change with stronger hurricanes, raging fires, earthquakes, tsunamis, droughts, floods, unbearable heat and/or cold, food and water insecurity, climate-induced displacement and migration, and zoonotic viral diseases—coupled with political upheaval and economic instability—has complicated any easy predictions of local and global sociopolitical futures. For instance, the decimation of crops by fire, drought, hurricanes, or pests in one place can reverberate across the globe's integrated financial regime, markets, and supply chains. If the COVID-19 pandemic has demonstrated anything about the current condition, it is that the human and nonhuman worlds are more interconnected than we wish to believe. Our blithe assumptions about environmental, sociopolitical, and economic stability have once again been undermined by viral forces beyond our immediate control.

Since the early 1970s, the nongovernmental sector, policy makers, academics, politicians, and the corporate sector have used scenario planning. Melinda Cooper explains that "Specialists from different disciplines are asked to imagine and unfold a series of alternative futures from a position of present uncertainty" (Cooper 2010, 171). In a world in which climatic, economic, and political uncertainties prevail, the scenario method presents a coherent, internally consistent and plausible description of a possible future state of the world (Carter et al. 2007, 145; cf. Cooper 2010, 172). As used by the United Nations Intergovernmental Panel on Climate Change, scenarios are "not predictions or forecasts but are alternative images without ascribed likelihoods of how the future might unfold" (Carter et al. 2007, 145; cf. Cooper 2020, 173). For its part, the National Intelligence Council explained on its website that "scenarios are plausible alternative views about how the future might develop" (Cooper 2010, 173). This methodology is designed to offer alternatives for "decision making under conditions of uncertainty," wherein the "focus is not on risk" but rather on "the radical uncertainty of unknowable contingencies" (Cooper 2010, 173).

Certainly, this method cannot account for all future possibilities. This has become particularly apparent in the era of climate catastrophe. Catastrophic events lead to other events and reactions, as was the case when the government's fumbling ineptitude after Hurricanes Irma and María led to hundreds, if not thousands, of preventable deaths and mass out-migration. After the 2017 hurricane season, ordinary citizens were left to fend for themselves and to pick up the pieces of their former lives. The Puerto Rican diaspora stepped in with aid to fill the vacuum left by the state.

Still, no scenario imaging could have predicted the simmering, accumulated rage that the populace in the archipelago and the diaspora felt at Governor's Roselló's incompetence and his complicity with the federal government's callousness. It could not have foreseen the flood of protests that swept the streets of San Juan in July 2019, to his eventual ousting. On August 2, 2019, ordinary citizens changed the course of the archipelago's immediate future by coming together and exercising their democratic right to protest the antics of an inept, careless government. They did this even in the face of great uncertainty, armed only with the knowledge that their current situation had become intolerable.

RESTORATIVE ALTERNATIVES TO RACIALIZED DISPOSSESSION

In this book I illuminate how Black women's lives have been marginalized and erased from Puerto Rico's historiographic and anthropological canons. I use as a guide Indigenous decolonial thought and the scholarly literatures on the afterlives of slavery to position the Puerto Rico archipelago and its diaspora in relation to Black and Indigenous continental thought. In doing so, I aim to challenge and contribute to the destruction of the cruel coloniality of historical and taken-for-granted knowledge about Black Puerto Rican women's lives. Chapter 1, "Surviving Matriarchal Dispossession," focuses on Black Puerto Rican women crafting livable lives for themselves and their families within an unjust system I call matriarchal dispossession. Their lives and the solutions they create to deal with everyday circumstances are sometimes imperfect, but they use the tools and options at their disposal.

To show what the lives in one dispossessed Black matriarchal family look like over time (intergenerationally) and across space (in Puerto Rico and in the diaspora), I engage an autobiographical example to chart an incomplete version of my maternal family's lineage. With this method I aim to show what a just anthropological ethnography might look like, one that leads with the ethnographer's skin in the game. My family is part of the history of Puerto Rico's southeast, a place where disposable Black people were brought to toil in the sugarcane plantations. After abolition, they were left to fend for themselves under conditions of extreme duress in a labor market that exploited them and left them with very little to build their lives. They lived in a virulently anti-Black racist social system and structure that left them with few other options but to eventually displace themselves to the frigid, urbanized continental North, where they could try their luck at making better lives.

In the second chapter, "Doing Home-Work in the Mother-Land," I engage with what it means for a so-called native anthropologist to conduct "home-work." I reveal layers of my own emotional complications and ambivalence toward the archipelago's political, elite, and intelligentsia class. Questions about diasporic and Black national belonging and perceptions of the devaluation of diasporic and Black Puerto Ricans emerge as a source of anxiety, sorrow, and ongoing hurt. In dealing with these challenging questions, I engage in "epistemic and political disobedience," as well as in *reparative narrating*, to take a step toward decolonizing and undisciplining myself and my ethnography (Mignolo 2009, 16; Sedgwick 1997).[7] This approach takes into account the partial nature of the ethnographic enterprise, and it centers loss and unknowingness as part of this herstory.

The role Black women have played in archipelagic and diasporic demands for environmental, climatic, and racial justice is documented in chapter 3, "Life-Affirming Practices." Demands for environmental justice began in reaction to deepening ecological ruination and capitalist extractivism. But the individuals, collectives, and communities documented here are not just making demands—they are busy creating restorative alternatives to dispossession. Solutions are imagined and tested through trial and error, solutions that sometimes work and other times don't. But temporary setbacks do not stop the women, collectives, and communities from continuing to fight against environmental injustice and racism or from demanding, conceptualizing, and building more just futures. Solidarity, reciprocity, and an ethics of care are at the center of the lives and communities I document here.

Chapter 4, "Living with/in Ecological Catastrophe," documents what I learned from the women I interviewed who experienced Hurricanes Irma and María and their aftermaths. Using matriarchal dispossession as a lens through which to view the documentary *After María*, I analyze its controversial reception. This chapter contextualizes racialized capitalism dispossessive logic within the framework of the archipelago's five-hundred-year colonial history. It documents how the wealthy have begun to plan their climate apartheid dreams in tandem with their growing fears of what climate catastrophe will bring. The chapter also focuses on the community volunteer work carried out mainly by women after Hurricane María with the Iniciativa de Eco Desarollo de Bahía de Jobos (IDEBAJO), a social and environmental community organization. Community members question what it was that "outsiders"—NGOs, academics, journalists, filmmakers, and disaster adventurers of all types who swarmed the archipelago in the aftermath of the hurricane—wanted from their communities. In this chapter I consider the political and economic systems that have characterized the global coloniality of power and offer a decolonial conceptualization of the archipelago's cultural history. In the book's epilogue, "A Word about Black Puerto Rican Ecological Knowledge," I detail briefly how, if heeded, Black Puerto Rican ecological knowledge and practices could help the archipelago become a more ecologically sustainable place for all.

EPISTEMOLOGY OF A DECOLONIZED ETHNOGRAPHY

My main ethnographic method consists of listening closely and attentively to what people say. I also observe what they do, their material conditions, and their engagement with the ecosystem around them. Put together, people's words, actions, material conditions, kinship and community ties, and how much they use the ecosystem that sustains them offer a holistic view of their lives. It is also important to pay attention to people's hopes, goals, aspirations, and dreams. Understanding and accounting for the futures people wish for and hope for affords them the dignity they deserve. I do not take for granted my cultural adjacency to the people I learn from and write about. As an "ethnographer of home," I feel a deep ethical responsibility to them. I care for the people and the stories they entrust me with.

In 2015, I began getting to know and interviewing environmental justice activists who were demanding the removal of the open-air mountain of toxic coal ash produced by the Applied Energy Systems (AES) coal-powered plant, which they stored on their grounds in Guayama. At the time, activists were also demanding an end to the dumping of toxic coal ash in the Guayanilla and Humacao landfills (Lloréns 2016). The Puerto Rico Electric Power Authority's plan to build a liquefied natural gas (methane) platform named the Aguirre Offshore GasPort to power the Aguirre Power Plant Complex was of concern between 2015 and 2018 (Kunkel 2018). Before the plan was withdrawn, activist and environmental attorney Ruth Santiago discussed with me what it would have meant for the health of the people and ecosystem in the Jobos Bay (Lloréns 2017). Between July 2015 and August 2017, I spent concentrated time with the women activists planning and volunteering at the El Coquí community center. At the time, it was the central headquarters for IDEBAJO where various community projects were planned and carried out. During those two years, I interviewed and volunteered alongside women and youths working on the community garden project, the children's summer camp, the Coquí Solar project, and the Convivencia Ambiental summer youth camp.

In 2016, I joined a group of ethnographers on a project funded by the University of Puerto Rico Sea Grant College Program (NOAA) led by Dr. Carlos García-Quijano titled "Coastal Forest Fisheries: A Study of Estuarine Forest Resource Dependency in the Southern Coast of Puerto Rico." We focused on understanding the lives and work of coastal resource users, fishers, mangrove and coastal foragers, crabbers, coconut harvesters, gardeners, and *cocineras* (women cooks) to learn about their relationship to the ecosystem and its animals and plants and about their uses of the coast throughout Puerto Rico's south (García-Quijano and Lloréns 2017; Lloréns and García-Quijano 2020). Headlines and national conversations were focused on the debt crisis and the deepening austerity politics at work defunding public health and education at the time.

I returned to Puerto Rico from December 2017 to January 2018, and again during the summer of 2018, this time funded by a National Science Foundation EAGER Rapid Response Research grant for a project titled "The Political and Moral Economies of Recovery from Hurricanes Irma and María in Puerto Rico and the U.S. Virgin Islands." I interviewed women, men, and children throughout Puerto Rico about the effects Hurricanes Irma and María had on their household's ability to cope and survive. I focused mainly on women's coping mechanisms and the practices of exchange, reciprocity, and solidarity that sustained them in the immediate aftermath of the storms. Water-, electricity-, and food-sharing practices were commonplace for several months after the storm.

Between 2015 and 2019, I conducted hundreds of hours of in-person interviews and conversations about environmental injustice as it pertained to energy production and water, the national debt crisis, school and hospital closings, the aftermath of Hurricanes Irma and María, poverty and migration, solidarity, reciprocity and care practices, and knowledge of, interactions with, and uses of the coastal ecosystem. I went on transect walks in the mountainous forests, along the coast, and in the mangroves; went to summer camp planning meetings; helped to cook at the youth summer camp; gave a presentation to Coquí Solar's youths about anti-Black racism in Puerto Rico; spent time gardening with the youths at the El Coquí community center; attended a weeklong Coquí Solar workshop; attended meetings at the anti-toxic coal ash camp in Guayanilla; gave a talk on environmental racism to toxic coal ash activists; attended meetings in Guayama led by the local anticoal activists who live near the AES plant; and traveled to the Cerrejón coal mine in La Guajira, Colombia, with attorney Ruth Santiago to fully understand the reach of the "coal death route" (Lloréns and Santiago 2018a). During this trip, we joined the Witness for Peace delegation led by Dr. Aviva Chomsky, Dr. Steve Striffler, and activist Richard Solly. We toured the mine and met with its management, as well as with the mine workers' union, and we visited several Indigenous Wayúu and Black Colombian communities affected by the mining operation.

In the aftermath of Hurricane María, I spent a substantial amount of time fundraising in coalition with colleagues Dr. Catalina de Onís and Dr. Carlos García-Quijano, whose scholarly work also centers in the Jobos Bay. Three weeks after the storm, we had raised enough funds to ship two solar generators to power the El Coquí community center to serve as an oasis for people in the community. We continued raising funds for the Coquí Solar Project through 2017–2018. As diasporic academic collaborators with IDEBAJO and the Comité Diálogo Ambiental, we have worked together to draft grant applications that would allow these community organizations to continue their grassroots work. In 2020, Dr. de Onís, attorney Ruth Santiago, and I were awarded $125,000 from JustFund for the Comité Diálogo Ambiental's Campaign for Clean Water and Electricity, 2020–2021. Our coalitional support for IDEBAJO and Comité Diálogo Ambiental projects is ongoing as we draft petitions; review, edit, and comment on documents for publication; offer research data and expertise; and assist in any capacity we can (see de Onís 2021).

This scholar-activist model is based on a commitment to places and people that transcends the extractive pursuit of academic knowledge for the sake of knowledge production. Rather, it is premised on the belief that

Puerto Rico's southeast is a place worthy of documenting for the exemplary ways in which the people there try to live sustainably in their desire to leave it a better place for subsequent generations. We believe that we have a lot to learn from them as we engage in the arduous fight against ravenous capitalist extractivism, racialized dispossession, and ecocide (García-Quijano and Lloréns 2017). After all, in the Americas and in the world over, the people at the margins of society who have long struggled against capitalism's dispossessive logic and the state's enabling have extensive experience confronting catastrophe. Of all people, they have the most to teach us "urbanized cosmopolitans" about how to survive the onslaught.

CHAPTER 1

SURVIVING MATRIARCHAL DISPOSSESSION

THIS CHAPTER UNFURLS A MATRIARCHAL STORY, TRAVERSING terrains of memory, oral history, temporality, affect, culture, ethnographic research, and history. It also explores complex and fragmentary kinship ties between people and places. By places I mean geographic, political, and emotional locations. In this chapter I aim to bring into relief the seemingly "raggedy and rickety spins" that emerge beyond the constraints of social and affective normativity that characterize the lives of dispossessed Afro-descendants in the Americas.[1] Here I engage with the historical and cultural memory of women from Puerto Rico's southeast region whose lives are marked by a social structure I call "dispossessed matriarchy." I have a personal stake in understanding the lives I aim to historicize and document because I am the descendant of such a maternal genealogy. In this chapter, I offer a scholarly critique to make visible the often hidden and frequently erased lives of Black Puerto Rican women.

This analysis centers on gender and race, Black Puerto Rican womanhood, mothering, and family life. It confronts the violence, rupture, and sense of loss and longing wrought by enslavement, colonialism, racism, and sexism. It recognizes the attendant consequences of poverty, economic marginalization, displacement, migration, and environmental injustice. In rooting this inquiry within matriarchy, I engage its generative and life-affirming potential. I formulate Puerto Rican matriarchy using Peggy Reeves Sanday's affirmative assertion that "matriarchy does not reflect female power *over subjects* or female power *to subjugate*, but female power (in their roles as mothers and senior women) *to conjugate—to knit and regenerate social ties in the here-and-now and in the hereafter*" (1998; emphasis in original).[2]

I focus in part on my kinfolk's life experiences—those of my mother, my grandmother, my aunt, as well as close, distant, and ancestral relatives, all of whom were born and who lived in Puerto Rico's southeast—to expose the coloniality of historical and taken-for-granted knowledge that has helped craft duplicitous prevailing tropes about their lives. If they are visible at all, the lives and lifeways of the women I discuss here are devalued, marginalized, and far from history, the state, and its nation-building projects. They are believed to be so unheroic, unremarkable, and valueless as to be uninteresting, unnoticeable, overlooked. Considered "unproductive," their lives are the stuff the social problems literature and its statistics are made of single, unwed mothers, living under the poverty line, chronically unemployed or underemployed, with little formal education, believed to have "bad" physical and mental health, sexually promiscuous with no regard for family planning, passing time in a state of idleness, lacking in financial security, reliant on social and economic welfare programs, unstable, and, as poor migrants to US cities, burdens to the state. Their "lumpen" lives unfold in "zones of indistinction," or, when analyzed through a social justice lens, they dwell in "zones of abandonment," left by the state to fend for themselves with only the police, social services, and the medical establishment as disciplinary witnesses to their "unruly" lives (Hartman 2019).

But the women whose lives I document here are neither heroic resisters nor passive victims of the systemic and structural oppression that constrains them. Instead, they deploy a series of daily improvisations and make decisions aimed at making good, livable lives for themselves and their families. Through the lens of a rational, profit-driven Protestant ethic, the middle and upper classes understand the lives of these women and their families largely as failures with little to offer the social body. Functionalists understand the marginal lives of these urban and postindustrial rural poor as necessary features of the capitalist system's built-in structural inequalities. Because they are not constituted as "workers," these women are deemed capitalism's "social refuse," whose existence necessitates an army of police and social service personnel to manage, surveil, and contain (Hartman 2019). Their "disagreeable" habits and lifeworlds must be kept at bay, even made invisible to the hardworking, productive, sanitized, and upwardly mobile strivers who live and build desirable social lives.

I assert that the supposed "matriarchal pathology" of the much-maligned Black matriarchal household is in fact a positive adaptive strategy in the face of dispossession. Furthermore, I contend that the strategies women in these households develop to weather the storms of uncertainty, such as unemployment and underemployment, austerity, illness, loss of family members, migration, and incarceration, are instead a form of resilience. In fact, I have found that in the communities in southeast Puerto Rico where my family is from and where I do my home-work, resilience strategies in the face of hardship include relying on extended household and fictive kin networks, cooking and feeding large groups of people, and sharing goods, services, and favors (Lloréns and Santiago 2018b). These strategies are part of a long tradition of Black women's solidarity and mutual aid networks. The networks sometimes include men, but women form their significant connecting nodes.

An overarching goal in this chapter, then, is to highlight the historical, lived, and imaginary counternarratives crafted by everyday Black women such as my own kinswomen and others I interviewed, as well as writers and scholars who focus on the "afterlives of slavery" and Black life in the Americas. In centering antihegemonic narratives of Black womanhood, family, and kinship, my goal is to undermine, upend, and contribute to the destruction of existing racist, sexist, colonial, masculinist, and Eurocentric narratives about the lives of Afro–Puerto Rican women.

DAUGHTERS OF "MATRIARCHAL DISPOSSESSION"

Saidiya Hartman's question "What did it mean to be a surplus human?" (2019, 187), as well as her assertion that "the mother's only claim [is] to transfer her dispossession to the child" (2016, 166), further motivated the exploration of my family's maternal condition. I am the "illegitimate" daughter of a "consensual union" between a young Afro–Puerto Rican woman and an elderly white Puerto Rican man. As an adult, I learned these sociological labels and their uses—by the state, policy makers, academics, social workers, doctors, and teachers—to describe my own life condition and family. My family certainly did not see itself mirrored in these externally imposed labels. When I shared with my mother what I had learned in my college sociology course—that I was an "illegitimate" child born "out of wedlock"—she voiced a strong rejection to the notion of illegitimacy. "I know who your father is, and you knew your father. That other stuff is nonsense," she responded. Her reaction was partly based on the visceral rejection of notions of wrongdoing on her part. As she sees it, she wanted to have children and become a mother, so she did. In her view, she did not need the state's permission to birth a family and, as far as she understood it, "God conferred his permission by blessing me with my four children." Even when the odds were stacked against her, birthing four children was its own achievement and has been a source of pride. My mother's experience resonates with Peggy Antrobus's assertion about gender and "the cycle of poverty" in the Caribbean when she explains, "The majority of the poor are women. While many of them have large families, they are not poor *because* they have many children. In fact, the reverse is true. They have many children because they are poor, which means they have very limited options in terms of education, training and employment, and see children as a source of wealth, perhaps the only source of affirmation" (1995, 56; emphasis in original).

My mother, Ana Hilda, is also an "illegitimate" daughter conceived during a passing fling between her mother and a man who was married with a family of his own. My mother has shared her story with me, in bits and pieces, over the course of my life. She told me that her mother, my grandmother Virginia Rivera, died an anonymous death and was buried in an unmarked grave in Arroyo's cemetery. Her burial site is forever lost to us, her descendants. My mother also said that before her death, Virginia had been caring for a sick girl, and when this girl died, the family gave my grandmother the girl's clothing. She cared for the sick girl in exchange for food and a place to sleep at night, because she and her young daughter, my mother, were homeless. A young child at the time, my mother does not know whether Virginia contracted the tuberculosis that presumably ended her life from this dying girl. This was in late 1940s Arroyo, Puerto Rico, and given the trauma of her living conditions, as well as the passing of time, my mother's memory about those early years of her life is blurry. Or maybe my mother is trying to spare herself and me from remembering "too much." Sometime before her death, Virginia gave my mother to a childless couple, Don Balbino Colón and Doña Teresa Santiago, who raised my mother as their own. The circumstances of Virginia's death and subsequent burial remain a mystery. Ana Hilda would meet her biological father after she'd already had her first child. About her father, my mother recounted,

> People always told me that you look just like Pedro Garcia and that he was
> my biological father. I would pass by his house on my way to and from

town, and I would wave at him, and he would wave back. One day, I was coming back from church, and I decided to finally go to his house and confront him. I asked him flat out, "Am I your daughter?" And he said, "Yes, you are." We hugged and cried and became close after that. He told me that my mother had wanted to leave me with him but he could not take me in at the time. Pedro and I built a good relationship, and I also became close to my half siblings. But I was not the only child Pedro had outside of his marriage. There is at least one other that we know about, and we behave toward each other as siblings. Things were not as orderly back then as they are now; people had children all over the place, and children grew up with other relatives, friends, and neighbors who would take them in. That's how it was back then. I know I suffered a lot because of this, but that's how life was back then. We were dirt poor, just making the best of it, I suppose.

As was common for rural girls of her race and class at the time, my mother completed only elementary education. She learned the very basics of reading, writing, addition, and subtraction. She had been left at her adoptive parents' door all those years earlier, so she had no birth certificate formally attesting to her existence. It was her adoptive parents' idea then to inscribe my mother in the birth registry when she was a teenager—the year of her birth is uncertain—because they believed that my father would marry her. They wanted to make sure that she had the documents needed for marrying Alejandro, the man over thirty years her senior with whom she had recently decided to go live as "husband and wife." They didn't know yet that my father had no intention of ever marrying my mother. For him, having four mixed-race children with my mother and "recognizing them" by granting them his last name was one thing, but legal marriage was another. He was not willing to share his money or bestow property upon these late-in-life children. He had divorced his first wife with whom he had four older children, two of whom were a few years older than his new "wife." The divorce from his wife nearly wiped out his savings even though he was the one who decided to get the divorce. But he was a miser, and having to share his savings with his ex-wife and older children was something he would not soon forgive and would resent for the rest of his life. For their part, my white half siblings would not soon forgive my father for taking as a "wife" that poor Black girl-woman and, adding insult to injury, fathering four bastard, mixed-race children with her. My father did not plan to ever enter a legal marriage again. His uppity white family believed that my mother was beneath them in every way. But his brothers and sisters were glad that their brother, now an old man, found that girl to take care of him in that forsaken town, in that *arrabal* (slum) of a neighborhood where he had chosen to open a general store.

My father's older children would go on to spread rumors about my siblings and me. They said things like "Those children are not really our father's," "Their mother is a loose, no-good woman who only wants our father's money," "The two boys are our brothers, but the two girls are not our sisters," "The youngest girl, the dark-skinned one, she is not our sister, she is not a Lloréns." I am the youngest daughter and the most Afrodescendant looking of my mother's four children. I am the only child who looks like her and her Black family. My mother's personal project of birthing "whitened" children that would *adelantar o mejorar la raza* (better the race) had been successful until I came along. This attempt at "erasing the stain of Blackness" from Black families was a common practice in her time. Today individuals who are part of antiracist and progressive social circles understand this practice to be an act of internalized racism and self-hatred. I understand that for my mother, a nearly illiterate poor Black woman, marrying a white man and birthing "whitened" children was a strategy to gain social status and privileges to which she would not have access otherwise.

Ever since I can remember, my paternity has been a source of rumors, contention, and jokes. Growing up, the joke I heard was that an older man nicknamed Limber, who was our close neighbor and a beloved part of my mother's fictive kin network, was my "real" dad. Even my father was in on this joke. Limber was a dark Black man, so I was said to look more like Limber than like my pale-skinned, blue-eyed father and my three siblings. My three siblings are light-skinned. They are much older than me. The third son, born nine years before me, is white and blond. When he was a baby, strangers would ask my mother if she was the child's nanny, and none would believe, even now, that she was his mother.

I was the fourth and last child. My mother blames my father's advanced age of sixty when I was conceived as having weakened his white genes, making her Black genes more dominant. My siblings were nearly grown when I was born. Unlike them, I only lived with my father until I was two years old, when my mother left him and began her life as a single mother. After separating from my father, my mother spent time with her family and with her new partner's family. These were Black folks who loved their Blackness and who were proud to be Black. Through them I learned to have pride in my Blackness and to respect and value Afro–Puerto Rican culture.

When I returned to Arroyo in 1998 to carry out dissertation home-work, I hoped to discover Virginia's whereabouts as a way to offer my mother a sense of knowing and maybe even some healing from the "mother loss," a profound, open wound that I believe permanently pains her. Along with this affliction, I have sensed that my mother experiences a deep *vergüenza* (shame) about her childhood and the circumstances of her mother's life and death. Perhaps she carries a kind of survivor's guilt cou-pled with the knowledge that in this world, to be dispossessed is to be devalued, written out of history, and invisible, leaving no trace of self in the social archive.

I dutifully and methodically searched for Virginia's grave. I walked the cemetery several times, marveling in the process at the well-preserved his-torical graves constructed with reinforced cement, surely no longer reposi-tories of bodies, but markers and inscriptions of the "illustrious" names of Spanish, French, and Corsican men and their families, colonial settlers who owned the town's sugarcane agricultural fields and commerce in the seventeenth, eighteenth, and nineteenth centuries. I wondered whether any of these men whose graves had withstood the passing of time had bought and owned one or more of my ancestors who had been abducted from their homeland in Africa. Sitting down near this cluster of "histori-cal" graves, their closeness signaling the segregation in death that they had lived in life, I jotted anthropological notes reflecting on a speculative gene-alogy of miscegenation in which, as a mixed-race woman searching at the end of the twentieth century, I was cruelly and permanently cut off from knowing who my Black ancestors were, much less where they had come from. They were left out of history, the details, the intimacies, the joys of their lives, all of it a gaping hole in the kinship and social fabric of my uni-verse. Yet the legacy of my white ancestors, my father's people, was every-where legible.

Finding no markings of graves where indigent individuals had been buried, I consulted the cemetery's keeper about accessing written ledgers, notebooks, or records, testaments to the materiality of the bodies interred there. Apologetically, he told me that the ravages of time along with storms, rains, and floods had damaged the records from the early part of the twen-tieth century. All my hopes of locating Virginia's whereabouts ended then and there under the smoldering heat of the southern sun. What stood out to me through the process of searching for my lost grandmother was how easily the lives of the poor and the marginalized could be lost, unaccounted for, literally erased from the face of the earth.

Much the same way as my mother, I have been haunted all of my adult life by the thought of my dispossessed and ill grandmother erased from the historical record. As a result, I live with/in an odd sense of intellectual discomfort, knowing that her fate was not unique and that, in fact, this was and still is the fate of millions of marginal, poor, dispossessed, Black, and Indigenous people, and of women and children in particular. For Black, Indigenous, and poor people, a marginalized existence was and still is a defining feature of the sociohistorical relations of this "New World" birthed by European colonialism, the Middle Passage, Indigenous genocide, racism, and sexism, the consequences of which we live with and grapple with today (Holland 2000).

Recently, a colleague I am acquainted with but do not know well sent me an e-mail saying that Ancestry.com had just expanded and had released a chunk of data about Puerto Rico. I had never told her I was interested in either genealogy or DNA data, but I imagine that Puerto Rico's post-2017, newly heightened visibility in the American mediascape must have reminded her of me, perhaps one of only a few Puerto Ricans she knows personally. I decided to log on and try my luck at locating my grandmother. I began by typing "Virginia Rivera" and specifying her location as Arroyo, Puerto Rico, but this search did not return any hits. I then typed my great-grandmother's name, Hipolita Rivera, and once again specified Arroyo, Puerto Rico. To my surprise, I found a few documents inscribing my great-grandmother's existence in the biopolitical management records of the state. By far, the most exciting find was my grandmother's birth certificate. She appeared as Carmen Virginia Rivera, born in Arroyo in 1912. Her race is described as "*trigueña*," a euphemism often used for Black. The girl's "natural mother" was Hipolita Rivera, whose estimated birth year is 1873, the same year enslavement was abolished in Puerto Rico. Hipolita's occupation is listed as "*domestica*" (domestic), and the girl's father is not listed. My great-grandmother's parents are listed as Pascual and Carmen Rivera from the town of Maunabo. They were deceased at the time of Carmen Virginia's birth. Carmen Virginia, father unlisted, appears to have also been an "illegitimate" daughter.

It was remarkable to have found information about both of my great-great-grandparents on Carmen Virginia's birth certificate. I immediately shared this information with my mother, whose response was, "We have family in Maunabo. That means we are like our old neighbor Nicio Curet because he once told me he came from Maunabo to Arroyo to work in the sugar fields."

Ancestry's site suggests hints to its users. These are documents of individuals who are possibly related to one's search. For Pascual, my great-great-grandfather, the hint was the Registro Central de Esclavos, 1872 (the slave registry), for a man listed simply by his first name and whose estimated birth year was 1852. This Pascual was registered in the municipality of Mayagüez, located about two hours by car to the west of Maunabo. His parents were Eduard and Andrea, and his owner was listed as Du Lenon Delorisse. I doubt that Pascual from Mayagüez was the same Pascual from Maunabo listed as Hipolita Rivera's father. But it is likely that Pascual, my great-great-grandfather who was born during enslavement, was also an enslaved man. Maunabo had a dense concentration of sugar fields and the Columbia sugar refinery owned by C. and J. Fantauzzi, the same French men who owned large tracts of land and the Lafayette Sugar Mill in Arroyo (Ramos-Mattei 1988, 388). The production of "king sugar" is embedded not only in the history and ecology of the southeast, but also in the region's ancestral and kinship history.

I later found Hipolita Rivera in the Social and Population Census of 1930, 1935, and 1940. In these documents, several members of my great-grandmother's household are listed, but there is no mention of Carmen Virginia Rivera, my grandmother. She vanished once again. These census documents reveal the number of household members, their educational and literacy levels, their relationships to each other, their race, and their occupation. My grandmother's adult siblings are listed, as are their spouses and children, offering a picture of the common Afro–Puerto Rican configuration of extended households.

In the 1935 census, Hipolita's household members are listed as "colored," and only the two adult men are listed as having occupations in the sugar industry. The occupation for women and children is listed as "*ninguna*" (none). Occupation must be listed for everyone over ten years old. Although Carmen Virginia is absent in the 1935 census, I notice my aunt Teresa, my mother's sister, who was one year old and who appears as an "*alojada*" (lodger), instead of granddaughter. In the 1940 census, Florentina, my grandmother's older sister, appears, listed as white. Hers is the only race to undergo a change from colored to white in the span of five years. In the 1940 census, Tia Teresa is no longer listed as a member of this household. When I asked Tia Teresa whether her mother, Carmen Virginia, had come to get her from her grandmother's house, she answered, "No, she left me there and never came back to get me." Pressed to understand Carmen Virginia's absence from these records, from the family, and from her children's lives, I thought back to 1998, when I interviewed the grandmother of one of my friends and she told me, "Yes, I remember that poor girl Virginia. She was sick, so sick, she was an indigent. I think she may have drunk too much. I would see her lying around on the ground around town . . . that poor woman." I mentioned this to my mother and asked her if she knew anything else, and she answered, "People said things like she was an alcoholic and a prostitute . . . but I don't know . . . she was sick and didn't have a place to live. Her family did not want her around. They shunned her. They were mean, hateful people. But I never knew what the truth about her was. I was just too young."

Tia Teresa, for her part, reports that the time she spent living in her grandmother's house as a child was a time of "beatings," "getting worked to the bone and being treated as a servant." Tia Teresa, the oldest of Carmen Virginia's three children, learned through Carmen Virginia's family that she had siblings. It was Tia Teresa who found Tio Juan and Ana Hilda, my mother, and who tried to give shape, however imperfect and fraught, to a nuclear family made of the three of them.

The administrative records from Ancestry.com opened up more queries than they answered. Certainly, these records are silent about the details of family life. An important consideration for my purpose was that these biopolitical administrative records mark the women as having no occupation. Under an intensifying capitalist regime, this also means that they are essentially considered to have "no constructive" social role. Yet oral history has revealed that the women in my family worked in the informal sector of the economy, caring for children, taking in clothes to wash, ironing for more well-to-do families, cooking, gardening and harvesting foodstuff, tending to animals (chickens, pigs, goats), and selling seasonal foods. They also created formidable exchange and reciprocity systems with neighborhood women that often survived intergenerationally and transnationally. Thinking specifically about the gendered dimensions of Puerto Rican migration to Chicago, Gina Pérez wrote that "*women's migration can also be understood as important 'kin work.'* . . . In the case of transnational migration, kin work frequently includes caring for sick or elderly kin, and for adolescents who may be sent to live with family members in order to protect them from actual or perceived dangers. This work is done by women in aggregate and is unremunerated labor. In this way, family members affirm ethnic and cultural identities through women's labor and networks connecting their households across different communities" (2004, 18–19; emphasis mine).

After locating the 1940 census, I have not found other family records. My mother was born in the early 1940s, but she was not inscribed in the birth records until 1961. As a child she worked alongside her adoptive parents, harvesting sugarcane, gardening foodstuff, helping tend their animals, cooking, and doing chores. As a teenager, when she started living with my father (who refused to share his money with her), my mother began to wash and iron for well-to-do folks in order to earn a living, and she cooked and sold seasonal foods. To survive financially and emotionally my mother, like her people before her, created strong exchange and reciprocity networks as well as affective bonds with several women in the neighborhood. During Christmas, a time when each household would make hundreds of *pasteles*, the women would create a *konbit* (combo)— that is, they would work as a group to help the women of each house make her *pasteles* before moving on to the next house to do the same. "Othermothering" has come naturally to my mother, who, as a young woman in her early twenties, began taking care of her increasingly numerous nieces and nephews. These children belonged to Tia Teresa, who, in her young childbearing years, was like her mother, Carmen Virginia, in that she would leave her children in the care of relatives, including my mother, for long stretches of time. My father was not pleased about my mother taking in even more children, but she ignored him because this was her family, and she would not deny them a place to live. My mother would also take care of neighborhood children. Some of them lived intermittently in our household for weeks or months at a time.

Throughout the twentieth century, people have migrated steadily from the southeast to agricultural fields and cities in the US north. Many of the affective or fictive kin networks continued in renewed formulations through changes brought about by migration. In northern cities, migrants often landed at the apartments of family or friends from their hometowns. When my mother moved to Hartford, Connecticut, we stayed with my matriarchal aunt (my mother's half sister on her father's side) who was the respected head of her extended household (Lloréns 2006). Later, when my mother established her own household, she, too, became a respected diasporic matriarch, lodging a stream of new arrivals in our apartment, particularly the young daughters of her friends. The arrivals eventually created an entirely new community of women's reciprocity and exchange networks in these northern settings. About these transnational kinship support networks, Pérez asserts, "Many Puerto Rican women migrants have engaged in these transnational practices . . . and they have continued to cultivate similar ties in the present" (Pérez 2004, 19). Citing Cecilia Menjívar's scholarship on Salvadoran immigrant women, Pérez cautions against romanticizing "immigrant women's networks," particularly because of the added burden, precarity, and hardship entailed in relational care and kin work. In line with Menjívar, Pérez reminds readers about migrant women's intersectional contexts in which "impoverished migrants live" and points to the "potential deleterious effects of poverty on their informal sources of assistance, and to their remarkable capacity to survive, even when they have very little, if anything, going for them'" (2004, 19; Menjívar 2000, 174).

WE KNOW LITTLE ABOUT THE BLACK PUERTO RICAN FAMILY DURING ENSLAVEMENT

In colonial America, white families were recognized as legitimate and were offered social, legal, and economic protections, whereas the Black family was often not permitted, encouraged, or recognized. Enslaved Black women's contributions to the building of the nation rested on their capacity "as laborers, breeders and entertainers of workers, not as family members" (Thornton Dill 1994, 25). As Bonnie Thornton Dill explains, "They were denied the societal supports necessary to make their families a vital element of the social order" (1994, 25). Under conditions of unbearable hardship, Black women, along with blood kin and fictive kin, still managed to produce families and extended kinship networks. In Thornton Dill's words, "They . . . had the task of preserving the human and family ties that could ultimately *give them a reason for living. They had to socialize their children to believe in the possibility of a life in which they were not enslaved*" (1994, 26; emphasis mine).

In the post-plantation Americas, Puerto Rico's Afro-Creole kinship groups, particularly those that are part of the lower socioeconomic strata and subordinate social groups such as my maternal family, have long been described disparagingly as "matriarchal," "matrilineal," or "matrifocal" (Spillers 1987; Doucet-Battle 2016). This coloniality of knowledge or authoritative master trope crafted by European colonial settlers about the "Negro" and Puerto Rican migrants to New York City, for example in Nathan Glazer and Daniel Patrick Moynihan's *Beyond the Melting Pot*

(1963) and Daniel Patrick Moynihan's *The Negro Family* (1965), drew from and built upon E. Franklin Frazier's concept of "disorganization" to characterize "the black family's" matriarchal female-headed households as a source of a "tangle of pathologies" reproduced intergenerationally (Spillers 1987, 66; Robinson 2003, 119; Briggs 2003, 175). Frazier's "disorganization" indexed the Black family's so-called divergence from the European patriarchal nuclear family norm (Robinson 2003; Hunter 2006). But scholars have pointed out that Frazier's conceptualization of disorganization was intended not to pathologize and judge the Black family but rather to point out that massive social disorganization, dislocation, and deracination were core features of the capture and transplantation of Africans and their subsequent conversion into enslaved property in the Americas (Semmes 2001; Hunter 2006; Platt 1991; Thornton Dill 1994). In fact, Frazier noted that enslavement made many African American women experts in self-sufficiency: "When emancipation came . . . women had to depend upon their own efforts for the support of themselves and their children" (Semmes 2001, 5; cf. Frazier 1939, 125–26). This self-reliance, argued Frazier, was an adaptation strategy deployed by women determined to survive in the face of the dehumanizing conditions wrought by enslavement (Frazier 1939; Semmes 2001; Hunter 2006; Platt 1991).

Offering an unflinching counterhegemonic analysis in "Mama's Baby, Papa's Maybe" (1987), Hortense Spillers argues against the discursive and politically motivated framing of the African American "'matriarchal' pattern" as a "state of social pathology" (66). Spillers describes the dehumanizing conditions of enslavement under which Blackness and Black life unfolded as a "New-World diasporic plight marked by *a theft of the body*" (67; emphasis mine). Enslavement created the condition in which the captive lost not only the ownership of her body but also her subject status and humanity. This loss transformed her into a type of property that was permitted only a not-quite-human social status (Spillers 1987; Hartman 1997, 2016, 2019).

In her analysis of "the modern/colonial gender system," feminist critic María Lugones asserts, "Women racialized as inferior were turned from animals into various modified versions of 'women' as it fit the processes of global, Eurocentered capitalism" (2007, 189, 203). Constituted as labor and as capital during enslavement, Black women and their families were exploitable (for work, sex, entertainment) and disposable (raped, left to die, killed), their subjective self-regard, kinship roles, obligations, and desires unknown or ignored by the colonial white man (McClintock 1995; Espiritu 1997; Collins 2000; Morgan 2004; Lugones 2007; Smallwood 2008; Fuentes 2016; Johnson 2020).

Under these sustained conditions of duress, "kinship" and "family" took on meanings and formulations different from the European's conception of nuclear and extended family. After all, the white nuclear family was protected, encouraged, and recognized under the law, whereas the Black extended family was believed to be a threat to the existing white supremacist social and economic order (Thornton Dill 1994; Morgan 2004; Smallwood 2008; L. King 2007; Fuentes 2016; Johnson 2020). In the context of African racial enslavement in the Americas, a core feature of which was the disarticulation and destruction of humanity, personhood, and by extension, kinship ties, the definition of who constituted family necessarily exceeded blood-based definitions (Spillers 1987; Hartman 2019). Spillers argues convincingly that within this brutal context, the creation of a "Black family" based on "powerful feelings of sympathy" and "networks of feelings" is "one of the supreme achievements of African-Americans under conditions of enslavement" (1987, 74; Thornton Dill 1994). About this affective achievement, Saidiya Hartman writes, "Flexible and elastic kinship were not a 'plantation holdover,' but a resource of black survival, a practice that documented the generosity and mutuality of the poor" (2019, 91). Black women birthed, built, and sustained families, all while refusing a nonhuman status, or "the inhuman in its codified state as property" (Yusoff 2018).[3] Acting as witnesses, memory makers and custodians, storytellers, healers, and caregivers, Black kinsfolk created ancestral (kinship) and ecological (place-based) knowledge in the new American motherlands.

Though the configuration of the Black Puerto Rican family in the context of enslavement in the archipelago has not received much scholarly attention—an omission that I believe directly results from the overwhelmingly white male authorship of much of the archipelago's historiography and that reveals a disinterest in the lives of women generally and Black women particularly—some of the critical historiography of enslavement and life in Puerto Rico has questioned the prevailing belief that under the Spanish, enslavement was "mild," "benign," or "humane" (López and Petras 1974; Findlay 1999; Roy-Féquière 2004; Figueroa 2005; Godreau 2015). For instance, López writes, "True, out of the Spanish metropolis there emerged a code of law that treated the slaves as rational human beings . . . designed to protect them against the rapacity of their masters"

(1974, 21). But López also notes a great distance between the law and the way the masters actually behaved on the ground: "In Puerto Rico, as in most societies where slavery has existed, the slaves were seen as chattel by their masters and were brutalized (physically and psychologically)" (López and Petras 1974, 21). Luis Figueroa cites Victor Schoelcher, a French abolitionist who visited Puerto Rico in 1841–42 and who observes this about the Spanish slave codes: "Unfortunately one does not see that [officials and planters] have ever wished to enforce them" (2005, 94). Similarly, writing at the end of the nineteenth century, local journalist Salvador Brau confirms the planters' "noncompliance with slave code regulations" (Figueroa 2005, 94). Significantly, Figueroa notes that Brau remarks upon the planters' lack of "encouragement of marriages" among the enslaved as well as their lack of "respect for the slave family" (Figueroa 2005, 94). In *Women and Slavery in the Caribbean*, Rhonda E. Reddock remarks, "Among slaves the housewife did not exist" (1985, 64). Marriage between the enslaved was not encouraged, and certainly, during enslavement the enslaved were not permitted to stay home and care for their own homes and families. Thus, in the context of the plantation, the "housewife" was a status reserved for women of European descent even when housework and childcare was carried out by enslaved women.

Documenting the political debates among elite white men regarding the expansion of female education in late nineteenth-century Puerto Rico, Eileen Suárez Findlay notes that they focused their attention almost exclusively on "female sexual morality" and "motherhood." To these men, it seemed that in their current state, all Puerto Rican women were "unfit mothers," a flaw they believed was a "cornerstone of Puerto Rico's weakness" (1999, 59). Regarding "previously enslaved and other Black women," they "could never be so effectively reformed. Slavery had left them, at best, stupid and brutish, 'reduced purely to a vegetative state' and, at worst, 'monstrous mothers who murdered their children'" (Findlay 1999, 60). The majority of the liberal reformers of late nineteenth-century Puerto Rico, tasked with the project of nation building, still believed that "'unwhitened' plebeian women remained inherently and permanently degenerate" (Findlay 1999, 60).

In many respects, the cursory understanding of how enslavement and anti-Black racism led to the disarticulation of kinship based on blood relations in Puerto Rico—which the enslaved and their descendants rearticulated in the shape of strong fictive and affective family networks—has in turn led to an inadequate understanding of how family is constituted among Black Puerto Ricans. Black Puerto Rican families characteristically include extensive blood and fictive-kin networks. In majority-Black Puerto Rican towns and neighborhoods such as San Antón in Ponce, El Bajo in Patillas, Yaurel in Arroyo, San Felipe in Salinas, Emajagua in Maunabo, El Pastillo in Juana Díaz, and in the town of Loíza, families often live in compound-style dwellings (Lloréns 2008, 2018a; Godreau 2015). This arrangement allows resource pooling and enables a strong reliance on family networks for emotional, physical, and economic support. Solidarity and mutual aid are widely practiced within Black Puerto Rican kinship, affective, and community networks (Lloréns 2018a; Lloréns and Santiago 2018b).

UNMASKING THE COLONIALITY OF KNOWLEDGE ABOUT THE AFRO–PUERTO RICAN FAMILY'S "PATHOLOGICAL MATRIARCHAL PATTERN"

The coloniality of knowledge about the presumed pathologies of the "matriarchal pattern" in descriptions of the Black Puerto Rican family, which in the continental United States mirrors narratives about Black, Indigenous, and Chicana women, persists and resurfaces with unsettling regularity in scripts about the "culture of poverty," welfare dependency, underachievement, juvenile delinquency, and the so-called resignation of the poor to their undesirable life conditions. Within the Puerto Rican sociocultural context, the racial democracy myth—that three equal races, the Taíno, Spanish, and African co-inhabit and mix without conflict, hierarchy, or erasures—is integrated into conceptions of the "matriarchal pattern." In turn, this has linked the so-called matriarchal family configuration with "raceless" poverty. In other words, poor women and their families surface as representatives of this "pathological" family configuration, but the correlations among enslavement, racism, poverty, and the Black family remain unspoken and unacknowledged publicly. Yet single-headed households and poverty are inextricably tied to the histories of enslavement, anti-Black racism, sexism, and classism that have marginalized the Black Puerto Rican woman—historically and in the present—almost above all others.

Much has been written about Oscar Lewis's sociocultural study *La Vida* (1966) and its characterization of the "culture of poverty," embodied by an urban, slum-dwelling young mother and head of household for whom prostitution was a way to make a living in the context of a rapidly modernizing wage economy. As Laura Briggs puts it, Lewis's "culture of poverty" is characterized by "absent fathers, matriarchal families, women having children while still very young themselves, poor work habits, violence and obsession with sex" (2003, 163). Following the sociological or "social problems" literature of the era, Lewis asserts that the culture of poverty is passed down and reproduced intergenerationally (1966). Thus, children born to this "degenerate" family structure have little chance of escaping it before going on to reproduce it. By far the most troubling and enduring judgment from Lewis's study is that poor, "too loose," "bad" mothers are to blame for the reproduction of poverty (Briggs 2003, 165). Tellingly, Lewis asserts that compared to the Mexican women he had studied, Puerto Rican women were much more aggressive, outspoken, and violent (1966, xxvii). I contend that these descriptors reveal more about Lewis's biases regarding the Afro-Caribbean sensibilities found in Puerto Rico in contrast to the Indigenous cultural lifeways that are dominant in Mexico. In this coloniality of knowledge schema, Blacks are believed to be aggressive and dangerous, and the Black woman is ungendered, rendered masculinelike, whereas the Indigenous are understood as innocent and childlike noble savages.

In *Puerto Rican Americans* (1971), an "interpretive essay" about Puerto Rican migration to New York City that seeks to contextualize the process of identity formation within a new sociocultural context, Joseph P. Fitzpatrick includes a chapter titled "The Puerto Rican Family." In it he identifies four major influences on family structure and kinship patterns that include the precolonial culture of the Indigenous Taíno, Spanish colonial culture, slavery,[4] and the post-1898 US influence (77). Fitzpatrick asserts that the Spanish colonial culture has been the most influential in the formation of the modern Puerto Rican family and society. He describes a "very clear distinction" between the "good woman," an unmarried girl protected by her father and brothers and later, as a married woman, protected by her husband and sons, versus the "bad woman," "who is available for a man's enjoyment" (81). Because the latter is sexually active, she is assumed to be "damaged," unmarriageable, and thus undeserving of male protection. Fitzpatrick's assertion about "good" versus "bad" women omits the ways in which the discourses about women's respectability, honor, and sexuality were, and still are, racialized (Findlay 1999; Carrasquillo 2008; Lloréns 2008).

In her work about Black working-class women at the turn of the twentieth century in Puerto Rico, Findlay explains, "Sexual norms and their enforcers regulated women's lives, demarcating the 'worthy' from the 'disreputable'" (1999, 2). Thus, threats to women's reputation and the possibility of public shame were a biopolitical strategy used to keep white women in their "proper place" while maintaining the racialized and classed politics of respectability that simultaneously maintained white patriarchal hegemony. Unlike white Puerto Rican women, Black Puerto Rican women endured racialized stigmas that marked them as tough, aggressive, manlike, not quite human, sexually "animalistic," and by virtue of their racialization, disreputable (Findlay 1999; Merino Falú 2004; Roy-Féquière 2004; Carrasquillo 2008; Lloréns 2008).

In his text, Fitzpatrick explains in two paragraphs the effects of enslavement on the Puerto Rican family. Regarding its influence on family life, he asserts the prevalent myth that enslavement was a milder institution in Puerto Rico than in the United States (1971, 82). "The usual consequences of slavery in the *broken* family life of Negroes have been as evident in Puerto Rico as elsewhere," he writes (1971, 82; emphasis mine). The reader ascertains a relationship between "slavery," Blackness, and the "broken," "mother-based family." The pathological leftovers of African enslavement, it seems, are still present in the Puerto Rican family. Fitzpatrick remarks on consensual unions, a family structure prevalent in the archipelago, and "illegitimacy," which refers to the children born from these unions. In a table comparing statistical regional change in the number of consensual unions over a period of three decades from 1930 to 1960 in the large island's northwest, north central, and southeast regions, Fitzpatrick finds the lowest rates of consensual unions in the northwest and the highest rates in the southeast (Fitzpatrick 1971, 86).

Interestingly, the statistics offered by Fitzpatrick map onto persistent claims about the archipelago's racial geography wherein the northwest region is believed to be whiter and the southeast Blacker. In line with how the coloniality of knowledge is generated and reproduced, this seemingly value-free regional statistical depiction of the consensual union family structure is laden with references to existing racialized notions. Puerto Rico's prevailing racial geography was a result of the labor landscape that gave rise to life in each particular region. In other words, the southeast *is Blacker*, and I argue that *it is also a culturally Black Caribbean region* because of its greater concentration of sugarcane plantations and toiling enslaved Africans, who became the region's current Afro-Creole Puerto Rican population.

The southeast region of Puerto Rico has been a center of activities exploitative of human labor and environmentally destructive since the seventeenth century—sugarcane agriculture, oil refineries, pharmaceutical manufacturing, and electric energy production. The point is that given the historical lack of regard for the families and blood relations of the enslaved, as well as the historically high levels of poverty after emancipation in the southeast, a Black Puerto Rican region, the numbers of consensual unions are representative of a history of the subjugation of Black families, which includes the denial of access to formal channels (i.e., the church and courts) for establishing legal marriage. These numbers also signal that Afro-descendants in Puerto Rico and the Americas have not depended upon the state to legitimize their lives and their families.

The coloniality of knowledge that has historically constituted Black Puerto Ricans as lacking has also been taken up by contemporary scholars. Consider this statement from a 1988 article titled "Child Psychology and Juvenile Delinquency in Puerto Rican Society," in which the author instructs readers about the social and historical formations of "modern" Puerto Rican society, writing that *a growing African population, brought in to work as slaves, contributed a more matriarchal social organization* (Porrata 1997, 173; emphasis mine).

Subsumed in this statement is a persistent misunderstanding about enslavement in Puerto Rico that *Africans were brought in to work as slaves.* This makes it seem as if they were "brought in" as migrant workers to fill the position of "slaves." This view is supported by the enduring belief mentioned previously that persists in Puerto Rican scholarship and popular culture alike: that enslavement in Puerto Rico was a benevolent institution devoid of the kinds of cruelty the enslaved experienced in places such as the United States (Godreau 2015).

This entrenched conception of Puerto Rico's "benign" racial enslavement is disturbing, first because it presumes that slavery can be something other than cruel and dehumanizing, second because it is nothing more than a discursive strategy for perverse ends that include assuaging collective white guilt about enslavement. In its most destructive form, this discourse refuses to confront and grapple with the historical violence perpetrated upon Black Puerto Ricans. And this *doxa* (common sense) helps to sustain the myth that because the enslaved were treated well, this system did not lead to the development of social antipathies and antagonisms such as antiwhite resentment on the part of Blacks or anti-Black racism on the part of whites. In Saidiya Hartman's words, "The fungibility of the commodity makes the captive body an abstract and empty vessel *vulnerable to the projection of others' feelings, ideas, desires and values"* (Hartman 1997, 21; emphasis mine).

It is precisely the forced and enforced silencing of the Black Puerto Rican person's rendition of his or her life that has allowed the "projection" of a story of a compassionate enslavement that upon emancipation naturally gave way to racial harmony. The claim of racial harmony does not broach, and in fact altogether evades, the persistent issue of anti-Black racism and the development of a social program of racial equality and rights (Franco Ortiz et al. 2019).

In *Ethnicity and Family Therapy* (2005), in a chapter called "Puerto Rican Families" that underscores the significance of kinship and community networks, Nydia Garcia Preto explains that because Puerto Ricans tend to rely on family, extended networks, folk healers, or medical doctors during times of stress or crisis, they use social services and therapists as a last resort, if at all (Garcia Preto 2005, 242). This chapter's explanation of Puerto Rico's "sociopolitical history" repeats some of the assertions made in previous texts. The Taíno are said to have passed down their "peaceable demeanor" and "tranquility" as well as their emphasis on "kinship and dependence on the group" to the modern Puerto Rican culture (Garcia Preto 2005, 242). Echoing Fitzpatrick's assertions about the Puerto Rican family—which as a central trope in the coloniality of knowledge about Puerto Ricans has been widely repeated—the author asserts that Spaniards contributed their "patriarchal family structure and a double standard regarding gender" (Garcia Preto 2005, 242–43). Though less is said about the contributions of enslaved Africans to the structuring of the Puerto Rican family itself, the author writes, "They also carried with them the *acceptance*, strength, and resilience of an enslaved race. Although there were fewer slaves in Puerto Rico than on other islands . . . Puerto Rican slaves suffered the same horrors as those elsewhere" (Garcia Preto 2005, 243; emphasis mine). While this author does not minimize the travails of enslavement, the notion that they accepted their fate is far-fetched. In fact, the enslaved in Puerto Rico, like elsewhere, actively resisted their predicament. They did so in small, everyday ways, by pretending to be ill, dragging their feet during tasks, rolling their eyes, gossiping, and spreading malicious rumors about whites (Scott 1985). They also resisted in big ways, by running away individually or in groups, setting fire to the sugar fields, collectively rebelling, and conspiring against their owners (Figueroa 2005; Baralt 2007).

THE BLACK AND NON-BLACK WOMAN IN SOCIETY

In the decades between the 1930s and 1950s, in a modernizing Puerto Rico, the state supposed that being a worker was a "masculine" and "masculinizing" pursuit; thus, the Black woman laborer remained as masculinized as she had been during enslavement (Spillers 1987; Muñiz-Mas 1998). According to Félix Muñiz-Mas, defining acceptable gender roles was a key program in the Popular Democratic Party's (PPD) midcentury colonial and patriarchal state. It sought to regulate female behavior by reminding women that their primary role in Puerto Rican society was motherhood and the maintenance of the household (Muñiz-Mas 1998, 198–99). In the gender context of colonial and Euro-settler Americas, femininity has been ascribed as the unique purview of white and "whitened" women, while "colored" and Black women have been rendered as "masculinized." Thus, I contend that in the eyes of the Puerto Rican colonial state, the regulation of appropriate femininity was centrally applied to white, Creole, and *jíbara* (rural peasant) women, otherwise imagined as the universal Puerto Rican woman or the standard, but not to the Black Puerto Rican woman, whose equal rights still remain only partially acknowledged and withheld.

Gladys Jiménez-Muñoz noted that in early twentieth century Puerto Rico, the ruling political, economic, and intelligentsia class believed that white and Creole woman's interest and involvement in politics and the demand for women's suffrage put her at risk of "masculinizing herself" (1998, 154). Her role, according to one observer, was "to live peacefully in a sacred home, nest of love and happiness, encouraging her husband in destiny's difficult struggles and modeling the heart of her sons for the service of her fatherland" (Jiménez-Muñoz 1998, 154). A socially liberal union leader who favored granting women suffrage and incorporating women into the labor market and in organizing efforts observed, "Woman with or without suffrage has the right to be a good wife and a good mother. . . . The duty of women is to mend men's pants but never try to wear them" (Jiménez-Muñoz 1998, 155–56; cf. Osorio 1928, 1). This latter stance, I contend, still reverberates in progressive men's attitudes toward women's participation in Puerto Rico's (still read as) masculine public sphere, an arena considered "sexually charged" and therefore unsafe for "good," "feminine" women. In Puerto Rico, the right to vote was granted to literate women in 1929, a move that excluded the majority of the archipelago's women, who hailed from the illiterate working and poor classes (Acosta Belén 1986, 8).

Arguably, this was a way to bar Black women from voting, the majority of whom had no access to formal education. In 1936, women's universal suffrage was passed in the Puerto Rican Legislature (Acosta Belén 1986, 8). Historically on the archipelago, the rate of participation at the voting booth has been high across gender, racial, and socioeconomic groups.

During the 1940s consolidation of the PPD's populist agrarian and industrialization reforms, the party constructed respectable Puerto Rican women "as mothers and wives, and not as workers" and at the same time bolstered the myth of the male breadwinner (Muñiz-Mas 1998, 182, 185). This was a move to reduce male unemployment. But the PPD's industrialization project would result in more women working outside the home in factories, offices, banks, hotels, and so on. As Puerto Rican women did this work, their more public face would be socially perceived as part of the process of "Puerto Rican Americanization" (Acosta Belén 1986, 13). This transformation—the archipelago becoming more like the continental United States in social values and practices, in mass consumerism, and particularly in women's roles, social behaviors, and attitudes—was seen as negative. Certainly, notions of feminism and women's liberation in midcentury Puerto Rico were viewed skeptically as a threat to the "traditional" family, to patriarchal authority, and to the naturalized order of male superiority and female subordination (Acosta Belén 1986, 14). But in a contradictory move, the PPD, under US counsel, introduced an aggressive family planning and population control campaign in the 1940s and 1950s. They believed that high levels of poverty coupled with the archipelago's overpopulation would stall progress and modernization, so the state encouraged and supported the medical practice of the mass sterilization of Puerto Rican women as a means of contraception (Acosta Belén 1986, 14). Edna Acosta Belén surmises that "a relationship can then be established between the sterilization of Puerto Rican women and market demands for their labor" (Acosta Belén 1986, 14).

Working-class and socioeconomically disadvantaged women were the main targets of *la operación* (the surgery), the everyday name given to the sterilization campaign, which was popularized in the documentary by the same title (García 1982; Briggs 2003, 145). Though it has been widely documented that poor women were specifically encouraged to undergo sterilization, the racial composition of the women sterilized during the heyday of *la operación* is not well-known. There are several reasons for this: one reason, mentioned previously, is that under the racial democracy myth, class eclipses race so that poverty is understood as raceless; a second reason is that when one views the archipelago from the vantage point of the continental US, Puerto Ricans are "people of color," without regard to the workings of island-side racial hierarchies that place Black Puerto Ricans at the bottom of the social ladder while granting privileges to white Puerto Ricans. Given the history of enslavement and anti-Black racism in Puerto Rico, poverty can be correlated to Blackness and to being Black Puerto Rican (Lloréns, García-Quijano, and Godreau 2017). This certainly does not mean that all Black Puerto Ricans are poor, but it does mean that if you are a Black Puerto Rican person, you are more likely to be socioeconomically disadvantaged. Significantly, among Puerto Rican women—on the archipelago and stateside—the sterilization rate remains one of the highest in the world (Roberts 2014, 94; Parrot and Cummings 2006, 49; López 2008).

As discussed earlier, in the context of the Americas, Black women have been categorized primarily as laborers, first as enslaved workers and, after emancipation, as underpaid, marginalized laborers. As Gerda Lerner put it, Black women "know they will have to work whether they are married or single; work to them, unlike to white women, is not a liberating goal, but rather an imposed lifelong necessity" (1972, xxiv). In this vein, Sueli Carneiro remarked, "We are part of a contingent of women that have worked for centuries as enslaved, tilling the land or on the streets as vendors or prostitutes. [We are] women who did not understand when the feminists said that women had to take over the streets and go to work" (2010; translation mine). Unlike white and Creole Puerto Rican women, the locus of (undesirable) significance conferred upon the Black Puerto Rican woman has been almost exclusively in the context of domestic labor and in the illegal, "amoral," and "unhygienic" sphere of sex work (Crespo-Kebler 1996; Matos Rodríguez 1998; Findlay 1999; Merino Falú 2004; Rodríguez-Silva 2012). This maps onto the wider stereotypes and prejudices in the Americas of historically tying a Black woman's visibility to her role as a productive worker, scorning her for her "idleness," and suspecting her fitness as a mother who, in that role, needs oversight and management. The burdens associated with the total devaluation of the home as women's "domestic sphere" take on additional problematic dimensions for Black women. First, domestic service, which for Black women has consisted mainly of cooking, cleaning, and taking care of children and the elderly, but not decorating, is belittled and perceived as unimportant, unskilled, bottom-rung work. Second, since mothering in itself is devalued, Black women's "motherwork" and their homes more broadly are lacking and suspect (hooks 1986).[5]

Writing about New York City at the beginning of the twentieth century, Saidiya Hartman notes the following presumptions and attitudes: "For state authorities, Black homes were disorderly houses because they were marked by the taint of promiscuity and illegality. The domestic was the locus of prostitution and criminality. Is this your husband? Where is the father of your child? Why is your child unattended?" (2019, 244). I contend that these attitudes and images informed state management techniques, mainly carried out by social work, medical, and educational institutions, and have been part and parcel of state intervention, both on the archipelago and the diaspora, in the lives of Black Puerto Ricans. Suspicion and oversight have been permanent features of the Anglo state's involvement in the lives of dispossessed and racialized Puerto Rican families stateside.[6]

In her important sociohistorical analysis of the past and present discrimination against Black Puerto Rican women, Aixa Merino Falú remarks, "Because it is sexist and racist, Western society has placed the Black woman in a position of invisibility" (2004, 106; translation mine). And, as Magali Roy-Féquière put it, "Hegemonic discourses have conceded very limited intelligibility to the Black Puerto Rican woman" (2004, 185). The Black Puerto Rican woman deals with an unacknowledged and unresolved social problem: the double discrimination of sexism and racism. If she is poor, she also has to contend with classism. In "Ennegrecer al feminismo" (Blackening feminism), Sueli Carneiro writes, "When we speak of the myth of feminine fragility, which has historically justified men's paternalistic protection of women, about which women are we speaking? We—black women—form part of a women's contingent . . . that never recognized themselves in that myth because they were never treated as fragile" (2010; translation mine).

The push for Black women's full equality in Puerto Rico and in the rest of the Americas will remain incomplete as long as it does not confront widespread anti-Black sexism and racism (Lassén and Crespo-Kebler 2001; Colón-Warren 2003; Merino Falú 2004; Alegría Ortega and Ríos González 2005; Alegría Ortega 2007; Carneiro 2010; Lassén 2016). Scholars who uncritically take for granted the coloniality of knowledge about the archipelago's sociocultural formation repeatedly link the "pathological matriarchal pattern" to Puerto Rico's African "presence." Simultaneously, many archipelago-based and diasporic Puerto Rican scholars, researchers, politicians, policy makers, and journalists habitually ignore, devalue, and thus leave as unmarked the significance that race, gender, and sexism play together in the structural inequalities unevenly shaping women's lives and their possibilities, trajectories, and outcomes (Alegría Ortega and Ríos González 2005; Alegría Ortega 2007). Rather than rendering everyone as equals, ignoring "the problem of the color line" has further marginalized and stigmatized Black families and communities in Puerto Rico and in the diaspora. This "color-blind" social system places the blame for past and present dispossession on the individual rather than on racist and sexist social structures and the systematic exclusion that constrains the life chances and possibilities for individuals marked Black. Acknowledging the place of race and Blackness in the marginality historically experienced by families whose ancestors were enslaved, or who were even "free Blacks" in an atmosphere thick with anti-Black racism, will reveal the ongoing centrality of racism and its corollary, racial dispossession, in the lives of Afro-descendants in Puerto Rico and in the Americas more broadly. Finally, the scholarly literature focusing on Black women's lives and activism has focused on urban areas, mainly San Juan and Ponce, while the lives and cultural practices of Afro–Puerto Ricans living in rural and hinterland regions remains scarce (Mayo Santana et al. 1991). Thus, there is a limited and incomplete understanding of the particular realities and challenges Black women face across the archipelago's nonurban geographies.

A PUERTO RICAN "POETICS OF ENSLAVEMENT"

If the historiography of enslavement in Puerto Rico is thin, the history of women's lives within this dehumanizing system and after abolition is barely present (Crespo-Kebler 1996; Findlay 1999; Jiménez-Muñoz 2003; Merino Falú 2004; Roy-Féquière 2004; Carrasquillo 2008; Rodríguez-Silva 2012; Moreno 2012). Certainly, a robust historiography and social science literature about the intimate everyday lives of Black women, family life, and mothering is absent from canonical accounts. Writing about Puerto Rican womanhood and race, Gladys Jiménez-Muñoz aptly remarked that the overwhelming majority of studies about the "race question" have reduced "racialized experiences and cultural representations to the male context" (2003, 72). She further asserts that the Puerto Rican social science literature on race has linked it to social class while completely omitting gender as a significant variable organizing the lives of those studied (2003, 73). This, I contend, is a feature of the potent sexist and racist practice of centering the white Hispanic male experience as universal and completely discounting the unique and specific experiences of women. The "sociological problems era" (roughly 1890s–1970s) coincided with the early decades of emancipation and with the "great migrations" of Blacks and Puerto Ricans to northern cities. This led to scrutiny of Black women's lives and their role as mothers (Hartman 2019). As Hartman put it, "This state of affairs—Black women as providers, heads of households, and wage laborers—transgressed what was deemed normal and proper. . . . A woman who didn't need a man or depend on one raised concerns and instigated doubts about her own status—was she a woman at all?" (Hartman 2019, 186). The question of "proper womanhood" is also raised in relation to childless women, lesbians, incarcerated women, transwomen, and other women whose lifestyles and choices mark them as subaltern.

In an effort to grapple with the gaping historiographical hole about the lives of enslaved Africans in Puerto Rico, literature scholar Zaira Rivera Casellas used the term "poetics of enslavement" (*la poética de la esclavitud*) to define the field of fiction authored by Puerto Rican women—Carmen Colón Pellot, Beatriz Berrocal, Yolanda Arroyo Pizarro, and Mayra Santos-Febres—in the twentieth and twenty-first centuries (2011, 100; 2015). This canon narrates the fictional details of the personal and affective lives of Black women during enslavement and after emancipation. Rivera Casellas notes that the voices and stories of enslaved persons could be a source of historical memory and continuity for Afro–Puerto Ricans. But "it is obvious that we cannot turn back time or reclaim those absent voices. And yet in contemporary Puerto Rican literature, I perceive texts that allow us to enter that silence through fiction to help us rethink the arbitrariness of images, values, and cultural representations shared by the members of the African diaspora in the Americas and Caribbean" (2011, 99; translation mine). Rivera Casellas calls attention to the silencing of Black life, which *is* a central feature of the racial democracy myth *and* of the historical practice of marginalizing Black Puerto Rican voices and cultural life. So inconsequential were their lives that the lack of information, voices, and stories by and about enslaved Africans and free Blacks during the Spanish colonial era has worked to typecast Black Puerto Rican culture as consisting *solely* of its external manifestations (i.e., music, dance, and entertainment). This profound historical void denies contemporary Afro–Puerto Ricans factual knowledge about the lifeways of their ancestors, and this void has been carved in Puerto Rico's social fabric. The silencing of enslavement experiences has made contemporary Black Puerto Ricans feel unmoored from their African provenance. For Black Puerto Ricans, this void is a source of pain and trauma. It is still not unusual today to ask a Black Puerto Rican elder the question, as I did in 1998, "Where did Black Puerto Ricans come from?" and receive a painfully uncertain response, as I did from eighty-three-year-old Doña Carmen:

> I am sorry . . . I don't know much about that. What I do know is that a long time ago there were slaves here and that the Indians were decimated, but I never did learn much about where my family came from. I think my mother once mentioned that her father came here from Vieques to work in the sugar fields . . . but I don't know much else about where we came from . . . I'm sorry, I don't know much about slavery, but I do know there were slaves here and I know that there is racism against us Blacks . . . that to be Black in Puerto Rico is to endure a lot of racism, but we don't talk about it much. We act like it is not there at all . . . you know, no one wants to think about pain and hurt. I'm sorry . . . but about where we come from other than Puerto Rico? I really don't know much about that."

Here I have exposed and challenged the masculinist coloniality of historical and taken-for-granted knowledge that has helped craft prevailing tropes about the lives of Black women and their families as defective. The term "matriarchal dispossession" describes the encompassing forces—social, economic, legal, and political—of dispossessive racialization at work against Black women from enslavement through the present. The historiography of Puerto Rican enslavement is almost completely devoid of the lives of Black women. But Black Puerto Rican women authors have been busy at work narrating what Zaira Rivera Casellas calls "a poetics of enslavement" (2011). Writers such as Mayra Santos-Febres, Yolanda Arroyo Pizarro, Carmen Colón Pellot, and Beatriz Berrocal, as well as social critics such as Marie Ramos Rosado, Idsa E. Alegría Ortega, Ana Irma Rivera Lassén, Aixa Merino Falú, Palmira Ríos González, Ada Lucía Verdejo Carrión, Mariluz Franco Ortiz, and Bárbara Abadía-Rexach, among others, have gathered and stitched together surviving shreds of historical and archival material into literary quilts that center the lives of forgotten and ignored Black women in Puerto Rico. Their undocumented lives are matters of (and for) our imaginations. But Black women, such as my maternal kinswomen, were neither victims nor heroes. They were living their lives doing the best they could for themselves and their families. Theirs/ours/mine is also a story of survival and perseverance.

CHAPTER 2

DOING HOME-WORK IN THE MOTHERLAND

why do I care so deeply for a place that doesn't care for me?

silenced.

ejected.

erased.

and still, i say:

"i am from that place.

i love that place."

ancestor worship.

earth. sky. plants. air. clouds. rain. rocks. water: salt & fresh.

its animals, my kin.

"how could i not love the only place i can say i am from?

i know no other earth to be from."

I WROTE THE EPIGRAPH AFTER RETURNING STATESIDE FROM fieldwork in Puerto Rico in January 2018. I had traveled to Puerto Rico in December 2017, with a team of anthropologists sponsored by the National Science Foundation to study the moral economy of Hurricane María recovery.[1] That trip marked my twentieth year returning to Puerto Rico as an anthropologist doing fieldwork. Because I study my own culture, American anthropologists call me a "native" anthropologist. Kirin Narayan defines these Other(ed) anthropologists as those "who are believed to write about their own culture from a position of intimate affinity" (1993, 671). This label no doubt problematically essentializes me. My family migrated from the archipelago to the continental United States for good when I was thirteen. Because I am a one-and-a-half-generation migrant, I am often labeled a "Nuyorican" when I return, an "outsider" (*de afuera*). Sometimes in Puerto Rico I am even called an "Americana."[2]

But my emotional relationship to the archipelago and its people has always been complicated, even before I left as a child. My ambivalent relationship to Puerto Rico is partly due to what I can only describe as an intergenerational feeling passed down through my maternal line of "motherlessness" and "territorial unboundedness," as well feelings of rejection and abandonment perpetrated against us by "our" homeland's political class. In "The Blood Stream of Our Inheritance: Female Identity and the Caribbean's Mothers'-Land," Anne Morris and Margaret Dunn explain that "for the Caribbean woman, the notion of motherland is especially complex, encompassing in its connotations her island home and its unique culture as well as the body of tropes, talismans and female bonding that is woman's heritage through her own and other mothers. *The land and one's mother then are co-joined*" (1992, 219; emphasis mine).

In fact, I believe this fraught relationship to that "small place" led me to become an ethnographer in the first place.[3] Added to this is the certainty that all anthropologists, indeed all individuals, possess what Renato Rosaldo termed "multiplex subjectivity"; that is, an embodied bundle of identities and affiliations (1989, 168–95; Narayan 1993; Chawla 2006). In relation to the archipelago's political and intelligentsia class, I am, at best, a partial insider. Though large numbers of Puerto Ricans hail from the archipelago's small hinterland towns, for the powerful few, the measure of "insiderness" is mostly tied to the cultural capital of family lineages and connections to institutions (i.e., schools, civic clubs) in Puerto Rico's "centers of culture" (such as San Juan, Ponce, and maybe Mayagüez).

Though I feel no affinity whatsoever to the archipelago's elites, I share gender, race, and class positioning with the women I conduct research with, as well as experiences of migration, living with and in poverty, intergenerational dispossession, and trauma. In fact, my strong desire to account for herstories of women like those of my own family—historically devalued, silenced, ejected, and erased—led me to the communities of women with whom I work in Puerto Rico's southeast and in the diaspora. These are powerful, courageous women unafraid to confront change, life's curveballs and uncertainties, in their search to make livable lives.

This chapter exemplifies what a decolonized ethnography might look like and the ways in which the "autobiographical example" offers insight into the epistemological usefulness of embodied knowledge. I discuss diasporic, Afro, and Black national belonging and consider ethical questions about the right (and privilege) to tell others' stories. I grapple here with what it means for a so-called "native" ethnographer to do fieldwork versus home-work. The chapter closes with a decolonized reimagining of the "ancestral motherland" in the context of the twenty-first century and a brief look at the contemporary demands for liberation that seek to build a more inclusive and just Puerto Rican society.

DECOLONIZING ETHNOGRAPHY, UNDISCIPLINING OURSELVES

In this time of radical reckonings with the naturalized Eurocentric and masculinist coloniality of knowledge, scholars of color—particularly women—whose knowledge has been marginalized historically and in traditional academic disciplines such as anthropology, must continue to undiscipline from the tyranny of positivist social science methods and theory not capacious enough to allow for or contain our storytelling (Collins 2000; McClaurin 2001; Pérez 1999; Tuhiwai Smith 1999; among others). The authors just cited, and many others, have called attention to the overwhelming experiences Black and Indigenous women face, as other women of color in traditional social science disciplines do, wherein their work often suffers from invisibilization and erasure, delegitimization and trivialization (Dinzey Flores et al., 2019). In refusing positivist, one-size-fits-all social scientific methodology and narrative "norm," as scholars of color we face the triple burden of doing field research, writing our stories, and then critiquing and creating methods through which to uncover and tell our stories.[4]

Here I follow in a long tradition of critical Black women and other historically marginalized women scholars in the North American and global Eurocentric academy who have actively called for and produced variations of a decolonial feminist ethnographic canon. To attempt to decolonize ethnography means to delink from deeply engrained practices in the anthropological canon such as theorizing and narrativizing with academese as a lingua franca and employing power-laden citational practices that are required to validate our claims and our informants'. Ultimately this means challenging or disregarding altogether as illegitimate the discipline's valuation of "decolonized ethnography."

To attempt to write decolonized ethnography, then, means to face the violence implicit in reducing people to abstract data, a process that disappears the embodied stories and experiences of people, our informants, the vast majority of whom already live marginalized lives that often render them extractable, disposable, and otherwise invisible to the academy and the elite sectors of society. In critiquing the extractive violence of traditional ethnographic practice, Mariolga Reyes Cruz explains that her "informant" Graciela was not someone she could cite as an authoritative source; rather, she was someone "to be talked about, not talked from. Graciela was data" (2008, 652).

A decolonized ethnography seeks to center our "informants'" knowledge, experiences, insights, and observations alongside our own. This is a particularly important exercise for those of us who are survivors of marginalization, or who come from lineages of invisibility and erasure and turned academic, as I did. I attempt to produce a decolonized ethnography, one that refuses the coloniality of knowledge as the central source of authoritative knowledge about the/our/my world. In decoupling colonialist authority and authoritative knowledge, I knowingly engage in acts and practices of "epistemic and political disobedience" (Mignolo 2009, 16).

A decolonizing ethnography requires sustained and critical introspection about self and other, history and knowledge. It means reckoning and working through sometimes contradictory, messy, incomplete, and painful stories, memories, and materials, such as photographs, landscapes, graveyards, ruins, archives (embodied, on paper, and online), and other objects and mementos. Significantly, it is an approach that allows the absences, silences, and gaps to emerge to the surface. In fact, it highlights the incompleteness of that which we do know and points towards ruptures, gorges, and gaping holes in our knowledge about the world our kidnapped and trafficked ancestors come from, and to which they arrived.

In this way, a decolonized ethnography is a method that stitches together scraps of knowledge to attempt to re-member and historicize, while pointing with equal intent to what remains *in*visible. These unknowns are witnesses to the ruptures and violence our ancestors endured. They underscore that knowledge—what is visible—is always incomplete. This method also reveals that among the many great losses our Black and Indigenous ancestors suffered was their ability to be fully known to us, their great-great-great-grandchildren. We can only imagine who they were, what languages they spoke, their cosmology and spirituality, their ideas about history, and their cultural knowledge.

Still, I wrestle with ethical questions about my right to represent and write about the lives of others, even if these others are my kinfolk or people who are "like me." For these reasons, I have practiced the "autobiographical example" since the inception of my anthropological career. As a source of deep, embodied knowledge and a narrative strategy, this approach connects my lived experiences and those of my ancestors to the wider community of Afro—and Black Puerto Ricans, to the Black Caribbean, and to the histories of those of us whose lives shape the Black Atlantic experience more widely (Chandler 2014; Spivak 1993; Lloréns 2006). As Saidiya Hartman has cogently expressed it, "It's not about navel gazing, it's really about trying to look at historical and social process, and one's own formation as a window onto social and historical processes, as an example of them. . . . I wanted to tell a story capable of engaging and countering the violence of abstraction. For me, that had to be embodied in physical story, and I was the one who had to hazard the journey" (Saunders 2008, 5).

Even as my life experiences allow for what I call a cultural adjacency to the women with whom I collaborate, our interactions are still marked by "positional contingencies" (Chawla 2006, 15). For instance, I was still getting to know Yesi, a woman who took me on a transect walk through the mangrove forest in Las Mareas, her community.[5] She shared that she had been released from prison recently, after serving six years on drug-trafficking charges. She was transferred from Puerto Rico to serve her sentence in a Florida prison. Being away from her family had been extraordinarily difficult. Two cousins my age with whom I was close as a child are now imprisoned, but otherwise I have no other experience with incarceration. I mentioned one cousin who is serving a life sentence and whose gang-related activities are the stuff of local lore. Yesi said she knew my cousin from "back in the day." She then told me her grown children had migrated to Massachusetts to "build better lives" because "there are no jobs here for us." And there are prejudices against hiring people from coastal communities like hers. When prospective employers see such an address on a job application, they immediately disqualify the person. She explained, "Employers believe that people from here are illiterate, too poor, or involved in drug dealing and trafficking. There is a lot of prejudice against us. You see, some of us become involved with the drug trade because there are not many ways to earn a living here." Yesi was excited about having recently become a grandmother. She talked about how spending time in the mangroves, hunting for crabs, and swimming in the hidden lagoons and beaches has always been a source of joy and a kind of therapeutic space for her and her family: "This is the place where we come to forget about our worries and problems."

The therapeutic effects of "contact with nature" have long been identified as important to job satisfaction and well-being by Puerto Rican and other coastal-resource users (i.e., fishers, crabbers, and foragers)

(García-Quijano and Poggie 2019; Seara et al. 2017; Griffith and Valdés Pizzini 2002). Coastal-resource users in general report that their jobs allow for more time for family life and community relationships (García-Quijano et al. 2015). But few researchers account for how women and children also benefit from their direct engagement with coastal nature. Often women and children fish, hunt, and forage, but they do so from the shore or on land, such as in the mangroves. In part, less is known about women and children's engagement and contributions to the culture of coastal-resource users because males are often the household's de facto fishers, crabbers, and/or foragers. Moreover, male anthropologists, who have largely produced the ethnography of coastal-resource users, follow prescribed rules of proper gender behavior and respectability and so have little access to the contributions of women and children.

Yesi is a dedicated community activist who defends her *comunidad marginada* (marginalized community) against developers. Southern coastal communities like hers are constantly threatened with displacement by government ambitions to sell the coast to tourism developers. If this were to happen, the community's access to the mangrove channels and the ocean, which members of these communities depend on for food, cultural identity, leisure, and well-being, would be restricted if not altogether forbidden (García-Quijano and Lloréns 2018; García-Quijano and Poggie 2019; García-Quijano 2006).

During that walk, Yesi and I discovered that we were exactly the same age, forty-three, with birthdays just a few weeks apart. Yesi stared at me in disbelief. "But Hilda," she said, "you look so young, you look twenty-eight! You are so thin, you look like a girl. . . . Well, I've never looked like a little fashion model, I guess." I laughed awkwardly, keenly aware of the ways my educational and linguistic experience, my weight, height, and skin color, and my middle-class privilege (relatively new to me) might mark me as a kind of "aspirational insider" in the eyes of the women and communities I work with.

In some ways my story of educational achievement is well-known in our poor communities. But as Nelson, a respected community leader, once shared, "Here in the community, we can't stand when someone from the community moves away to attend university. They make it professionally as a lawyer or doctor, and when they do come back to visit, because they never move back to live in the barrio [neighborhood], they come driving a fancy car and boasting about their income, buying everybody rounds of drinks at the local bar, and showing off their material wealth." In my case, as a matter of enacting my ethics and living by my personal values, I have always practiced respect, compassion, and humility, behaviors which have not gone unnoticed or unremarked on by community members. "You are a *persona humilde* [humble person]," they say, or "It is nice that you don't forget about us and always come back," and "It is good to see how proud you are to be from here." In other words, my core cultural values are congruent with those practiced by community members with whom I conduct ethnographic research, and my presence has been rewarded with their acceptance (Smolicz 1981; García-Quijano and Lloréns 2019). This is noteworthy because Puerto Rico's southeast region is notoriously unreceptive to outsiders.

OUTSIDERNESS: ON BEING *DE AFUERA*

Ever since I can remember, I wanted to make sense of the feeling that I did not fully belong and was not fully accepted in Puerto Rican society. My family's socioeconomic position as dispossessed poor, our Black and Afro–Puerto Rican cultural identity, and our residence in a household headed by a single mother who relied on *cupones* (food stamps) to survive marked us as undesirable to the aspirational middle class and elites. Our skin color, where and how we lived, how we dressed and spoke, the music we listened to, the time spent waiting our turn in government welfare offices on the island and later in the diaspora, revealed our small-island-town-poor-folk provenance. We still speak a little too loudly, our joy is rambunctious, we become easily familiar and solidary with other poor folks, and we curse at the inefficiencies and disrespect of the social workers who lose our paperwork or make us wait hours only to tell us to come back the next day with little regard for our time or, indeed, our lives.

We have little in the way of money and material possessions, but we are quick to share what we have with others more needy. Where we are from, there are always needier folks. For instance, there are friends and relatives who arrive stateside from the island in the middle of New England winters—running away from unemployment, destitution, drug addiction, or a violent husband or lover, ill and hoping for medical care—wearing T-shirts and without a coat to their name. There are those whose heating is shut off for lack of payment and who need a few extra thick blankets and a space heater to get by. We keep each other company. We go to the supermarket, to the emergency room, to doctor's appointments; we go everywhere together. In the diaspora, when a relative's or friend's mother, husband, son, or daughter is sick and dying in the county hospital, at home, or in hospice care, we rotate visiting, so they are never alone. We sneak each other and our children in to see our loved ones in the emergency room, in intensive care rooms, in palliative care facilities. These rooms often get so crowded and loud that the fed-up nurses and staff remind us of the rules, ask us to take turns visiting, or plead for quiet and tranquility for the patient's well-being. But they don't know that we believe that too much quiet is bad for sick and dying folks, that life, noise, chatter, and the laughter of intergenerational visitors is the proper way to be present for our loved ones. Wherever we live, we live as a community, knowing that without each other, life would be unbearable. Much more than poverty, the biggest curse in the life of the Puerto Rican poor is loneliness and the lack of a community to count on. If we know or suspect someone is lonely, our job is to show up for that person to make sure they know that we care. Culturally appropriate behavior entails we show up in good times and in bad, when our loved ones are alive and when they die.

There are many ways people can build social capital and goodwill. For the poor, being present for others, sharing time and resources, and practicing solidarity and mutual aid are some of those ways. My mother earns a fixed income of less than US$8,000 a year, and yet she considers herself a prosperous woman. Recently my adult niece, her grandchild, exclaimed, "Grandma is the richest poor woman I know!" As is culturally expected, her four children, including me, make sure her basic needs are covered, and she reports "not needing anything and having more than I need." But because we have families and needs of our own, we can provide her with only a modest amount of income each year. Partly because she has spent her life figuring out how to make do with very few resources and partly because she is a naturally empathetic person, among my mother's many talents is her ability to locate resources such as free food, clothing, and/or furniture, which she collects and redistributes among relatives, friends, and friends of friends. As a result, she in turn receives a constant stream of food, gifts, and favors. She also barters services; for instance, when her longtime mechanic calls her to consult her about a family dilemma, she takes the time to listen and give him advice. At Christmas she brings him some of the special seasonal Puerto Rican foods she makes to give to her network of friends. In exchange, when her car needs repair, he fixes it for the price of the parts. She connects emotionally with others with ease, and as a result, her friends seek her out as a wise woman, a kind of "street therapist" to consult on problems and dilemmas and to ask about available resources. Anthropologist Ana Y. Ramos Zayas defines the "street thera-pist" as an individual who uses an "emotion-based theory of practice that is grounded on relational affect and knowledge sharing" (2012, 7).

In the continental United States, the ubiquitous question "Where are you from?" reminds Puerto Ricans and other people of color that they are seen as perpetual outsiders. This question usually comes immediately after someone hears us speaking so-called accented Latinx English. It does not matter that some of us were born here or have lived in the continental United States for twenty, thirty, forty, or more years. It doesn't matter that the archipelago itself and the small towns we left are now distant memo-ries, if the homes and neighborhoods we grew up in still exist at all. Recently, a diaspora-born-and-raised friend told me that he brought his children to Puerto Rico for the first time in their young lives to show them the places in Puerto Rico where his parents, the children's grandparents, were from. His parents had met, courted, and married in New York City, not in Puerto Rico. He said, "Before migrating to New York, my mother lived in an old workers' barrio called *el fanguito* [the little mud]. It doesn't exist anymore, and so I showed my children where it used to be located, and then we looked up historic photographs online. We enjoyed our time visiting, but I could not really live on the island."

Another friend visited her hometown for the first time since migrating thirty years ago. "I didn't know anyone; I didn't recognize any familiar faces," she said. "It was disorienting. I used to know everyone. The place looks so run down and sad, the streets so narrow, the businesses shut down. Visiting my hometown felt like I had been to a loved one's funeral, and I don't want to return there anytime soon."

Another friend, a woman who travels to the island every chance she gets, remarked, "I need to get home to Puerto Rico as much as I can. Hope-fully I can move back very soon. The greenery, the warm ocean water, the sounds, all of it makes me feel whole again. It's like half of me goes dor-mant when I am up north, and when I return, I get to be my whole self."

For some diasporic Puerto Ricans, the archipelago remains an idyllic homeland, but for others, it is a place of no return. Stateside Americans often assume that "outsiders," migrants of color from the Global South or, in the case of Puerto Rico, US colonial citizens, fit neatly and coherently into their societies of origin. This is in part because they mistakenly attri-bute a coherence or unity to the nations of the Global South. But the US does not stand alone in the Americas as a divided nation that believes itself to be mainly composed of, and governed by, Euro-American immigrant-settlers who have long subjugated Native Americans and African Americans, in which racism is a core social feature, and where Indigenous and Black citizens are excluded, discriminated against, and have to fight for their rights at every turn. In fact, this is a shared reality in the Americas, both North and South. Therefore, those of us who are Indigenous and Black in Latin America and the Caribbean are as likely to be dispossessed and poor, silenced and erased as are Indigenous and Black individuals and communities in the Global North. Thus, my childhood feelings of not quite belonging to Puerto Rican society are not a figment of my imagination but are in fact real feelings shared by many. This is because Puerto Rico's political nationalist project, co-constructed by the archipelago's elite and intellectual class, has constituted the polity as a homogenous Creole nation made up of urbanized whites and rural *jíbaros*, a polity whose motherland is Spain and whose authentic national language is Spanish. Thus, all the people who do not fit into this mold, such as poor single mothers, Afro–Puerto Ricans, gender and sexual minorities, returned diasporic Puerto Ricans, and racialized migrants such as Dominicans, have been historically marginalized in the name of "national unity" (Ramos Zayas 2003, 28; Díaz-Quiñones 1993; Sandoval Sánchez 1997; Dávila 1997; Guerra 1998; Duany 2002; Zentella 2000; La Fountain-Stokes 2002; Pérez 2004; Dinzey Flores 2013; Lloréns 2014; Godreau 2015; LeBrón 2019a). Due to my family's and my own experiences of exclusion from the Puerto Rican social body, when Puerto Rican scholars assert that the archipelago's pervasive nationalist discourse is as "exclusionary and oppressive as U.S. colonialism," the statement rings true to me (Ramos Zayas 2003, 29; Pabón 1995; Negrón-Muntaner and Grosfoguel 1997).

I am a culturally Black, Afro-racialized woman from a family whose ancestors were illiterate and dispossessed poor, and whose belonging to the national body was tenuous at best. This picture becomes even more complicated for those of us labeled diasporic Puerto Ricans, an identity with its own complexities. Historically the diaspora, as Ramos Zayas asserted, "was generally portrayed as dark, young and displaying mannerisms and dress styles that some Puerto Ricans on the island associate with Black youth in the United States" (2003, 23). The prejudiced, negative characteristics assigned to the Puerto Rican diaspora by islanders has made returned migrants feel rejected.

There are differences within the diaspora itself—there are the folks in what I call the "deep diaspora," who were born stateside, whose families have resided on the continent for more than one generation, and whose ties to the archipelago are emotional or based on cultural identity rather than on direct connection. Then there are those in the "new diaspora," who have migrated more recently (in the last thirty years), who return to the archipelago regularly to visit relatives, who might still own property, and who still plan to return to Puerto Rico someday. Though cultural nationalism expressed by the Puerto Rican diaspora is strong regardless of the amount of time individuals have spent "deterritorialized" from their homeland, neo-locality has led people to create and nurture a sense of community in their current home places. Many of the "deep diaspora" folks I have interviewed have shared that while their families initially planned to return to the archipelago "to retire," as family life took its course in their new homes, their children married, their grandchildren were born, and relatives moved from Puerto Rico to join these established communities, it became increasingly clear that home had become reconstituted in the form of affective ties. In the process, the definition of home as land or as geographic location became less salient.

DOING THE HOME-WORK OF FIELDWORK

I returned three months after Hurricanes Irma and María battered the archipelago on September 20, 2017. The destroyed Spanish colonial–era buildings and houses that lined Arroyo's *malecón* (seaside district) and Calle Morse (the town's main street) left me stunned. These had seemed grand and indestructible in my youth. Made with reinforced concrete, the seemingly permanent structures fell apart because they had been abandoned long ago. The historic buildings had slowly decayed, their walls had cracked without witnesses, and the paint had chipped off with each tropical rain and wind gust emanating from the Caribbean Sea on the southern edge of town. Three months after the storm, slabs of cement and pieces of wooden roof were scattered exactly where they had fallen the day of the storm. No one, it seemed, concerned themselves with cleaning up the debris.

I thought of the present state of each of these structures, where the Spanish sugar barons and their families had once lived and, later, where their descendants had lived, this small town's moneyed Creoles who appeared to taunt the rest of us from their wraparound verandas and lush gardens nourished by the salty breeze from the nearby sea. We walked by under the punishing sun and wistfully admired the beautiful woodwork, the wrought-iron gates, and the pastel colors, envying their luck to have

FIG 2.1 Damaged Spanish-era colonial building in Arroyo, Puerto Rico, in the aftermath of Hurricane María, December 2017.

been born privileged. The rest of us, the town's many dispossessed poor, struggled to make a go of life before *having to* migrate to cold-weather stateside cities with gray skies and bleak tenement buildings filling the landscape in all directions (Lloréns 2006; Lloréns 2018b). The Spanish-era colonial structures were just the latest to collapse amid the ruination in the southeast and other rural areas that had begun long ago. In the early twenty-first century, the decay took hold of the entire archipelago (Lloréns 2018c). To me, the creeping decline I witnessed in Puerto Rico during my lifetime, first from close-up and later from afar, was a kind of blight, an infestation brought on by the relentless forces of capitalist greed, political corruption, neoliberalism, disinvestment, austerity, and government abandonment (Lloréns 2018b).

Over the years, my feelings have wavered between melancholia, sadness, and hurt, as well as anger, resentment, and righteous indignation toward the archipelago's political class and the intelligentsia. This is because I understand firsthand—it has been my lived experience—that the archipelago has been ruled by wealthy white (and off-white) families and their descendants whose Hispanophile and more recent Euro-American aspirations have left no room for people like my family and me. The archipelago's intelligentsia, like the political class, hails from lineages of mainly white upper-class intellectual families. Ensconced in their metropolitan university posts, they, too, have devalued the dispossessed poor in the archipelago and in the diaspora.

Puerto Rico's dispossessed poor—people who own no land or who have no proper title to property, who have no connections to the archipelago's political or educated classes, and who rely on government assistance—have historically been and continue to be ejected from the archipelago. In other words, the archipelago's poor have been purged to stateside cities, where they often live similarly marginal and segregated lives marked by inadequate housing, education, employment, health, and environment. Our stories, told from a sociological problems angle, are a source of embarrassment to the aspiring middle classes, while the upper classes try to ignore our existence. When they acknowledge us, it is only to complain that we are eyesores, that we are lazy and lack motivation, and that all we do with our lives is live off the government's charity. They do not attempt to understand how the dispossessed poor manage to forge good lives for themselves and their families or how they survive in the face of multiple systems of oppression. They focus only on their deficits or what they lack, never on their assets or what they build.

As a so-called native ethnographer, I engage taken-for-granted notions of anthropological fieldwork and instead use the notion of home-work to signal a *complicated familiarity* with my anthropological "field sites." I aim to call attention to the gender dynamics associated with the "field" versus the "home" site. In 1998, when I first began to do fieldwork in my mother's hometown, the place where I lived throughout my childhood, I was repeatedly warned by relatives, friends, and neighbors that I should not walk alone around town. I told them that I liked to exercise, and that walking was a great way to observe and get to know the people I was planning to interview. I mentioned that I did not want to buy a car and would rather take public transportation to get around. They insisted that these were unsafe choices for a young woman in Puerto Rico. They told me that even during the day, the town's streets were dangerous and that I was putting myself in grave danger. I could end up abducted, raped, or even murdered. They told me I had been living *afuera* (outside) for too long, that I had forgotten how unsafe the streets were for young women.

These warnings frightened me. I soon gave up walking through town because whenever I walked, I was offered rides, catcalled, and sometimes even yelled at from passing cars. Maneuvering through groups of men liming on street corners, in front of stores, and at gas stations was taking its toll. Within a short time, it became clear that walking alone was indeed unsanctioned behavior for young women. I gave in and bought a barely working old car. Still, my focus on festivals, celebrations, and public commemorations of Black cultural traditions required that I enter public spaces during the day and at night. These spaces were safer for women during the day, but without a group of family members or friends, or a husband or boyfriend, I needed to go home after prime time. A woman going to nighttime events risked being labeled "loose," sexually available, and possibly depraved. Because my gender (and outsider status) produced concerns for my safety, I attended public events with relatives and groups of friends. So, for me, fieldwork was not, and more importantly could not be, a period of distant and solitary immersion. Instead, it was a period of intense *convivencia* (cohabitating) with my female kin and friends. From then on, my gender would direct the kinds of research I could do. Through these experiences, I realized early on the importance of my gender, race, class, and age in my academic and scholarly work.

In a book review titled "A Hero of Our Time," Susan Sontag wrote that "for the anthropologist the world is divided into 'home' and 'out there,' the domestic and the exotic, the urban academic world and the tropics. The anthropologist is not simply a neutral observer. He is a man in control of, and even consciously exploiting, his own intellectual alienation" (1963). In anthropology, as Sontag signaled, the field has been rendered historically as a masculine site. In contrast, ideas of home index constraint, enclosure, the internal and private realm, the womb as "first home" and, in its pedagogical dimension, the private work of the mind. This indexing maps onto established notions of gender, space, and belonging. These include the notions that the bodies of men belong in the field, and women's bodies belong in the home, or that men's bodies can be exposed to the "elements" while women's bodies should be protected from these "elements." Women's bodies simultaneously require enclosure and act as enclosures.

American anthropology and academia more broadly are inhospitable to people of color, and to women of color in particular (Harrison 1997, 2008; McClaurin 2001; Dávila 2008; Navarro, Williams, and Ahmad 2013; Pandian 2019; among others). Anthropology has a long history of excluding women of color from its ranks, as the outsider status of anthropologist Zora Neale Hurston exemplifies (Visweswaran 1994; Hernández 1995). Faye V. Harrison wrote, "This professional homelessness is reflected in Hurston's being scorned at Columbia University for her so-called lack of rigorous techniques" (1997, 235). Today, the continued "subtly racist" tendency to treat people from "elsewhere as objects of study, rather than as thinkers and theorists in their own right" is still prevalent in anthropology (Pandian 2019, 1). Anthropology has historically reproduced mainstream notions of gender in actual ethnographic fieldwork, as well as in the development of theory and methods. In Ruth Behar's words, "Why is it that anthropology—the discipline whose legitimacy is so wrapped up in the multiplicity of languages and worlds—continues to be conceived in such resolutely patrilineal and Eurocentric terms?" (1995, 12). Fieldwork about external, public, sociocultural matters, such as warring, politics, and ecology, has been the purview of white men. For instance, in what is regarded as a "classic" of anthropological functionalism, "The Nuer of the Southern Sudan," E. E. Evans-Pritchard explained matter-of-factly, "We regard the family, the household, and the hamlet *as domestic*, rather than political, groups, and do not discuss them further in detail" (McGee and Warms 1999, 189; emphasis mine). With this brief explanation, Evans-Pritchard discounts the significance of the world of women and of family life in the sociocultural, political, ecological, and emotional *functioning* of the Nuer of the Southern Sudan.

When white Euro-American female ethnographers finally began to "head out" to the anthropological field, Othered brown and Black women, their children, and their homes became almost exclusively their purview. In their depictions, Euro-American female ethnographers created a cultural Other in their renditions of "third-world" and minoritized US women of color (Behar 1995, 6). Still, even the anthropological interventions of women such as Margaret Mead, anthropology's most popularly known twentieth-century scholar, have been largely left out of the theoretical and methodological canons (Behar 1995, 9). Evans-Pritchard must have believed that women were daft and contributed little to the sociocultural worlds they lived in. A major detractor of Margaret Mead's ethnographic work, he said Mead belonged to the "Rustling-of-the-Wind-in-the-Palm-Trees School" (Behar 1995, 9).

Though feminist ethnography has been a vanguard subfield in anthropology with its calls for inclusion of the marginalized voices of women ethnographers in the discipline's canon, it faced its own marginalization practices belatedly. Calling attention to how white feminism is privilege over "Third World Feminism" in the academy, Catherine Lutz writes that "when theory is gendered, then, it is simultaneously raced and classed. . . . Theory has acquired a gender in so far as it is more frequently associated with male writing, with women's writing more often seen as description, data, case, personal, or as in the case of feminism, 'merely' setting the record straight" (1995, 251).

With its "deep concern" "with the politics of authorship," *This Bridge Called My Back* (1981) heralded a turning point in the American feminist canon when it was published (Behar 1995, 7). Behar states that the anthology's authors "pondered the question of who has the right to write culture for whom" (1995, 7). And, if it can even be referred to as a right, does being from a particular place or claiming familial or national adjacency to a place bestow upon the researcher more of a right to write about a place and its people? The anthology's section "Entering the Lives of Others: Theory in the Flesh" begins to think through answers to these difficult questions. The following excerpt sheds light upon them: "A theory in the flesh means one where the physical realities of our lives—our skin color, the land or concrete where we grew up on, our sexual longings—all fuse to create a politic born out necessity. . . . We do this bridging by naming our selves and by telling our stories in our own words" (Moraga and Anzaldúa 1981, 23).

With this statement, the authors confront the "multiplex subjectivities" within their already liminal subject positions, in relation not only to gender, but also to race, culture, class, education, and sexuality. For them, a way to *bridge* liminality's "neither here nor there" distance was to quite literally use their bodies and life experiences as *source material*, *site*, and *vehicle* for storytelling, narrating, and theory making to reckon with and against the Cartesian limits of Euro-American disciplinary boundaries (Cervantes-Soon 2014, 98). In this way, Cherríe Moraga and Gloria Anzaldúa charted a path for feminist scholars of color to move beyond the constraints of objectivity imposed by (masculinized) disciplinary borders to reveal the ways in which our (womanist) work is "grounded in emotional investment" (Moya 2002, 49; Walker 1983). Here was a call to "undiscipline" ourselves from the tyranny of centering our abstract minds over the physical, sentient, relational, and worldly realities and contradictions in and of our bodies. And the anthology was an example of how to do it.

Kamala Visweswaran wrote that "homework" refers to "the actualization of what some writers have termed 'anthropology in reverse'" (1994, 102). Understood literally, anthropology in reverse would entail the so-called native anthropologist leaving their home to study the West. Instead, Visweswaran calls attention to the complex layers of "anthropological homework" to remind us that the "field" and "home" are interdependent and that their borders are blurred (1994, 113). It becomes clear from this reading, however, that for the "native anthropologist," home indexes a multiplicity of locations. One is the ancestral home, where we might have grown up or from which we are removed by a generation or more. The diasporic home is where our families migrated, or the universities where we arrived to study and later to work. Here I heed Visweswaran's apt remark that a feminist ethnography characterized by a kind of home-work that redirects its gaze homeward might assist in producing a decolonized ethnography (Visweswaran 1994, 104, 113). *Doing* home-work as a theoretical, methodological, and analytical practice opens up possibilities for a radical and liberating rendering of the home, which in patriarchal society is the quintessential women's space.

In this work, I *gaze homeward* from an "accountable positioning" that foregrounds my "situated knowledge" (Haraway 1988). I gaze homeward in *relation to* my home(s) in the diaspora, Puerto Rico, in between these two places, and in the academy, as well as quite literally looking at/into the homeland of the people with whom I work. Science and environmental theorist Donna Haraway said, "Vision is always a question of the power to see—and perhaps of the violence implicit in our visualizing practices. With whose blood were my eyes crafted?" (1988, 192). This provocative statement is my guiding force as I delve deeper into an examination of how and what *we are even able to see* in the world. About the West's elevation of the "ocular function," Saidiya Hartman wrote, "Sight is the sense elevated above all others in apprehending the world. Not being able to see clearly is tantamount to ignorance" (2008, 174–75). I tackle questions of memory, vision, visualizing practices, and their narrative constructions using multiple lenses. I apply an autoethnographic lens because this work is the result of my enduring interest in understanding the greater factors that shaped my family's—particularly my kinswomen's—life experiences.

My early childhood memories are marked by life in a sugar-producing town in Puerto Rico's southern Caribbean coast. I am the great-granddaughter and granddaughter of individuals who worked the cane and whose life rhythms were closely tied to sugarcane seasons. For my ancestors brought in shackles from Africa, mercantile capitalism was a disaster. The lives of my Afro–Puerto Rican mother and her siblings were marked by displacements and dispossession. My mother and her siblings were orphaned as young children. My grandmother, their mother, died of tuberculosis and was buried in a pauper's grave. Racism in Puerto Rico, poverty, and deprivation led each of them to eventually migrate from the island. My uncle Juan was the first to leave, in the early 1960s, never to return. My aunt Teresa migrated in the late '60s. Then, in the late 1970s, my mother decided to try her luck.

Memories of my childhood on the island are marked by my family's poverty. Sometimes we did not have food to eat or money to buy food. Sometimes we did not have a place to live. We spent the decade between the late 1970s and late 1980s caught up in the *vaivén* (revolving door), moving between our hometown of Arroyo, the San Juan metropolitan area, and *el barrio* in New York City, over and over again. This migratory circuit is not an unfamiliar one to the archipelago's poor, who often follow the ebbs and flows of the job market. Because my mother has a sixth-grade education, her job prospects have been limited to janitorial work, childcare, and cooking, jobs she performed, often simultaneously, throughout her life. To make ends meet, at seventy-six years old my mother still sells food and sometimes works as a nanny for brief periods.

Dispossession follows the dispossessed. From where I stand, with eyes crafted from the blood of my courageous ancestors, I attest that capitalism has been a great source of suffering for us nonwhite Others (Afro-descendants and/or Indigenous people). In Cedric Robinson's "racial capitalism," racism is a core structure in the logic of capitalism (1983). Thinking through racial capitalism leads us to question whether it is possible to imagine the history of the Americas or the history of capitalism without enslavement. Doesn't nearly every aspect of political, social, and cultural life in the Americas reflect the crippling inhumanitarian features of capitalism and the legacies they leave behind? Sylvia Wynter asserts that in the current era's coloniality of power, the Caribbean has been (mis)understood as an "archipelago of poverty" (2003). This misunderstanding resonates throughout my work as the motivation to restore the humanity of those who forge good lives and even thrive on the margins of the current neoliberal, capitalist logic.

Thus, the "complicated familiarity" with my home/field sites stems from my liminal subject positions and multiplex subjectivities making relationalities and expectations across social fields a multidimensional undertaking. For me, doing homework in Puerto Rico and in the diaspora entails a series of negotiations beyond my control. This, of course, is not a unique experience. Doing fieldwork entails negotiation and serendipity. But markers such as race, gender, age, family lineage and connections, and institutional affiliation confer a person's social capital and therefore grant or limit access to certain social fields and segments of the ethnographic population. These markers even influence the outcome and subsequent visibility of one's anthropological work.

Because I "live between worlds" and "belong neither here nor there," home for me is not a location from which to draw a neatly packaged identity nor a place I can easily locate on a map. When I am asked the proverbial question "Where are you from?" no doubt triggered stateside by my distinctive "Latinx accent," I most often acquiesce to the asker's curiosity by offering a generic "Puerto Rico." Rarely do I bother explaining that I have not lived continuously in Puerto Rico for extended periods of time since I was child, well over thirty years ago. And that even as a child, my mother and I shuttled regularly between Arroyo, San Juan, New York City, and, later, Hartford, Connecticut (Lloréns 2006). I do not bother to explain that while living in Puerto Rico and later stateside, we moved so many times across state lines and neighborhoods that I lost count. That my family's most comfortable dwelling place might be in the *vaivén*, the comings and goings, that have characterized the lives of Puerto Ricans—especially the lives of archipelago-born, working, and dispossessed-poor-turned-diasporic Puerto Ricans—since the early decades of the twentieth century (Duany 2002).

In Puerto Rico, when people realize that my Spanish is a bit rusty at times, or that I often insert the English word "so" to mean *entonces* (therefore) in between my sentences, I am often "unmasked" as being from *allá fuera* (out there), a local reference to those who live in the continental US. Anthropologist Gina Pérez defined and explained the culturally contextual uses of the label "*los de afuera*," the outsiders, as "usually employed pejoratively, connoting a culturally distinct group whose values, behaviors, language, and dress directly challenge dominant understandings of 'authentic' Puerto Rican culture" (2004, 111). Those of us who live "between worlds" also live with the repeated reminder that we don't quite belong or fit in the mainstream of either the continental US or Puerto Rico. Yet, the margins of society, where the dispossessed poor dwell, are populated by massive numbers of individuals who have never been allowed in or who have been permanently expelled there. Because home is completely out of reach or simply does not exist, home as a location of belonging is for many an embodied, relational, or spiritual experience. In her reading of Cristina García and Loida Maritza Peréz's New York–produced literary work, Vanessa Valdés wrote that these authors, originally from Cuba and the Dominican Republic respectively, reconfigure a notion of home through their engagement with African diasporic spirituality and religion: "The authors employ the religion as a metaphor for liberation: they come to understand that they carry their homes within themselves" (Valdés 2014, 59–60). Home and community, then, are not external but are rather intimately inhabited and acted upon.

In my case, negotiating this perpetual "unbelonging" has in many ways opened up a larger world and has taught me to feel at home in my body. But my home-body is also a social body; that is, like all social bodies, it is imbricated within an already circulating set of prescriptions and social scripts both within and beyond my control. For instance, during fieldwork I met a friend of a friend in San Juan, the city, whose family also hailed from the southeast, the rural hinterland. Upon meeting me he said, "Oh yes, you definitely are from the southeast," and, as if not talking to me, went on: "Look at her skin color and hair; models like these aren't made anywhere else in Puerto Rico." As I appraised him, his skin color and hair texture almost identical to mine, I replied, "You look like you could be my cousin." This friendly exchange took place far away from home and confirmed that we both belonged somewhere else, not San Juan, and that in the place where we belonged there was a recognizable "type." Another time, I met a young man in Arroyo who asked me what I did for work. I told him I was an anthropologist conducting fieldwork about environmental injustice. He answered, "I am always surprised when outsiders take interest in our town." I explained that I was not quite an outsider, that my family was from "here," that I was born and spent part of my childhood "here." He said, "Yes, but you left a long time ago." For this man, who was born, raised, and still living in Arroyo, my diasporic position marked me as an "outsider."

PUERTO RICO'S SOUTHEAST AS A BLACK EXPLOITATION REGION

First, the racialized history of Puerto Rico's southeast is intimately connected to its sugar-producing past. This legacy plays an outsize role in the landscape, the memories, and the lives of its inhabitants today. Second, after the abolition of enslavement, the limited market in which men, women, and children in this region could sell their labor has had lasting pernicious environmental and social effects. Third, the geographic distance between the San Juan metropolis, as the center of government and power, and the southeast, as a Black exploitation region, cast the southeast historically as an out-of-the way hinterland in which to situate polluting and contaminating industries.

In Puerto Rico, enslaved African men, women, and children were the first sugarcane workers. By the late nineteenth century, sugarcane workers were mainly coastal residents, descendants of enslaved and free Blacks, and poor peasants who came from other parts of the island to work in the fields and in the mills. Writing about the southeast in 1938, historian Rafael Picó explained that "everything from Ponce to Patillas is connected with sugar" (Figueroa 2005, 94). Today, sugarcane stalks still grow wild in the fields, attesting to a long-gone past alongside the ruins of the sugar mills (Lloréns 2018b). At the center of this region's "landscape of memory" are the sugarcane fields, the sugar mills, and the Caribbean Sea (Schama 1995).

The transformation in the late nineteenth century from enslaved to wage labor also meant women and girls left the cane fields and the sugar industry proper (the mills). The all-encompassing world of the sugarcane became reimagined as an exclusively masculine labor and social site. This meant that poor and working-class women were largely left out of the formal labor market. In Puerto Rico, agricultural work has been imagined generally as men's work. Despite a vast literature on the world of the sugarcane industry in Puerto Rico, the Caribbean, and the Americas, there is hardly any literature illuminating its gendered and its particularly masculine ethos (Mintz 1974; Ramírez 1999; Whalen 2001; Figueroa 2005; Findlay 2014). Writing about the Salinas labor force at the beginning of the twentieth century, historian Carmen Whalen explained, "Employing primarily men, the sugar industry shaped women's options. Very few women worked in agriculture, and because of the predominance of sugar processing, few worked in manufacturing. Those who did, worked in the home—needlework and other apparel. Instead, with only 13 percent of women in the labor force, half worked in the nonprofessional services, where the overwhelming majority (96 percent) were domestics" (2001, 110).

The San Juan metropolitan government has historically adopted a laissez-faire approach to "the island," the term Sanjuaneros use for the rest of Puerto Rico. This approach prevails even when San Juan is less than two hours away by car from the southern coastal plain. In Puerto Rico, local town politics are often complex and, at times, vicious. There are multiple layers to the story of San Juan's ruling government and elites' uneven interests and involvement in and with the hinterland. Metropolitan interest has largely depended on the historical value of a place or region (e.g., Spanish colonial architecture, sites of historical importance), its natural resources and industries, and any natural beauty that might be of interest as an enclave for leisure or tourism (Valdés Pizzini 2006). Towns that rouse metropolitan interest have usually been led by charismatic mayors who are both respected politically and well liked by constituents, typically down-to-earth, strong-willed populist patriarch types (two deceased mayors, Ponce's Rafael Cordero Santiago, affectionately known as "Churumba," and Caguas's William "Willie" Miranda Marín come to mind).

A town's ecosystem and its natural resources also play a part. Jobos Bay neighborhoods comprise mainly wetlands and mangrove forests (García-Quijano 2006). In Puerto Rico, the Caribbean, and the Americas, descendants of enslaved Africans have historically inhabited what Brazilian sociologist Antonio Carlos Diegues calls "mangrove civilizations" (Diegues 1995; Glaser 2003; García-Quijano et al. 2015). Mangrove ecosystems still make up a *racialized geography* (Cordero Giusti 1996; Lloréns 2008, 2014). During enslavement, mangroves served as a refuge for runaways and free Blacks, who built makeshift communities without much interference from the state. Mangrove habitats have traditionally been undesired as places to live. They are swamplike, they flood easily, and they have dense vegetation and mosquitoes. The soil is fickle for the cultivation of agricultural crops. Their inhabitants have been associated with Blackness, backwardness, primitivism, criminality, contraband, and poverty. Like the perceptions about the mangrove ecosystem, its inhabitants are imagined as mysterious and suspect.

Extractive and contaminating industries were established in this region over a century ago. After Spanish conquest, the fertile soils and easy access to a calm Caribbean Sea in the southeast proved desirable for the development of protoindustrial sugarcane plantations. At first, enslaved Africans toiled in these plantations and populated what would, with the passing of time, become a predominantly Black cultural zone (Findlay 1999; Figueroa 2005; Lloréns 2005). Though enslavement on the island was officially abolished in 1873, plantation agriculture, with its staggering racial and wealth inequalities, continued there well into the second half of the twentieth century, until the Aguirre Sugar Mill closed its doors in 1990. Sugar mills were a source of contamination, too. Wood was burned to boil the sugarcane, and in many cases the charcoal used was made from local mangroves. Later on, as the mills modernized, there were oil spills of various sizes. Particularly important for the local environment were the molasses spills that caused massive fish and shellfish mortality in the bays (García-Quijano 2006).

In this context, "fugitivity," the act of running away from oppressive conditions—either physically or linguistically, by using strategic or evasive language—points to the historical and socioracial realities of Black life in Puerto Rico's southeast (Lloréns 2005). In the centuries after Spanish conquest, Puerto Rico's southeast comprised a Black cultural zone characterized by intense heat and desert-arid conditions to the west, dense forests and steep mountainside to the north, and oceanside ravines to the east. The region's "uninhabitable" wetlands, mangroves, and steep, dense rural mountainsides, out-of-the-way places where the European settlers did not want to live, became Black communities where residents lived, unencumbered by whites (Lloréns 2005). These undesirable "Black places" became home to fugitive Blacks running away from the harsh constraints of plantation life. But they ran even closer to "natural" or "wild" spaces and places because they found a sense of freedom in the density of the steep mountainside, in the expansive view of the sea from the shore, or when the mangrove lagoon, bordered by a tangle of trees, opened up to a blue sky. These "out-of-the-way" places protected residents, left to fend for themselves, from the relentless force of Puerto Rico's brand of anti-Black racism (Lloréns 2018a). This geographic and spatial segregation nurtured the creation and maintenance of Black Puerto Rican cultural traditions, ways of life, and local ecological knowledge (Lloréns 2005, 2018a).

The archipelago's mid-twentieth-century modernization project sited many of the large, heavy, contaminating industrial projects in these "wild" places far away from San Juan, in the island's southern "hinterland." The Commonwealth Oil Refinery Company (CORCO) in Guayanilla began operations in 1956, the Chevron Phillips Chemical Puerto Rico Core opened in Guayama in 1967, and in 1971 the Shell Yabucao Oil Refinery opened its doors. The landscape and history of southeast Puerto Rico make it a "sacrifice zone," and knowing this helps us understand the relationship between the community and the environment (Lerner 2010; Lloréns 2016). In addition to the three, now-closed, refineries, continued threats to the environment and to the people who live in Jobos Bay come from the island's two largest power plants in the Aguirre Power Complex, built in the region in the 1970s. They serve the growing electricity needs of newer factories established in the region and supply 30 percent of the energy consumed on the island today (Lloréns 2016). These colossal plants are located in the town of Aguirre, the same community that houses the ruins of the defunct Aguirre Sugar Mill. The privately owned Applied Energy Systems, which operates in Guayama, what has been the island's only coal-burning power plant since 2002, is also located on the Jobos Bay, Puerto Rico's second most significant estuary and a National Oceanic and Atmospheric Administration (NOAA) reserve. As a result, residents of this socioeconomically disadvantaged region endure disproportionate environmental harm compared to other regions of the island.

THE HOME-WORK VERSUS FIELD-WORK ARCHETYPE

When I was thinking about archetypal locations of laborers during enslavement, Malcolm X's distinction between home-work versus field-work embodied in the "house negro" and "field negro" came to mind.[6] For X, the acculturated "house negro" behaved as his master's tool because he was too close to the hearth to have the distance needed to develop a critical analysis of his own oppression. The "house negro" was under the spell of hegemonic white supremacy, often exhibiting class aspirations that mirrored those of his master. These behaviors distanced him even more from the ethos and aspirations of his rebellious field-working kinfolk. The opposite of this worker, the "field negro" represented the masses, the majority of the laboring enslaved. This latter group hoped for the master's demise and for the end of the dehumanizing institution. X characterized himself as "field negro" because in the fields, among the field-workers, there was a modicum of freedom, where he believed the seeds of rebellion were sowed. Perhaps referring to the open skies above, the closeness to the earth, the fresh air and the wide, open spaces, Fred Moten said, "There's something in the field; that even in deprivation, there's an opening" (Harney and Moten 2013, 141).

While the field is a place that cannot be totally controlled, the master's house is a locus of total control over the bodies of the enslaved. But Malcolm X's characterization of the "house negro" embodied in Uncle Tom does not account for the female domestic laborer. This is largely because while Uncle Tom was expected to fade into the background, he did not disappear from view, and in fact was hypervisible. But Patricia Hill Collins has noted the female domestic worker was only visible in the kitchen and was expected to be invisible in all other areas of the house (2000, 57). Thus, another expectation: Black women make themselves visible only when needed for laboring. Here laboring refers to the day-to-day work expected of Black women, and to the labor that goes unseen, work that is in effect invisible, such as sex work, childbirth, child rearing, and sustaining family life—both the master's and her own. Thus, home-work also evokes enslaved women's work toiling in the "big house" and later, after emancipation, work as nannies, cooks, maids, and companions to elders, jobs such as the ones held by my mother and other women in my extended family. The duties performed in the private sphere of the home have been historically racialized and entail different yet still devalued spaces, housewife for white women, worker for Black women. As Collins remarked, "The 'iron pots and kettles' symbolizing Black women's long-standing ghettoization in service occupations represents the economic dimensions of oppression" (2000, 4). For Malcolm X, the white master's home represents a dangerous source of acculturation that dulls the spirit of rebellion and the desire to flee or rise up against the dehumanizing institution.

Yet it is important to underscore that during enslavement there was a porous border between field-work and home-work. In fact, the culture and materials that flowed in both directions, from the fields and homes of the enslaved to the master's house and vice versa, flowed mainly through enslaved women. It was the enslaved women who cooked in the main house, who brought her recipes in, but who also brought scraps and left-overs home. She quilted bedding and sewed clothing for her own family using leftover or gifted fabrics from the master's house. She observed white cultural norms of femininity that contributed to her understanding of her-self in relation to her community, as well as her oppressor's community. Examples of exchange, refusal, and the rearticulation of gendered cultural practices, norms, and expectations are bountiful. Bonnie Thornton Dill explains, "The intensification of reproductive labor made networks of kin and fictive kin important instruments in carrying out the reproductive tasks of the slave community" (1994, 8). It is no surprise that Afro-descended families in the Americas, in order to survive a system designed to work them to the bone and then dispose of them, developed "extensive systems of kinship ties and obligations" to help lighten the load (Thornton Dill 1994, 28).

bell hooks, deeply aware of the particularly heavy burdens Black women endured in service to white folks in a "patriarchal white supremacist soci-ety," thought of the Black home as a balm against white supremacy. She posited the "homeplace" for Black people as a "site of resistance," a place of safety away from the glare, management, and aggression of whites that historically served as a place of refuge and solidarity (1990, 42, 47). hooks was careful to denaturalize the sexist idea that a woman's place is in the home. She elevated the value of the homeplace without romanticizing or discounting its contradictions: "In our young minds, houses belonged to women, were their special domain, not as property, but as places where all that truly mattered in life took place—the warmth and comfort of shelter, the feeding of our bodies, the nurturing of our souls. There we learned dignity, integrity of being; there we learned to have faith. The folks who made this life possible, who were our primary guides and teachers, were black women" (hooks 1990, 41–42).

Applying this to my own family and life, it is noteworthy that for reasons unknown to us, my maternal grandmother seems to have been denied a homeplace throughout her life. This lack of homeplace is central to why my mother was separated from her mother, as discussed in the previous chapter, and it looms large in my mother's memories of her early childhood. My mother has never owned a home of her own. Actually, aside from experiencing chronic joblessness, another reason for my mother's decision to migrate stateside was that she lacked a place to live. The daughter of a dispossessed, poor, single mother who grew up with a fractured family life, my mother inherited neither land nor a house on the island. For low-income people, owning property and having a place to live is sometimes a safeguard against displacement. In the diaspora, my mother has rented subsidized housing using her Section 8 voucher, but her small apartments have always been nurturing, open-door safe spaces for her children, family, and friends. During the prime of her life, my mother's home was the center of extended family life. It was the place of birthdays, Christmas parties, births and baptisms, graduations, and all manner of celebrations. She cooked large meals and blasted music, and everyone ate, danced, drank, and spent time together. New arrivals from the island or other states could count on staying at her apartment until they got on their feet. My siblings could land there with their families during transitional moments such as a divorce or a move. I could not have made it through college and graduate school without the ability to save on rent and food by living with my mother. Though my mother often came home from her kitchen jobs exhausted and worried about making ends meet, she still found the strength to rejoice, to celebrate our family's accomplishments, to teach us to value our culture and practice it with pride, and to offer us a place where we unquestioningly belonged.

Silvia Federici has aptly critiqued the pervasive capitalist idea that housework does not count as work because it has been constituted as a natural, internal impulse of the "female physique and personality." She argued that the transformation of "housework into an act of love" has in turn categorized it as undeserving of wages (2012, 16). Furthermore, by

not admitting that housework is in fact a job, capitalism perpetrates a
"pervasive manipulation" and "the subtlest violence against any section of
the working class" (2012, 16). In regard to my mother's life, it is fair to say
that she feels prosperous even when her income is considered that of an
extremely poor person. But during her prime working years, one of her
survival strategies was providing a nurturing home for her children and
extended family clan. At that time, she also took care of her grandchildren
for free so that her children could work full-time jobs. She often gave
family members, friends, and relatives a place to live, feeding them and
celebrating life in the process.

This "helping" disposition is a strategy that circumvents the money-
centered capitalist economy with the logic of solidarity and mutual aid, in
which Black women, such as my mother, learned to use the limited
resources and tools at their disposal to build social capital and goodwill to
ensure prosperity, not in the form of capital accumulation, but in the form
of the exchange of time, goods, and services. This does not mean that
women like my mother do not suffer from the kinds of deprivation and
violence that the poor are forced to suffer in highly economically stratified
and unequal societies such as the United States. Rather, it means that she
operates by a different value system in which the accumulation of wealth is
not the end goal. Instead, the goal is accumulation of relationships and
social ties. The strategies and mechanisms passed down to her intergenerationally softened the blow of living as a dispossessed poor person in a
capitalist society.

Applying the home-work versus field-work analogy to my own anthropological work, as a "native" ethnographer studying "my" culture from the
"inside," my homeplace, home-work, and fieldwork are porous and border-
less as I move, at times uneasily, between locations. I will indulge in an
imaginative exercise to explain what I mean: Imagine the master's house,
the place where I engage in home-work, as the university and academic
world of anthropological theory and methods. Now imagine my homeplace as the metaphorical enslaved shack in which my maternal ancestors
dwelled and as the emotional location of my kinswomen's homes. I travel
between my homeplace and my home-work and I am conversant in both
worlds. My homeplace is a safe place, but is misunderstood and devalued
by the dominant classes, including the intelligentsia, which often labels it
as a "social problem." In anthropological home-work I experience unease,
and my belonging is often questioned because "real anthropologists" do
not look like me and they do fieldwork far away from their own homes, in

foreign, distant places. My chosen fieldwork aims to bring me closer to my homeplace, as I engage in acts of epistemological refusal to follow pre-scribed positivist forms of "reporting my data." Instead, I center my family and the women who would otherwise go missing from history, like my maternal grandmother did. In this work, then, I engage in the rebellious act of herstoricizing and visibilizing my kinswomen—both my family and the women from southeast Puerto Rico, the region that is my ancestral home in this "new world" to which we were forcefully brought to toil in long-gone plantations, then left to fend for ourselves in the face of the rav-ages wrought by racial capitalism.

ON BLACK PUERTO RICAN UNBELONGING

> "Where are you from?" The lady stood behind me in line to buy mangrove oysters in Cabo Rojo. She asked us this in English. At first, I looked around wondering, if she was talking to someone else, then I realized she was talking to my husband and me. She saw that we were confused, smiled at us, and clarified her question. "Like, what island are you from?" We answered in Spanish. "Oh, we are from *this island*, we are from Arroyo, a few towns to the east from here." The lady said, "Oh, you look like you are from somewhere else in the Caribbean, like Jamaica or Antigua. . . . It must be your braids; you don't often see Puerto Ricans wearing braids."

Karla and Roberto, an Afro–Puerto Rican couple in their forties, laughed politely at the lady's assertion that they must be from elsewhere, not from Puerto Rico. They are used to being asked this question, particularly when they travel away from Puerto Rico's east coast. Roberto said, "In San Juan everyone thinks I am Dominican. It doesn't bother me that people think this. But I am not. I am Puerto Rican. This is where my family is from, where I grew, and where I live." He explained that when he tells people that he is Puerto Rican, some people go as far as to say, "'No, you are not. You know, you don't have to hide that you are Dominican.' . . . This is when people go too far, and I get angry." When I asked Karla and Roberto why people believe they are not Puerto Rican, they both laughed. "Because we are Black. White Puerto Ricans act like there are no Black Puerto Ricans here, or that all Blacks are from, and live, in the town of Loíza." Given that Black Puerto Ricans have historically endured national invisibility, era-sure, and marginalization in the genealogical manufacture of the Puerto

Rican family's lineage, it is not surprising that they are perceived as out-siders to the archipelago. Regarding the contemporary consequences of national origin stories, Dionne Brand has argued that "country, nation, these concepts are of course deeply indebted to origins, family, home. Nation-states are configurations of origins as exclusionary power structures which have legitimacy based solely on conquest and acquisition" (2001, 64).

Caren, a young woman in her early twenties, told me, "Whenever my dad goes to stores in Old San Juan or to restaurants in El Condado, people speak to him in English. He then answers in Spanish, and often the sales-people respond in English again, like they don't realize that he is even speaking Spanish." I asked Caren why they don't hear his Spanish. She said, "Because they only see his dark complexion, and they assume he is not Puerto Rican, and it takes them a while to realize that he is. I am lighter skinned than my dad, so it is only when I wear my hair in braids or in a natural Afro that people think that I am not Puerto Rican. But if your skin color is chocolate brown complexion or darker, people here automatically assume you are not from here."

Sandra explained:

> When I went to the continental US to attend college, at first everyone
> thought I was African American, until I spoke. Then they heard my
> Spanish accent and would at first guess that I was Dominican, Panama-
> nian, and sometimes Colombian. Or they would flat-out ask, "Where are
> you from?" I'd tell them that I am from Puerto Rico, and they would be
> stunned because most people who asked me said they did not realize that
> Puerto Ricans could be as Black as me . . . I guess. . . . All my life, outside
> of my community in Maunabo, I get the same question, and it feels like in
> people's mind Black people can only be from certain places.

I asked Sandra where people assumed Black people in the Americas were from, and she answered, "Well, it depends where you are. But the assumption is that if you are Black, you are from the continental US, Haiti, the Dominican Republic, Panama, Colombia, Brazil, and the islands in the English Caribbean, like Jamaica and Barbados. . . . If you are in Puerto Rico, people assume you are from Loíza, maybe Ponce or Guayama . . . but that's about it."

For Black Puerto Ricans, the complexities of home and motherland manifest when these individuals are deemed as *unlocatable*. The transat-lantic slave trade—in which millions of Africans were kidnapped and trafficked to the Americas to build and to work in the extractive industries of the so-called new world—upended and reconfigured notions of home for the captives. As Fred Moten eloquently put it, they and their descendants live as if they "are not quite here" in this time and place; they are forced to become "cosmic hobos."[7] This assertion coincides with Christina Sharpe's poignant observation: "We are Black peoples in the wake with no state or nation to protect us, with no citizenship bound to be respected" (2016, 22). Thus, the Black Puerto Ricans I interviewed grappled with the frequent question about their provenance: "Where are you from?"

For Afro-descendant peoples in the Americas, "motherland" refers to Africa (Nasta 1992; Cliff, Dabydeen, and Adisa 1998; Alexander 2001; Adams 2006; Hartman 2008; among others). And this motherland represents an irrecoverable loss (Adams 2006; Hartman 2008). The Caribbean's "earliest mother" is the Amerindian, but with the decimation of the island's Indigenous inhabitants, this "mother/land, too, was lost" (Adams 2006, 4). In the Puerto Rican archipelago, the resurgence of individuals who claim a Taíno cultural identity and ancestry is often met with skepticism, and sometimes with ridicule or with the assertion that many who claim such an "impossible identity" are mixed-race Blacks who are trying to flee their Blackness (Brusi and Godreau 2007; Martínez-San Miguel 2011; Feliciano Santos 2011). For Black Puerto Ricans, however, the Puerto Rican nation-building project has blurred Africa as motherland and has marked them as perpetual outsiders to the "Spanish" Puerto Rican motherland. If they question the racism embedded in "Puertoricanness," Black Puerto Ricans are branded traitors, betrayers of the pervasive myth about the archipelago's racial democracy. Or they are "Americanized" outsiders who lack proper etiquette on how to practice and talk about race (Vargas Ramos 2005; Rodríguez-Silva 2012; Godreau 2008, 2015; Lloréns 2008, 2018a; 2018d; among others).

In Puerto Rico, the long history of biases based on race that excluded Black Puerto Ricans from the "imagined nation" is well documented (Cruz 1974; González 1980; Rodríguez-Silva 2012; Dinzey Flores 2013; Vargas Ramos 2005, 2014; Godreau 2008, 2015; Lloréns 2008, 2014; LeBrón 2019a, among others). As Black Puerto Rican scholar Yarma Velazquez Vargas noted, "I come from a territory influenced by colonial conquests, where the negotiations and conceptions of knowledge, beauty, and power have been historically mediated through Western aesthetics" (2008, 953). Therefore, for Black Puerto Ricans, the myth about a harmonious and unified "Puertoricanness" is a source of oppression. Where is the motherland of

Black Puerto Ricans when their homeland has long been withheld? Dionne Brand's evocative reflection on the lives of Black people in the Americas, including her grandfather's and her own, resonates: "We were not from the place where we lived and we could not remember where we were from or who we were" (2001, 5). To this point, I add Fred Moten's succinct observation in *The Undercommons*, "Fuck a home in this world, if you think you have one" (2013, 140).

The modern condition, inaugurated by seafarers-turned-merchants and colonists, opened the way to voluntary and forced mass movement and displacement of people and goods across the globe. This movement continues unabated in our era. In *Post-Nationalism Prefigured*, anthropologist Charles V. Carnegie explains that "transnational modes of dwelling are not only a recent fad but have historical depth in a region such as the Caribbean" (2002, 65). Citing Orlando Patterson, he writes, "The Caribbean is one of the few cases in which migration has become 'a basic means of individual and societal survival'" (Carnegie 2002, 65; cf. Patterson 1978, 106). Indeed, similar to almost every region of the world today, the Caribbean's defining characteristic historically has been its multilayered assemblage of peoples, histories, cultures, and traditions, a palimpsest predicated on its insertion into the global political economy. The multiple and complex migrations to and within the region that led to the creation of the new societies' cultural and economic arrangements led anthropologists such as Sydney Mintz, Eric Wolf, and Michel-Rolph Trouillot to argue that the Caribbean region has been modern "since its early incorporation in various North Atlantic empires" (Trouillot 1995, 228). The region's significance in the establishment of early global economic markets as well as the multicultural societies that developed there exemplify Mintz's, Wolf's, and Trouillot's claims of a centuries-old modern Caribbean.

The Caribbean's earliest citizens were aware of worlds—Africa, Europe, Asia, North and South America—beyond their shores. As the generations passed on and multiplied, particularly for the Africans brought there against their will, the memories of previous lives in these worlds as well as the passage from the old into the new world receded into historical memory, but they did not disappear completely. In the American Black diaspora, the reconception and remembering of Africa as motherland has been a steady, if at times muted, feature of Black life. As Saidiya Hartman eloquently put it, "It is only when you are stranded in a hostile country that you need a romance of origins; it is only when you *lose your mother* that she becomes a myth; it is only when you fear the dislocation of the new that the old ways become precious, imperiled, and what your great-great-grandchildren will one day wistfully describe as African" (2008, 98; emphasis in original).

Arguably, the mid-twentieth-century postcolonial and decolonial turns invigorated and made public a strong desire by Blacks in the Americas to re-member and affirm their African provenance. The hemispheric movement in the Black Americas to recover Africa as motherland while claiming "new world" national and ancestral allegiances meant in some cases (the Garifuna, for instance) rightfully declaring their status as Indigenous Americans while upholding their African ancestry and cultural traditions. Unquestionably, the cultural and artistic material created by members of each society (language, music, art, dance, festivals, food) and the materials' symbolic content are laden with references to the African past in the present (Harris 1999; Velazquez Vargas 2008; Abadia-Rexach 2009; Mohammed 2010; Lloréns 2014; among others).

José Luis González asserted in his cultural historiography and analysis, "Puerto Rico: The Four Storeyed Country" (1980), that

> the first Puerto Ricans were in fact *black* Puerto Ricans. . . . What I *am* claiming is that it was the blacks, the people bound most closely to the territory which they inhabited (they were after all slaves), <u>who had the greatest difficulty in imagining any other place to live</u>. . . . *negros criollos* or creole blacks, the name given to blacks born on the island before it became customary to recognize them as *Puerto Ricans*. (1993, 10; emphasis in original, underline mine)

> These blacks and mulattos, historically speaking, constituted the cement of Puerto Rican nationality because they were the first to *feel* Puerto Rico as their true home and <u>because they had no roots</u> in or loyalty to Spain, Corsica . . . or indeed anywhere else. (1993, 39; emphasis in original, underline mine)

González's bold, protodecolonial assertion about the place of Black Puerto Ricans within the nation is still today a radical, unsurpassed proposition. With this claim, he confronts several taken-for-granted and hidden sociocultural characteristics in the creation of a modern, post–Spanish conquest Puerto Rico. First is the transition of the big island once known by its Indigenous Taíno name, Borikén, into a Spanish colony that included

Vieques, Culebra, and a number of tiny islands and atolls that compose the archipelago, and its renaming as Puerto Rico. The so-called disappearance of the archipelago's Taíno inhabitants, which, to be accurate, was extinction through decimation and genocide, refashioned the territory as a blank slate from which the Spanish colonizers could extract resources. The archipelago was poor in minerals but rich in fertile soil and amenable tropical weather. By the seventeenth, eighteenth, and nineteenth centuries it was primarily a producer of sugar, with small sectors dedicated to tobacco and coffee. The enslaved worked the land at first, and later it was a large, poor, peasant class largely made up of Blacks, mixed-race people, and poor Creoles who became known as *jíbaros*, the quintessential "people of the land" and the "peasant heart" of Puerto Rico (Dietz 1986; González 1980).

The claim González makes is twofold. On the one hand, because they were the first to till and cultivate the land and to harvest its fruits, Africans brought to toil in the archipelago—now reconfigured as "rootless," without the ability to return to Africa—constituted the first colonial "native" inhabitants of the refashioned territory. On the other hand, the European colonial settlers and their descendants claimed Spain as their motherland and, indeed, claimed it as Puerto Rico's motherland. Therefore, they could name a place of provenance and imagine a place to return to in Europe. I differ from González only in his assertion that the Africans transported to Puerto Rico could not imagine an African motherland, particularly in the early decades after their arrival. I believe that they could not imagine *a viable way to make the journey back to Africa* but likely could imagine the motherland itself. For González, the stolen Africans brought to Puerto Rico were "rootless," that is, they were unbound to a territory of provenance. He proposes their reconstitution as the first postconquest "outsiders" to have no choice but to plant their roots in the colony, now their motherland. Their "rootlessness" was not chosen but forced and a source of pain and trauma for those Africans who would, with the passing of time, become Black Puerto Ricans.

The archipelago's colonial settler class that populated modern Puerto Rico mostly from Spain and some from Corsica have, since its inception and in no uncertain terms, claimed Europe as their motherland. This was the case even after Spain ceded the archipelago to the United States in 1898. The refusal to accept the United States as the archipelago's new colonial master is most apparent in their insistence on the Spanish language as the archipelago's authentic "mother tongue." Certainly, the existing colonial relationship to the United States, which casts Puerto Ricans as minoritized colonial subjects, is an ongoing source of political and economic upheaval for the Puerto Rican archipelago. Its fate rests in the hands of Washington-based politicians who seem to lack understanding of the island's history and culture. Yet it must be said that modern Puerto Rico, like the rest of the Americas, is a colonial settler society. In this regard, the hierarchies based on race and the attendant consequences of racism are alive and well in the archipelago.

The majority of the Black Puerto Ricans I have interviewed in the last two decades, both in Puerto Rico and in the diaspora, say they are proud to be Puerto Rican. In fact, time and again, my interviewees comment that calling Puerto Rico their home makes them different from others in the African diaspora. Antonia, for instance, a Black Puerto Rican woman in her sixties living in Puerto Rico, said, "I am proud to be Puerto Rican. I love my island, our food, our music. These are uniquely Puerto Rican creations and flavors, and I would not want to be from anywhere else or live anywhere else." Nora, a dark-skinned Black woman in her midthirties living on the island, said, "I am Puerto Rican first and foremost. This is where I am from, where my family is from. This is my nation, and I could not be prouder to be from here. I am Black, but I am not African American, or Jamaican, or Dominican. I am a Black Puerto Rican, and that is a unique culture in itself." Juana, a Black Puerto Rican who grew up and lives in Boston, said, "I am very proud of being a Puerto Rican, but I grew up around Black Americans and Jamaicans, and so I also know that even though my cultural heritage is unique, that here in the United States, when people look at me, I know they see just another Black person, and that is also fine with me because Black is beautiful." Janet, another Black Puerto Rican woman in her forties who was born in the Bronx but who grew up in New Haven, Connecticut, said, "I love being Puerto Rican. My family is proud of our culture. But to be honest, I can't imagine living there, and also, whenever we visit the island, we feel a lot of racism. . . . When I am in Puerto Rico . . . it is strange I guess . . . but I feel like I am more African American than I do when I am here in the States."

The significant voices of Black, Afro–Puerto Rican diasporic women, and women of Dominican descent who have lived in Puerto Rico but now reside in the United States have long been at the vanguard of calling out anti-Black racism as well as the common practice of making them feel as if their destiny is to forever "unbelong" in Puerto Rico, among Puerto Ricans and Latinxs. The noteworthy critiques of Black and Afro-Latina scholars and writers such as Angela Jorge, Marta Moreno Vega, Miriam Jiménez

Román, Tanya Katerí Hernández, Dahlma Llanos-Figueroa, Marta I. Cruz-Janzen, Maritza Quiñones, Zaire Dinzey Flores, Milagros Denis-Rosario, Alaí Reyes-Santos, Vanessa K. Valdés, Jaquira Díaz, and Yomaira C. Figueroa Vásquez, to name only a few, are significant for their radical uplifting of Black women's voices as well as for their sustained critique against Latinx anti-Blackness. Embodied and ancestral knowledge has offered these scholars a unique perspective on what it means to live and think as Black women in and across a multiplicity of political and territorial landscapes (Hernández 2021; Figueroa Vásquez 2020a; Dinzey Flores et al., 2019). Their voices and work, which tends to frame Puerto Rico, the Caribbean, and Latinxs as part of a larger node in global anti-Blackness, have paved the way for younger generations of Black Latinx scholars and writers to unapologetically claim their belonging in both the American territories their families call home as well as in the global African diaspora (Figueroa Vásquez 2020b).

REIMAGINING THE ANCESTRAL MOTHERLAND

Saidiya Hartman explains that even when the millions of Africans forced into the American diaspora faced the monumental task of building and creating new worlds, new homes in the midst of a profound dispossession, they still forged a narrow path, an opening to a new set of possibilities (2008, 97). Hartman writes, "For those bound to a hostile land by shackles, owners, and the threat of death, an imagined place might be better than no home at all, an imagined place might afford you a vision of freedom, an imagined place might provide an alternative to your defeat, an imagined place might save your life" (2008, 97; emphasis mine).

Remarkably, the winding path that European colonialism forced upon those born into this "new world" has led its descendants to imagine ever-novel ways to colonial liberation and freedom. For Puerto Ricans, the 1898 possession of the archipelago by the United States has been a source of trauma, and for many this unwelcomed recolonization is still an open and oozing wound. This is because by the end of the nineteenth century, the "old" worlds—Indigenous, African, and Spanish—that had coalesced to shape modern Puerto Rico had reconfigured the island as the daughter-land of the Spanish motherland. Understood as a political and economic invader, the United States has not been imagined, and for many Puerto Rican nationalists will never be imagined as Puerto Rico's motherland because, as mainstream nationalists argue, Puerto Rico remains culturally Spanish.

But another nationalist path tends to be practiced by Othered Puerto Ricans who reject Spain *and* the United States as motherlands, along with the archipelago's Catholic and patriarchal respectability politics. In this other rendition of Puerto Rican nationalism, its practitioners meld a political and cultural nationalism that affirms and centers the archipelago's Indigenous and African ancestry, cosmology, and spirituality. Its practitioners tend to be Blacks and mixed-race individuals, the dispossessed poor, diasporic Puerto Ricans, New Agey artists, environmentalists, decolonial intellectuals, as well as nonbinary and gender-nonconforming individuals (LGBTQI). For these diverse practitioners, the object of veneration is the motherland, the ancestral home comprising the very ground, the nature, and the ecology of the archipelagic territory itself. This holistic view includes the archipelago's bodies of salt- and freshwater, its plants, the sky and winds, and nonhuman animals. The psychic and embodied emancipation sought by the practitioners of this syncretic and mythical Puerto Rican "decolonial nationalism" aims to heal the "broken" and/or "fractured" bodies of its practitioners as well as the wounded body of the motherland, its waters, plants, animals, environment, and ecology. In this view, the island as ancestral motherland has endured a continued assault on her body that began in 1493. This assault originated when Spain usurped the island, then decimated the Indigenous population, trafficked and enslaved Africans, and established agricultural extractive industries. Later the United States appointed American governors, quelled the Puerto Rican nationalist movement, persecuted and incarcerated some of its leaders, installed military bases, and used the El Yunque rainforest and the islands of Culebra and Vieques as military weaponry testing and experimentation sites. It tested the birth control pill on Puerto Rican women and ran a mass sterilization campaign. It captured parts of the coast as tourist destinations, and it oversaw the ongoing contamination of the island's earth, water, and air by multinational corporations and the continued ejection of thousands of Puerto Ricans. In the twenty-first century, Washington's botched response in the aftermath of Hurricane María painfully brought to the fore its near-complete indifference.

A major impact of the US colonization of Puerto Rico has been the creation of a robust Puerto Rican diaspora in the continental United States (Flores 2009; Lloréns 2018a). As discussed previously, in Puerto Rico this diaspora has been cast negatively as Americanized, urban, Black, and poor, and its members denigrated as a degenerate kind of Puerto Rican (Rodriguez 1989; Whalen 2005; Flores 2009; and Thomas 2010; among others). In other words, the diasporic Puerto Rican is a transfigured, unoriginal version of a true island-born-and-bred, culturally adept Puerto Rican. Yet, in a decidedly postmodern twist of events, the Puerto Rican diaspora clings to its island roots with intensity. In part, this has to do with their minoritized ethnic positioning in the continental United States, where they are understood as perpetual outsiders. And it is partly because, as a "country made up of immigrants," it is the norm in the United States for individuals to identify using their ancestral provenance in offering mathematical explanations of ethnic identification, such as "I am a quarter Lakota and 75 percent English." In the context of the United States, even though Puerto Ricans, too, have a nuanced European, African, and Indigenous ancestry, they will for expediency's sake declare that they are just Puerto Rican.

Though Puerto Ricans travel back and forth between the continent and the archipelago with regularity, a practice known sociologically as the "revolving door migration" or the *vaivén* (the coming and going), through the years I have met individuals who decide to "rematriate" to Puerto Rico (Hernández Quirindongo 2019). Together, they make up a small but growing group of first- and second-generation US-born diasporic Puerto Ricans. These children and grandchildren of Puerto Rican parents or grandparents, who were born and raised stateside, decide as adults to permanently move to Puerto Rico, a place they consider their ancestral homeland. Christina Sharpe's queries about dreams of a return migration of African Americans to Africa are apropos: "What does it mean to return? Is return possible? Is it desired? And if it is, under what conditions and for whom?" (2016, 60).

To think through Sharpe's questions as they relate to Puerto Rico as motherland, I draw on the opus of Brooklyn-born, mixed-race Puerto Rican artist and writer Yasmín Hernández Quirindongo, whose noteworthy "Rematriating Boriquén" website documents through written reflections and visual art her ongoing rematriation and self-decolonizing journey. Hernández Quirindongo writes about her decision in 2014 to "return to the home of her ancestors." She learned from her father "the hidden history of Puerto Rico—stories of Indigenous warrior ancestors; legacies of West Africa; Pedro Albizu Campos, Lolita Lebrón and the Nationalist Party; *la masacre de Ponce* and the murder of two young independence supporters in *Cerro Maravilla*."[8] She explains that after years of visiting Puerto Rico to work on various projects, during a 2013 trip it became palpable to her that "parting with this land had become unbearably painful." A year after that epiphany, she moved to Puerto Rico with her family. She writes, "Coming home to Borikén taught me that in order to be of any service to this land, I first had to free myself . . . rebirthing myself renewed, liberated on the sacred land of my ancestors."[9] Inspired by Steven Newcomb's definition of rematriation as a process that seeks to "restore a living culture to its rightful place on Mother Earth," or "to restore a people to a spiritual way of life, in sacred relationship with their ancestral lands," Hernández Quirindongo invokes the Indigenous Atabey and the African goddesses Yemaya and Oshun as spiritual guiding mothers in her territory-bound self-actualization journey (Newcomb 1995; Hernández Quirindongo 2019).[10]

Rematriation, the word and the process, emerged from the decolonial thought of North American Indigenous women belonging to matrilineal societies (Mihesua 2000; Maracle 2006; Tuck 2011). For instance, for Haudenosaunee women, "rematriation" means "returning the Sacred to the Mother," and furthermore, for them Mother Earth and women are spiritually interrelated.[11] Eve Tuck remarks that in colonial settler societies, Indigenous rematriation is an inherently decolonial process encompassing "Indigenous land and life" (2011). As Tuck and Rubén A. Gaztambide-Fernández explain, "Rematriation can be described as . . . an ethical relationality, an 'ecological' understanding of human relationality that does not deny difference, seeks to understand mutual implication, puts Indigenous epistemologies at the forefront, and requires a more public form of memory" (2013, 84).

In the twenty-first century, Puerto Rico has faced an unrelenting economic recession, the 2016 imposition of a federally mandated fiscal board known locally as "la Junta," austerity measures, and incompetent local governance, as well as the environmental effects of the climate crisis. Together, these have contributed to the ejection of thousands more into the continental United States. This newer diaspora, like those of earlier eras, includes the dispossessed poor, but it has broadened to include members of the middle and upper classes, who, in earlier decades, would have found employment and a safety net on the island. In our present historical era, it is rare to find a Puerto Rican family untouched by stateside migration or one that does not include relatives in the diaspora. Apparently, it took an unnatural disaster the magnitude of the Category 5 Hurricane María to begin to thaw and reshape the prejudiced view of the diaspora by island-based Puerto Ricans. Upon realizing that the local and federal governments appeared woefully unprepared to assist the island, individuals, groups, and organizations in the diaspora sprang into action. The storm's aftermath showed that the island's most indispensable ally is its diaspora (Alicea and Toro-Morn 2018; Lloréns 2018c; Lloréns and Stanchich 2019).

Puerto Rico has been experiencing a number of notable sociopolitical shifts. Among these appears to be a historic demographic change in which the "Black and Afro voice" of Puerto Rico's island-based population is making itself heard. By this I mean that I have detected an emergent and possibly radical shift in the racial self-identification of Puerto Ricans, particularly among the youth, on the island. This is a population that has overwhelmingly identified as white and mixed race, but at the turn of the twenty-first century, an increasing number of this population appear to be shifting its racial self-identification to Afro-descendant and Black only. For instance, the 2000 census reported that only 8 percent of Puerto Rico's population self-identified as Black or African American. Ten years later, the 2010 census reported a four-point increase to 12.4 percent (Lloréns 2018a). This represents an increase from 302,933 to 461,498 individuals who identified as Black or African American only.[12] The net gain of 158,565 persons self-identifying as Black is remarkable given that in this same decade, Puerto Rico suffered a population decline of 82,821 persons (Lloréns 2018a). The 2020 census will be revealing. If this trend continues, Black Puerto Ricans might finally—five centuries after their arrival—find themselves centered as the rightful heirs of the Puerto Rican motherland.

As we near the close of the second decade of the twenty-first century, Puerto Rico is undergoing profound political and societal changes. Dubbed as the island's "political awakening," the multisectoral and multitudinous protests in July 2019 culminated in the ousting of the New Progressive Party's pro-statehood governor, Ricardo Roselló. These protests were spurred in part by the ongoing social justice work carried out over the last decade by university students, workers, feminist collectives, and LGBTQI organizations (Bonilla 2019; LeBrón 2019b; Morales 2019a, 2019b). These groups represent long-neglected segments of the population whose demands for gender and racial justice coalesced with broader popular concerns over austerity practices that led to massive cuts in pensions and social services, including the closing of hundreds of schools and hospitals and the dismantling of the public university, as well as police corruption and brutality (Brusi, Bonilla, and Godreau 2018; LeBrón 2019a). Demands for the auditing of the island's debt and for environmental justice have marked this as a watershed moment in the island's history. As a way to draw stateside attention to the events unfolding on the island, the diaspora organized parallel protests in over a dozen stateside cities, including New York, Boston, Chicago, Hartford, Los Angeles, and Orlando (Aratani 2019; Jaipuriar 2019). After the protests waned in late July 2019, public meetings known as *asamblea de pueblos* (town assemblies) emerged throughout Puerto Rico and in the Puerto Rican diaspora to democratically foster community discussions about Puerto Rico's political and economic future (Villarubia-Mendoza and Vélez-Vélez 2019).

Certainly, as a Puerto Rican cultural analyst, I can easily understand how the island's history has paved the way for the people to demand accountability from their government and demand that it work on the daunting but necessary tasks of imagining and building a functional, just society for all. It is a history in which generation after generation has suffered the profound traumas of colonization, dispossession, displacement, and careless and corrupt governance at the hands of both island and federal politicians. As Hurricane María made catastrophically apparent, it is time to find solutions to the more recent gripping reality of the current climate emergency. The youth of the island and of the diaspora, particularly the fearless young students, feminists, and LGBTQI individuals, some of whom are looking to/at the fierce global movements waged by Black diasporic, global Indigenous, and Palestinian anti-oppression fighters, dared to put their bodies on the front lines during the summer of 2019 in the archipelago and stateside streets to dream about and demand socially just societies where they can forge sustainable, meaningful, and safe futures for themselves wherever they choose to live. They deserve the opportunity to birth and nurture the kind of justice-minded future they imagine.

CHAPTER 3

LIFE-AFFIRMING PRACTICES

We don't wait for anyone, like the government or private entities, to
do what we have to do. We use what we have, or what community
members give us, and we try to be a completely self-sustaining group.

—LETICIA RAMOS

THE EMERGENT LITERATURE ABOUT ENVIRONMENTAL JUSTICE
struggles in Puerto Rico has for the most part neglected women's significant leadership and activism. This chapter centers on women who contribute
to social and environmental justice in Puerto Rico's southeast. Although
women are on the front line of environmental justice movements, they
remain marginally acknowledged in the scholarly literature as well as in
local environmental policy making. Intersections of gender, class, and race
coalesce to further marginalize the women themselves, their work, and the
communities they represent. In their scholarship about women's community work, community psychologists Mayra Muñoz Vázquez (2000) and
Roxanna Domenech Cruz (2015) assert that Puerto Rican women, and
mainly poor women, have historically played central organizing roles in
the archipelago's environmental struggles (Domenech Cruz 2015, 16).

Women who collaborate with the Initiative for the Eco-development of
the Jobos Bay, Inc. (in Spanish known as IDEBAJO) have created and sustained sites of resistance through community work.[1] I began conducting
ethnographic research mainly, though not exclusively, with women and
youths in estuarine Jobos Bay communities in Salinas, where I focused on
El Coquí, Aguirre, Las Mareas, and San Felipe. In Guayama, I focused
on the communities of Puerto de Jobos, Puente de Jobos, and Las Mareas.
Many, but not all, of the women I interviewed, spent time with, and
sometimes just had fleeting conversations with, between 2015 and 2019,
collaborated in some capacity with community-based social justice equity

initiatives and environmental grassroots organizations that were "mobilizing to protect their own communities" (Valdés Pizzini 2006, 45).

In the essay titled "The Greater Common Good," Arundhati Roy writes, "We have to support our small heroes. (Of these we have many. Many.) . . . Who knows, perhaps that's what the 21st century has in store for us. The dismantling of the Big . . . big dams, big ideologies, big contradictions, big countries, big wars, big heroes, big mistakes. Perhaps it will be the Century of the Small" (1999).[2] The women I interviewed in Salinas and Guayama were the kind of "small heroes" Roy describes in this passage. They were wives, grandmothers, married and single mothers, students, retirees, heads of household, unemployed and underemployed workers, community activists, environmental activists, respected elders, volunteers, fishers, gardeners, and foragers. The majority lived at or below the poverty line. All of them were Afro-descendants, and most were born and raised in the communities in which they lived. They ranged in age from eighteen to eighty-four, and the majority had completed high school or an equivalency diploma. A small fraction held associate or technical degrees, fewer had attended some college or had completed four-year college degrees, and one held a postgraduate professional degree.

Many, though not all, had migrated to northern US cities and had lived there intermittently throughout their lives. Some were born in US cities but decided to live in Puerto Rico. Glenis, for instance, a forty-three-year-old heavyset single mother of a seventeen-year-old son and a six-year-old daughter, lived in a frail-looking wooden, zinc-roofed house in Mosquito, a neighborhood adjacent to the mangrove.[3] She told me that she had returned to Puerto Rico a year ago from Springfield, Massachusetts. She came back to Mosquito because her son, Leny, was experiencing racism and bullying at his school in Springfield. The bullying worsened his learning disability. He was diagnosed with posttraumatic stress disorder, and the move was to help him recover from the schooling trauma.

Leny was doing much better in Puerto Rico. He felt safe there, and he could spend more time outdoors, crabbing and fishing and hanging out with family and friends. "The environment here in our neighborhood is better for him. He is a different person here. He is much happier and calmer. We will not move back to Springfield. We'll stay here even if we are poor," Glenis explained.

A respectful, tall, and lanky teen, Leny had recently become involved in youth activism through IDEBAJO initiatives, and I often saw him hanging out with other community teenagers at the El Coquí community center. He learned from volunteers in their summer courses about the basics of house construction, solar energy panel installation, and battery systems. That summer he was also part of IDEBAJO's house-building mutual aid brigade, which paid a small stipend of $25 per day. The brigade was composed of two teenagers and five men who ranged in age from seventeen to seventy-three. They were rebuilding a community volunteer's house, which had been destroyed by Hurricane María. That summer Leny and his mom, Glenis, were also active participants in the community collective of parents and their children that helped plan that summer's Convivencia Ambiental camp.

Marta, who was thirty-eight years old with three children, aged seven, ten, and fourteen, lived in a borrowed house with her husband, children, and two dogs while their roof was repaired. The zinc panels had been torn off by the storm, and their new roof would be made out of cement. She was unemployed when I talked to her but was volunteering to cook daily lunches for IDEBAJO's construction brigade. In the past, she had done seasonal work. Her last job involved processing seeds at Pioneer, one of several agrochemical and GMO multinationals located in the area, but these jobs were only temporary.

A few years earlier, along with several other community women, Marta fought and won against the first wave of school closures to hit the archipelago. Her eldest son had graduated to middle school, but her two youngest attended the community school in Las Mareas, walking distance from their house. It was the only bilingual school (English and Spanish) in all of Salinas. Las Mareas neighborhood was located deep in a Salinas mangrove forest and had a reputation for being a node in a vast network of drug-trafficking points along Puerto Rico's coast. "We are a poor community here," said Marta, "and we have a bad reputation because people say this is a dangerous community, and that's not true. For instance, our elementary school is among the best around here, and we live peacefully here. We watch out for each other, and we protect our community."

In this ethnographic chapter, I discuss the central role of local women in Puerto Rico's southeast social and environmental justice movements. I document how they use the tools at their disposal to resist subjugation and build meaningful and sustainable lives. The women I introduce work on projects with community organizations such as the Coquí Community Center, Diálogo Ambiental, and Coquí Solar, all which form a part of IDE-BAJO. Others, though, work independently, often with neighbors who share their plight. Even the women who work as part of localized neighborhood efforts consult with IDEBAJO's community organizers, volunteers, and attorney for advice and help, or they to ask them to act on their own or their community's behalf when interacting with representatives of the government or local multinational corporations.

BRIEF HISTORICAL BACKDROP OF AGUIRRE: PUERTO RICO'S SEGREGATED COMPANY TOWN AS EXEMPLAR OF A PLANTATION GEOGRAPHY AND CAPITALIST RUINATION IN THE JOBOS BAY

In 1899, the Central Aguirre neighborhood became an American company town after Henry Ford and other investors bought the sugar mill there. The new owners modernized the mill and built a town suited for its American employees. To this end, they built houses, a hospital, a hotel, churches, a theater, social clubs, schools, roads, stores, and a golf club. The town was racially segregated according to the US mainland's social conventions. The American managerial class lived in large, old-style hacienda houses away from the mill building and the bay, while some of the workers lived adjacent to the mill and to the bay in small houses near the center of town. The mill town is located in a mangrove, and mangrove inhabitants flank it on all sides. A great number of workers, however, lived outside the neighborhood limits altogether, across the street from the entrance to the "company town." Workers traveled from nearby neighborhoods such as El Coquí and San Felipe and towns such as Guayama and Arroyo to work at the mighty Aguirre sugar mill in Salinas.

The mid-twentieth century was a period of renewed hope in Puerto Rico as a result of the election of Luis Muñoz Marín, the island's first native-born governor. But this period also witnessed the steady decline of sugar production on the island. Regarding the Aguirre Sugar Corporation, Carmen Whalen explains that "it remained profitable until 1967, when it changed ownership. Between 1967 and 1970 the company lost $14 million, losing $6 million in 1969 alone. In 1970 the owners closed the factory, leaving 3,000 workers unemployed. . . . The government expropriated all of the property and assets and reopened the Central as part of Puerto Rico's Sugar Corporation, operating the mill until 1990 when they closed it, citing losses" (2001, 112).

The decline and eventual closing of the sugar mill in Salinas affected primarily men (Whalen 2001, 122). It is important to note that during Puerto Rico's drive to industrialize and modernize the economy with the enactment of Operation Bootstrap projects beginning in the late 1940s, women were recast as ideal factory workers. At that time, thousands of Puerto Rican women began to staff factories that had moved their operations to Puerto Rico to take advantage of tax incentives. These developments, declining agricultural production, and women's incorporation into factory work contributed to a crisis in men's labor force participation, a crisis that has only deepened in the first decades of the twenty-first century.

As the men's world of work in the sugar industry disappeared, the island's rapid modernization meant building energy-generating plants. The two largest complexes are situated in Aguirre, and they powered the growing number of pharmaceutical and manufacturing plants. The electrification of the island also meant powering the thousands of middle-class subdivisions built for the increasingly urbanized workers of a modern Puerto Rico. Significantly, desirable civil servant jobs in electricity generation and grid maintenance have been scarce, too few to employ the significant number of men who once worked in agriculture. State-sponsored mass migration of agricultural workers to the continental US aimed to alleviate the unemployment crisis besieging men (Meléndez 2017; García-Colón and Meléndez 2013). Hundreds of thousands of agricultural workers and their families migrated stateside during the first sixty years of US colonization. The largest migration per capita followed in the postwar era of industrialization, when nearly 850,000 left between 1940 and 1970. By the 1970s, migration was part and parcel of Puerto Rican reality and public policy (Nazario Velasco 2014). With the island's agricultural sector decimated, Puerto Ricans became consumers of imported foods.

FROM ENVIRONMENTALISM TO ENVIRONMENTAL JUSTICE

In the decades following Operation Bootstrap, the policy that promoted the industrialization and urbanization of the island, king sugar and the smaller coffee and tobacco sectors declined (Dietz 1986; Levy 2015). At the same time, the local Puerto Rican government encouraged the migration of agricultural laborers to stateside farms (Meléndez 2017; García-Colón and Meléndez 2013; García-Colón 2020). Environmental scholar Carmen Milagros Concepción explained that "Operation Bootstrap shifted to capital-intensive industries in the early 1960s. The allocation by the US government of special quotas which allowed Puerto Rico to import lower-cost foreign oil and feedstocks provided a critical incentive (added to low wages and tax exemptions) for the expansion of the petrochemical industry. This shift marked the start of an intensive use of energy, water and land and subsequent industrial pollution" (1995, 113).

By the mid-1960s, a budding environmental movement formed in reaction to the island's unhinged industrialization (Concepción 1995). A small sector of the educated public began to voice their concerns about air, water, and land contamination (Concepción 1995). At first, these early environmentalists were worried about the toll of pollution on the natural environment, rather than on human health, but in time they would realize that the pollution also threatened human health. According to Concepción, 1966 was a pivotal year for Puerto Rico's emergent environmental movement when, in February, Puerto Rico's House Resolution No. 152 led to the establishment of a Special Commission on Natural Resources and Beautification, and in March the governor appointed a Citizens Committee on Aesthetics and Natural Resources (Concepción 1995). In March 1968, the SS *Ocean Eagle* spilled 3.7 million gallons of crude oil from Venezuela after splitting in half in San Juan's harbor. The same year, Puerto Rico's Department of Public Works created an office of natural resources (Concepción 1995, 114). This environmental disaster propelled the government to create Puerto Rico's first environmental law and regulatory agency, the Environmental Quality Board, in 1970 and two years later, to establish the Department of Natural Resources (Concepción 1995, 14). A second massive oil spill occurred in March 1973, when the SS *Zoe Colocotroni*, on its way to CORCO in Peñuelas, went aground near La Parguera. To lighten the ship and dislodge it from the reef, the captain discharged 1.5 million gallons of crude oil into the Caribbean Sea (Gelabert 2013). In what became known as the *Zoe Colocotroni* case, the Commonwealth successfully proved environmental liability in Boston's First Circuit Federal Court, leading to the Environmental Quality Board's creation of an Emergency Plan for Oil Spills in Puerto Rico in 1981 (Gelabert 2013).

Still, the island's industrialization continued unabated. To aid the ailing US economy, Section 936 of the US tax code offered US corporations tax exemptions in 1976 on income originating in US territories (Bram, Martínez, and Steindel 2008). Large pharmaceutical companies that relied on a small number of highly skilled, well-paid workers took advantage of the exemptions and brought further environmental degradation. In addition to federal tax exemptions for firms operating in US territories, "recruitment tools" included the 1947 Puerto Rico Industrial Incentive Act, in which the local and federal governments gave industries local tax breaks for ten to fifteen years and "less stringent enforcement of environmental protection laws" than in the States (Berman Santana 1996, 62, 67; cf. Concepción 1990). This had great environmental consequences, as those attracted were overwhelmingly "dirty industries" (Lloréns and Stanchich 2019).

Puerto Rico's environmentalism has been historically tied to debates over the island's political status, with environmentalists overwhelmingly supporting the island's decolonization and independence (Atiles Osoria 2013). But there are historical and ideological differences between the early environmentalism of 1960 to 1990 and the explicit struggles for environmental justice that emerged after 1991. Early environmental struggles were concerned with protecting the ecosystem against unregulated and widespread contamination and pollution and safeguarding the environment against government-backed, extractivist enterprises such as open-pit copper mining in the mountains of Lares, Adjuntas, and Utuado (Concepción 1995; Massol González, Andromache Johnnidis, and Massol Deyá 2008; Colón-Rivera, F. Córdova Iturregui, and J. Córdova Iturregui 2014; García López 2015; Massol Deyá 2018). The renowned Casa Pueblo, an environmental organization founded in 1980, emerged from the work of two activists protecting what they named the Bosque del Pueblo forest reserve.[4] Tinti Deyá and Alexis Massol, 2002 winners of the Goldman Environmental Prize, continue to act as guardians of the very mountains and forests that would have been razed in the mining operation (Massol Deyá 2018; Lloréns and Stanchich 2019).

In 1977, another vanguard terrain of environmental struggle began, this one between the US Navy and the fishermen's association and people of Vieques (McCaffrey 2002; Baver 2012; Zenón 2018). Lasting until 2003, the nearly three-decade effort illustrates early environmental justice struggles that preceded, by over a decade, the emergence and codification of the Principles of Environmental Justice (1991). It also demonstrates that affected communities, particularly communities of color, had long advocated for environmental equity and for the health and survival of their ecosystem against increasing environmental degradation and harm (Bullard 1990). The environmental justice framework in the United States was born from early, pioneering environmental struggles waged mainly in poor African American, Native American, and Latinx hinterland communities (Bullard 1990). The demands and gains of the civil rights movement sparked a flame that led to the coalitional creation of the Principles of Environmental Justice (Bullard 1990). For instance, at the height of the movement, Cesar Chavez's advocacy and organizing on behalf of the United

Farm Workers concerned not only wages but hazardous working conditions, too. In 1969, Chavez stated that "the real issue is the dangers that pesticides present to farm workers. . . . We have come to realize . . . that the issue of pesticide poisoning is more important today than even wages" (Taylor 1975, 242; Gordon 1999, 51).

Comparably, the egregious state of sanitation and concerns about the health of the largely Puerto Rican community in East Harlem motivated the Young Lords Party (YLP) to launch their "garbage offensive" on July 27, 1969, to force the sanitation department to contend with its neglect of the city's poor neighborhoods (Gandy 2002). In Matthew Gandy's words, "For the residents of the barrio, uncollected garbage had become a poignant symbol of the indignity of poverty, political invisibility and municipal neglect" (2002, 736). The YLP also called attention to the risks of lead poisoning, to which poor children in East Harlem and other New York City boroughs were disproportionately exposed (Horvath n.d.; Gandy 2002). In "The Health Initiatives of the Young Lords Party," Theresa Horvath explains, "Some of the long-lasting contributions of the Young Lords' health initiatives include the Emergency Repair Program (1969), which obligated landlords to remove lead-based paint from apartment buildings" (n.d.).[5]

In the United States, what would later become the environmental justice movement emerged in the early 1980s (Lee 1987; Pulido 2016, 1). By the early 1990s, pioneering Latinx environmental scholars had begun producing scholarship that was explicitly environmental justice-minded. It aimed to document Latino environmentalisms and counter racist stereotypes about Latinos as "lacking a conservation ethic and destroying the environment" (Peña 2003, 55; Pulido 1996). Civil rights–era Latinx initiatives were some of the precursors of post-1991 efforts explicitly framed as community-led struggles for environmental justice. The environmental justice terrains of struggle of Puerto Rico, the US Virgin Islands, Guam, the Northern Mariana Islands, and American Samoa, all United States colonial possessions, have yet to be fully integrated into the US continent–focused history of movements for environmental justice (Lloréns and Stanchich 2019).

Overwhelmingly, environmental activism in Puerto Rico since the 1960s has been the purview of a certain segment of the island's intelligentsia whose members tend to be great admirers of nature's beauty and who are concerned about the continuous assault on the island's environment. They tend to be university-educated and often middle- or upper-class. In my ethnographic work, I have found that these activists rarely recognize the links between socioeconomic class (i.e., poverty) and race (i.e., Blackness), or how these demographic variables are intricately tied to the siting of environmentally polluting industries. When I ask, they flat-out deny such connections. They argue instead that the siting of polluting industries is connected to socioeconomic class and poverty but not to race or anti-Black racism. In their view, racism does not exist and therefore does not play a part in Puerto Rico's socio-spatial arrangements. They believe in environmental conservation and often espouse fortress conservation ideals. This conservation model is couched in the belief that it is important to protect ecosystems from human disturbance, but it is a problematic model because it does not often account for, and in fact tends to undermine, the ways in which local communities, who rely on ecosystems to survive, also act as frontline stewards and protectors.

They tend to be primarily concerned with nonhuman environmental function and use language markers such as "biodiversity" and "endemic species." Their decisions are reached through the understanding of scientific evidence as the preeminent domain of knowledge. They tend to express support for the island's political independence, and they collaborate with traditional American environmental organizations (e.g., Sierra Club). Contemporary environmental activists strive to prevent contamination and pollution and to restore, conserve, and protect the local environment (not necessarily with people's access to it). They tend to espouse a top-down approach that relies on scientific language and does not always prioritize the knowledge of local resource users and community members.

In Puerto Rico, the environmental justice framework has only recently been used to describe community-led environmental movements and their demands (Concepción 1995, 2010; Santiago 2012; Lloréns 2016; Torres Abreu 2016; López, Concepción, and Torres Abreu 2018; de Onís 2018; Lloréns and Stanchich 2019). Noting the absence of environmental justice research in Puerto Rico, Carmen Milagros Concepción suggested that researchers investigate the experiences and the struggles against contamination of the communities at the forefront of environmental injustice (1988, 2006). To be clear, although the conceptual category of environmental justice has been largely absent from the island's lexicon, demands for environmental redress fall squarely within the environmental justice agenda (Concepción 1995; Valdés Pizzini 2006; Santiago 2012; Atiles Osoria 2013; Torres Abreu 2016; Lloréns 2016; de Onís 2018; García López

2018; García López, Concepción, and Torres Abreu 2018; Lloréns and Stanchich 2019; de Onís, Lloréns, and Santiago 2020b). Since the island's population is classified almost entirely as Hispanic (98.7 percent), the whole of Puerto Rico qualifies as an environmental justice community.[6] Furthermore, 43.5 percent of the population lives in poverty, according to the United States Census Bureau.[7]

In 1991, the First National People of Color Environmental Leadership Summit defined the basic principles of environmental justice. These include the right to be free from ecological destruction, discrimination, or bias; the right to sustainable use of land and resources and protection from toxic or hazardous wastes; the fundamental right to clean air, land, water, and food; the right to self-determination; the demand for strict accountability and compensation for environmental harm; the right to participate in decision-making; and the right to a safe and healthy work environment without being forced to choose between working in unsafe conditions, being unemployed, and demanding that employers comply with environmental rights under international law (Lee 1992).

The summit participants called for the cleanup and rebuilding of cities and rural areas in balance with nature, the maintenance of cultural integrity in communities and fair access for all to the full range of resources, and enforcement of the principle of informed consent. Here they specifically mentioned testing experimental reproductive and medical procedures on people of color.[8] The summit opposed the destructive operations of multinational corporations and military occupations. The principles of environmental justice state that individuals must make personal choices to consume as little of the earth's resources and produce as little waste as possible and to make conscious decisions to challenge and create lifestyles that ensure sustainability (Lee 1992; de Onís, Lloréns, and Santiago 2020b).

Prompted by this movement, then-president William J. Clinton issued the Executive Order 12898 on Federal Actions to Address Environmental Justice, which instructed federal agencies to make environmental justice "part of their mission, by identifying and addressing, as appropriate, disproportionately high and adverse human health or environmental effects of its programs, policies and activities on minority and low income populations in the United States and its territories and possessions" including Puerto Rico.[9] Robert Kuehn offered a four-part taxonomic categorization that breaks down environmental justice into distributive justice, procedural justice, corrective justice, and social justice (Kuehn 2000; Pellow 2000; Zerner 2000; Pulido 2000; Pellow and Brulle 2005). More recently, environmental justice scholar David Schlosberg added "recognitional justice," and EJ scholar Ana Baptista contributed "structural justice" and "structural processes" to the four foundational taxonomic categorizations (Schlosberg 2007; Baptista 2008). David Pellow underscored that the era of #BlackLivesMatter requires the integration of an intersectional approach that critically centers race, processes of racialization, gendering, and socioeconomic class in the environmental justice framework (2018). According to Charles Lee, one of the pioneers of the EJ framework at the level of the federal government, the practice of EJ is entering its second generation in the context of the United States (2021). Simultaneously, the EJ framework has gained international traction, as globally activists and communities demand that their governments acknowledge and ameliorate the disproportionate impacts of contamination, pollution, extractive industries, land dispossession, gentrification, ecological collapse, and species extinction affecting Indigenous, Black, peasant, and low-income marginalized communities with little political representation (Debbane and Keil 2004; Claudio 2007; Brunnée 2009; Martin et al. 2020). The aforementioned authors and others propose that the future of the environmental justice movement, its practice and EJ-based policy making, must be global, plural, decolonized, and intersectional, and it must be one that enacts just transformation for workers (Martin et al. 2020; Lee 2021; de Onís 2021; García López 2020; Pellow 2018; Bullard 2008).

According to environmental activist Ruth Santiago, at the end of the second decade of the twenty-first century, the battle against the impacts of fossil fuel generation in Puerto Rico's southeast is the archipelago's most significant environmental terrain of struggle. As in Vieques, Jobos Bay communities have been engaged in safeguarding their environment since the late 1960s, when it became clear that the region was nationally marked as a site in which to place heavy industries such as energy-generation plants, pharmaceuticals, military bases, and manufacturing plants (de Onís 2021; García López 2020; Lloréns et al. 2018; Berman Santana 1996).

Local environmental justice activists understand fossil fuel–electricity generation as an agent of death for humans and the natural environment, and as a main contributor to the climate crisis (de Onís 2021). These activists tend to live in communities affected by environmental pollution. They are not always university-educated and tend to come from socioeconomically disadvantaged and working-class families. They tend to have an intersectional understanding of the ways in which race and class are inextricably linked and tied to the uses of space and to the siting of polluting

FIG 3.1. Children bathing in the Laguna de las Mareas with the toxic coal ash mountain in the background, Guayama, Puerto Rico, July 2018.

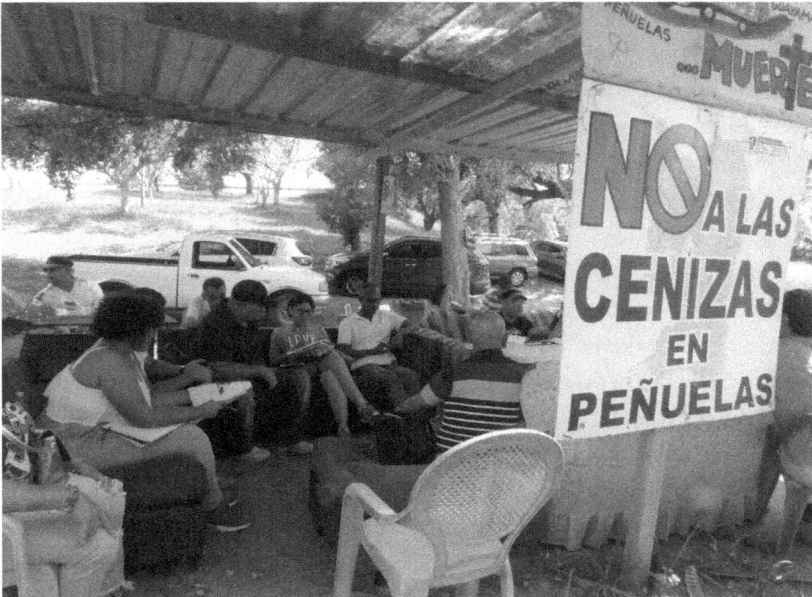

FIG 3.2. Planning meeting of anti–coal ash activists in Peñuelas, Puerto Rico, July 2018.

industries. Because of this, they tend to have a holistic view of environmental issues. They rely on scientific and firsthand community knowledge, experiences, and observations to build their account of environmental harm. In Puerto Rico, these activists do not always express support for the island's independence. They collaborate with stateside and transnational activist coalitions of Indigenous people and Afro-descendants on environmental issues affecting minoritized populations (e.g., Environmental Justice Alliance) and are guided by the Principles of Environmental Justice as well as the Jemez Principles for Democratic Organizing. They want the AES–Puerto Rico coal-powered plant to close definitively, and they want to transition to renewable sources of electricity generation. They hope to prevent contamination and pollution and to conserve the local environment and the people's right to live there and use it. They call attention to racist and classist practices in the siting of polluting entities and want to be included in the decision-making about the future of their communities. They espouse a bottom-up, collective approach to decision-making and planning.

SOLIDARITY, SOCIALITY, AND MUTUALITY ARE RESILIENT PRACTICES, BUT COERCIVE RESILIENCE IS TIRING

It is widely agreed that "resilience," a term that describes the ability of disrupted systems to quickly bounce back or adapt to new conditions, has been co-opted by neoliberal governance, which has turned it into a one-size-fits-all discourse that calls on individuals to "pull themselves up by the bootstraps" in the face of the Anthropocene's ever-mounting catastrophes (Walker and Salt 2006; Walker and Cooper 2011; Evans and Reid 2014; Chandler 2014; Tierney 2015). Policy makers, development workers, and engineers call it "engineering resilience" or "elastic resilience" because a rubber band was used as an early metaphor.

A different take is "ecological resilience," the amount of disturbance a system can take before it is forced to become a "different kind of system" (Holling 1973). Usually something is lost when this happens. So, for example, people want their household economy to be resilient, not to be forced to become a "homeless" or "jobless" household. But they might *not* want the system that oppresses them to be resilient, because they want it to be flexible to meet their needs. This is illustrated in chapter 4, when we meet Ana living in a homeless tent encampment and publicly resisting the state's prescription for her and her family. In that instance, Ana was balancing household economic resilience with putting pressure on the political system's resilience.

The contemporary case of Puerto Rico, a site emblematic of colonial abandonment and of local people as forsaken colonial subjects, offers a unique case study about the increasingly coercive nature of the neoliberal resilience discourse. The novel ways in which the rural, coastal, environmental justice–minded women with whom I collaborate attempt to forge good lives amid the turbulence of the present are an example of resistance to the discourse of neoliberal coercive resilience. It is important to underscore that the neoliberal "discourse on resilience" gets resilience wrong. Neoliberalism mistakes "bootstrap" self-reliance for resilience. Resilience does not have to be self-reliant. Households can be resilient by relying on others or by relying on the government and protesting and pressuring it when it fails.

The women and families presented here live in a geography where the material remnants of earlier capitalist labor regimes are still visible in the landscape in the form of memories and physical ruins. The ruins of the Spanish colonial plantation world coexist with the ruins of the failed nineteenth- and early twentieth-century attempts to industrialize sugarcane agriculture for global export. And these coexist with shuttered mid-twentieth-century oil refineries and manufacturers that promised and failed to bring financial prosperity to the archipelago, alongside present-day contaminating electricity-generating plants and shopping plazas (Lloréns and Santiago 2018a).

Over and over, these women have witnessed firsthand the failure of capitalist economic policies to deliver prosperity to the region's populace. Because extractive resources are finite, capitalism's resilience rests on its ability to create ever more fields of extraction, and as capitalism evacuates extractive fields and regions, it leaves ruination in its wake (Lloréns 2018b). This economic ruination will affect those who were most dependent on its jobs. In rural coastal areas such as the Jobos Bay, where the sugarcane plantation economy employed laborers only seasonally and left the majority of the laborers unemployed for six months out of the year, people have long had to figure out alternatives to paid employment (Figueroa 2005; García-Quijano 2006).

The residents' insurance and main source of resilience is their land, the coast with its natural resources, and the social relationships forged in this context (García-Quijano et al., 2013). Their ability to withstand the inevitable hazards of this chaotic world depends on having a healthy environment and access to its resources: clean water, fertile land, and fish in the sea. Economic catastrophe is not the end of communities such as those on the Jobos Bay. After all, they have lived through such catastrophes several times by now. The end of their resilience (what García-Quijano et al. call "a catastrophic loss of resilience" [2015]) would occur if a permanently damaged climate and ecosystem took away their ability to subsist from the ecological bounty around them.

Afro-descendant communities such as those in Jobos Bay have always lived simultaneously at the center and on the margins of the capitalist and neoliberal economic systems. They are at the center because their labor built capitalist wealth for the owners of production. They are on the margins because their homes, communities, and ways of life have persisted on the fringe of metropolitan governance. For the state, this rural populace is only visible as labor, votes, and needy wards, as defined in census data. Living in the shadow of the state and its top-down policies has meant that Black individuals and communities have historically relied on kinship and social solidarity networks to provide for basic necessities like food, care, and material goods. Black and Indigenous systems of sociality, solidarity, and mutuality predate the formation of the US nation-state's democratic governance in the Americas. These mutuality systems, though they were vulnerable in their early stages to the whims of the plantation owners and the anti-Black and anti-Indigenous state and police, began to take shape as soon as enslaved Africans began the transatlantic journey that continued through enslavement, into post-emancipation, and to the present. In short, sociality, solidarity, and mutuality are themselves resilient systems; that is, these "grassroots" practices persist even in the face of the whims of modern capitalist and neoliberal governance.

In this era of savage neoliberalism, it has become painfully obvious that post–World War II liberal notions of democratic governance enshrined in human rights, wherein the state acts as a benefactor to its citizens, have become so degraded as to have become undone (Walker and Cooper 2011; Chandler 2014, 2019; Evans and Reid 2014; Joseph 2013). Black subjects, arguably, have been left out of liberal democratic notions of protection from the start. In fact, Black individuals and communities throughout the American hemisphere have long experienced the state's disdain, outright racist violence, and terror, and they have been blamed for their "poor" living conditions (McKittrick 2006; Sharpe 2016; T. L. King 2019; Hartman 2019).

Even so, something has changed in the current era. The mid- to late twentieth-century myth that liberal democracy was a benefactor to its citizens has collapsed. The COVID-19 pandemic has made clearer that all citizens are affected by the state's withdrawal, left to their own devices regardless of race. This is particularly felt by the proletarianized working, urbanized masses dependent on export/import chains of food and other material goods, as well as those who make their living in the service sector and wage-earning economy. In light of this, people who are most able to be organically resilient in order to withstand the state's retreat and adjudication of its responsibilities are those who have lived unprotected for a long time already, on the margins and in the shadows of the liberal state. Rural coastal communities that have long ensured a degree of self-sufficiency through food cultivation, foraging, fishing, and sharing practices are prime examples (García-Quijano and Lloréns 2017; Lloréns 2019; Lloréns and García-Quijano 2020).

Still, in the present era of climate catastrophe and ecocide, Black, Indigenous, and low-income communities across the globe are increasingly pushed to the brink of their ability to cope, adapt, and bounce back—or "bounce forward" in the language of "emancipatory catastrophism"—what the president of the Rockefeller Foundation, Judith Rodin, called the "resilience dividend" (Rodin 2015; Beck 2015; cf. Chandler 2019, 305). With "the growing loss of natural ecological system reliance," communities find themselves unable to respond to catastrophe in organic, self-generated resilient ways (Chandler 2019, 307). They no longer have the tools at their disposal, such as healthy ecosystems, to cope and craft good lives.

In Jobos Bay, for example, the Applied Energy Systems coal-powered plant has contaminated the southern aquifer, on which thousands of local residents depend for potable water (Santiago 2012; Alfonso 2018, 2019; de Onís, Lloréns, and Santiago 2020b). Their resilient strategy in the face of a contaminated water supply has been, for those who can afford it, to buy expensive water filtration systems or, more often, to rely on bottled water for consumption (Lloréns and Stanchich 2019). Alberto, a retiree and resident of Puente Jobos, a mangrove community near the coal power plant, told me, "Here in our house, we only drink bottled water. In fact, I have been doing so since Hurricane Georges, because back then I saw how everything flooded and there was sewage everywhere. And since then, I have known the water supply here was contaminated, and I don't trust anything that comes out of the tap."

But this kind of resilience depends on artificial conditions, such as the capture of faraway water by multinational corporations, export/import chains, and the ebbs and flows of pricing and availability. And it does not even account for plastics manufacturing, itself a fossil-fuel industry. Individuals consume the toxins the bottles leach into the water, which affects their health (Mason, Welch, and Neratko 2018). Additionally, single-use bottles create massive amounts of waste. Puerto Rico has no effective plastics recycling program, so the bottles end up in overfilled landfills or, worse, littered across the territory or in the ocean.

Though Alberto's response is an adaptive, resilient one, it is "coerced resilience" because it responds to the federal and local state's negligence. The political authorities allowed AES to contaminate the region's water, air, and soil. As a result, residents are forced to forfeit their rights to clean and safe water, which turns them instead into dependent consumers. Ironically, this is the opposite of self-reliance. Self-reliant peoples everywhere have always relied on natural resources to survive because nature, the ecosphere, is itself a system of life support, which also points to the impossibility of "pulling yourself up by your bootstraps." This setup bodes well for the multinational corporations that sell water, for big pharma, and for the health-care industry. In Guayama alone, there are three dialysis centers operating seven days a week just to keep up with the surging cases of renal dysfunction and failure, to say nothing of cancers. In recent years, Walgreens and CVS have expanded throughout the southeast. Their pharmacy counters are always busy dispensing medicines to a frail, aging, and sick population. Unable to compete, locally owned town pharmacies have shut down.

The state is implicated in both the destruction of the ecosphere and in helping multinational corporations destroy ecosystems unabated while accumulating capital (Lloréns and Stanchich 2019). As the previous examples illustrate, coerced resilience "enables high levels of production" by relying on "'anthropogenic inputs' as the external 'replacement of specific ecosystem processes by inputs of labor and manufactured capital (e.g., fossil fuel, technology, nutrients, pesticides, and antibiotics)'" (Rist et al. 2014; cf. Chandler 2019, 306; Taussig 2018). In turn, this "artificial" source of resilience weakens organic, self-created, and self-directed sources of resilience that rely on local ecosystems for adaptation. Coercive resilience is destructive because it contributes even more anthropogenic inputs into the atmosphere that, in turn, speed up climate catastrophe and ecocide on a local and global scale (Chandler 2019, 308). In other words, the state is directly responsible for enabling multinational corporations to maximize profits over the health of people and the ecosphere.

As Anna Tsing writes, "We are stuck with the problem of living despite economic and ecological ruination" (2015, 19). Thus, Black and Indigenous communities continue their "survival" against great odds, often relying on the solidarity and mutuality of kin and community members who are equally strapped. In this sense, the state, with its repressive policies and outright neglect of these same communities, is a source of violence. In order to have a fighting chance, communities on the Jobos Bay continue to organize their own community well-being initiatives in the shadow of the state.

A woman from New Orleans in the aftermath of Katrina had poignant words for journalist Beverly Bell: "I am tired of being resilient" (2013, 175). Her words resonate as Black and Indigenous individuals and communities are pushed further into marginal wastelands. Their lives are sacrificed in the name of progress and the wealth accumulation of a tiny number of White owners of global enterprise. In the American hemisphere, Haiti, the Americas' first Black republic, stands as an exemplar of a place pushed beyond the brink. Yet writing after the catastrophic 2010 earthquake, Bell observes, "Haiti serves as a reminder of the lesson we in New Orleans got after the levees broke: the capacity of humanity to survive, create positive change, sustain culture, and hold joy is fierce. Except in the most extreme, sustained cases of oppression, it is unsinkable, like a cork that won't stay underwater" (2013, 168).

WOMEN'S SOCIAL AND ENVIRONMENTAL JUSTICE INTERVENTIONS IN THE EARLY DAYS OF THE NATIONAL DEBT CRISIS (2015–2017)

The 2010 US Census reports that Salinas had a total population of 31,078 people and Guayama had 45,362. However, a March 2016 Pew Research Center report states that between 2010 and 2015, Puerto Rico experienced a 7 percent population decline.[10] During the early phase of ethnographic research for this project, in 2015–17, several informants estimated that some neighborhoods of Salinas and Guayama had lost 65 to 70 percent of their residents. As of September 28, 2016, Salinas held the record for the highest unemployment rate on the island, with a structural unemployment rate of 30 percent and a 54 percent poverty rate.[11]

In 2016, I spent several weeks during the summer on the Jobos Bay interviewing resource users, collaborating on a NOAA–Puerto Rico Sea

Grant research study that sought to understand the links between use of and access to estuarine forest resources and the well-being of local residents. When I asked residents how the national debt crisis was affecting them, they often said things such as "Here in the south, we have always lived in crisis" and "Now everyone is learning to live the way we poor people have long lived" (García-Quijano and Lloréns 2017). They felt that the national crisis was a social and class equalizer.

On a hot and humid July afternoon, I sat on the balcony of Casa Aguirre, a fledgling community-led eco-lodge venture, to interview local community activists Ruth Santiago, Nelson Santos, and Roberto Thomas about the first annual mangrove festival recently celebrated in Aguirre. They told me about several "socio-productive" community-based projects in the estuarine communities. When I mentioned my interest in understanding how gender intersects with environmental activism, Santiago, Santos, and Thomas all agreed, "In the Jobos Bay, women compose about 70 percent of community activists and cultural workers." Nelson Santos, an esteemed elder and community organizer, told me that when it comes to community work, "women in Puerto Rico have taken the initiative that men have left behind." Similarly, Ruth Santiago remarked, "There has been a gender reversal in our communities, and sadly, many men have given in to self-destructive habits." Ruth Santiago and Nelson Santos invited me to several upcoming community events where I could meet community members, youths, and activists.

In Aguirre, I attended Convivencia Ambiental (in English, Environmental Cohabitation), a one-week summer camp for community youths ages twelve to eighteen. In 2016, the camp was in its tenth year and was themed "Solidarity and Resilience." To pay for the expenses of running the camp, Comité Diálogo Ambiental (the Environmental Dialogue Committee), one of the groups that compose IDEBAJO, relies on donations and volunteers. That year, Puerto Rico's Sierra Club chapter donated $500, local farmers donated fruits and produce, and Environmental Dialogue Committee members and a few parents donated their time as chaperones, cooks, and drivers. During its early years, the camp was held on the premises of the Jobos Bay National Estuarine Research Reserve (JBNERR), located in Aguirre, but the reserve's administration was traditionally fickle in granting permission to Diálogo Ambiental to use its facilities. This meant that Diálogo would only learn if they had received permission to host the camp on the premises a few weeks before the camp started. In 2015, new administrators at the reserve changed the lending policies for the reserve's lodging facilities. The facilities are available to researchers who come from all over the world to study the Jobos Bay ecosystem, but community members complained that the new administration seemed less interested in collaborating with community-led initiatives, particularly those that needed their recently renovated lodging facilities. In 2016, camp organizers were denied permission to host the community youths on the reserve's premises. They scrambled to find another place, and the camp was held at the Casa Aguirre eco-lodge.

Casa Aguirre was a brand-new IDEBAJO initiative that sought to offer modest lodging quarters to visitors along with various touristic offerings, such as guided walking historical tours, guided kayaking tours of the bay, and fisher-led trips to the offshore cays. The owner of the house where Casa Aguirre was located had not been using the property, and it was in disrepair. It was a historic wooden plantation house that once housed Aguirre Sugar Mill's upper management. Fearing that the house would fall apart, like many of the neighboring historic houses had, the owner had allowed IDEBAJO to renovate the house to use as an eco-lodge for a modest monthly income. That summer Casa Aguirre allowed the camp to be held on its premises free of charge.

When I arrived at Casa Aguirre on a sweltering July afternoon, the house was empty but for stray dogs on the premises. The camp's organizer had sent me the itinerary, so I knew the campers would be back soon from a scheduled "nature walk" in the mangroves led by JBNERR staff. I took the opportunity to lie on a hammock and listen to the wind. My short slumber was interrupted by the laughter and raucousness usual to groups of teenagers. They came in and immediately began complaining about the heat, about being sweaty and dirty, and about all the walking they had been doing this week. Yet they looked joyful. The eighteen campers were almost evenly divided between boys and girls. I sat on the balcony and listened to them talk about craving pizza and which pizzeria they liked best. A young woman mentioned a popular inexpensive pizzeria in Isla Verde, one of San Juan's tourist districts, while a boy mentioned that he liked Pizza Hut but that it was expensive and to eat there a family would need at least $60.

These teenagers, some holding modest phones, were much like other teenagers today. But statistically, they were among the island's poorest. They lived in some of the most marginalized communities and attended similarly underfunded and under-resourced schools. Ruth Santiago, one of the organizers, told me that the camp was aimed at giving these young people, who might otherwise never attend a camp, an opportunity to have the camp experience with positive adult role models. There were five adults present that day, and three of them—two women and a man—called themselves the "three musketeers" because, as the core organizers, they had staffed the camp every summer for ten years. One of the adults was the mother of one of the youths, a woman actively involved in community environmental causes. Another was a thirtysomething community organizer originally from San Juan who began working with IDEBAJO after graduating from the University of Puerto Rico and working on several other social justice community initiatives throughout Puerto Rico.

The Convivencia Ambiental camp teaches local youths about the environmental riches in their own communities and promotes stewardship and pride. It also exposes them to the environmental threats with which they live and teaches them about the importance of volunteer work and solidarity. During their one-week stay, the youths attend workshops about social and environmental issues related to ecology, traditional knowledge, fishing, arts and crafts, food making, and gardening. That evening, I sat down to dinner with the youths and the community volunteers who give their time to this important cause. I was heartened, as I would often be that summer, knowing that the lack of financial resources would not stop the community environmental and cultural workers in the Jobos Bay from doing this good work.

The Central Aguirre neighborhood, where the camp was traditionally held, is not only the site of the sugar mill ruins and the company town remnants. It is also the site of Puerto Rico's largest power plant complex. When I asked some of the youths from the community how they felt about the power plant, they told me that it was "really loud" and that "many community members suffer from hearing loss." The power plant is so large that its shadow is inescapable. On September 21, 2016, a fire at this power plant left most of the island without electricity for over forty-eight hours. The alarm sounds and the fumes were felt all over the community. Maria, a resident whose backyard faces the power plant, took a video of the fire with her phone. In the video, plumes of black smoke spew from the plant's smokestacks and extremely loud alarms blare in the background. She thought an explosion was imminent. The stress of the event and the high-pitched sounds of the alarms gave her a month of headaches and ringing in her ears, for which she had to seek medical treatment. She reported that her family lives in constant fear of fires or explosions.

The day after the fire, a youth who had attended the Convivencia Ambiental camp wrote this on his Facebook page:

> It is evident that the majority of the population suffers from dependence on electric power. And I suffer because of the lack of peace and pollution. I suffer because everyone is now complaining that there is no electric power. Ah! But when Puerto Rico's largest power plant explodes it degrades our community with its flares, its sound, the hot water it emits into the bay, oil spills, and because of their negligence. But no one does or says anything. It doesn't matter because only a minority suffers and what really happens in the community is not told in the media. Maybe this compares to Capeco [another oil refinery fire in Cataño, 2009], with the difference that this power plant will not end its operations, and the ones who live close to it, literally within 20 feet, will continue to suffer. I am writing this because I live it and I suffer. If you don't understand this, I invite you to come take a walk with me around my neighborhood.

On September 22, 2016, a day after the fire, two photos taken by NASA made headlines around the world. One was taken the day before the fire, with the island shining bright in the night sky. The other, taken after the fire, shows most of the island in the dark. The juxtaposition of the island at full electric capacity and then at reduced capacity was a visual reminder of the fragility of the island's deteriorating infrastructure before Hurricane María landed a year later on September 20, 2017. Puerto Rico at full electric capacity stands as the Caribbean's most electricity-dependent island. The reduced-capacity photo also reveals class stratification on two levels. San Juan shines brighter than the rest of the island, and those who have generators at home, usually the wealthy, continue to generate electricity to run their lights, air conditioning, and other appliances (Lloréns 2018c).

WOMEN'S COMMUNITY WORK IN EL COQUÍ

El Coquí neighborhood, where many Aguirre mill workers lived, is located just outside the main gates and across the street from the old, now defunct, Aguirre company town. El Coquí is populated by the descendants of sugar workers, as well as newcomers. On July 11, 2016, I attended the first day of a weeklong workshop held at the Coquí neighborhood's modest community center. In Puerto Rico, it is customary for neighborhoods to each have their own *centro comunal* (community center), where each neighborhood can host events such as weddings, *quinceañeros*, and parties of all sorts, as well as political meetings and workshops.

I attended a workshop that was part of a larger, ongoing project named "Coquí Solar." The workshop offered the attendees, who were mostly unemployed community youths, an introduction to the ambitious plan of, first, installing solar panels on the roof of the community center and, subsequently, on all the houses in the neighborhood, with the end goal of becoming a self-reliant solar community. The workshop was in part a volunteer recruitment effort and an informational session for youths who might be thinking about studying to become electricians at the local trade school. This effort to achieve community-led energy independence and to promote energy democracy emerged from IDEBAJO volunteers' search for solutions to the problems of contamination faced by Jobos Bay communities as a result of being the site of three electric power plants (de Onís, Lloréns, and Santiago 2020b).

El Coquí was designated as a "special community" in 2001 by Sila Calderon, Puerto Rico's first female governor. The Law for the Integral Development of Puerto Rico's Special Communities was created to combat widespread poverty in rural and urban areas across Puerto Rico. This law aimed to secure resources for low-income communities. Among those resources was the assignment of a community caseworker who would consult and enable communities with their own development initiatives and efforts. It did not escape me that Puerto Rico's first female governor was the person to create a law aimed at promoting the well-being of the island's most marginal communities.

The community center, which is currently the heart of IDEBAJO's community organizing efforts, sat idle for many years. It was "rescued" and put to work for the community with the efforts of the energetic and hardworking president of the El Coquí community board. Now the community center houses several core community cultural and environmental projects. The current president of the community board, Ismenia Figueroa, told me she got the keys of the community center in 2007. During our conversation at the modest one-room cement building, she recounted that

> I received the keys to the center from the "special communities" worker in
> March 2007. The people who had the center before us would rent it for
> parties but did not invest any money in fixing the building, so when we got
> it, it was in terrible condition. The bathrooms were destroyed. There were

no doors, and there was only $50 in the center's account. And so, the first
thing we did was fix the bathrooms, install doors, and paint the place. We
did all this work quickly because our first order of business was starting
a summer camp for community children when school let out in May.
I applied for free summer breakfast and lunch programs through the
Department of Education [*comedores escolares*], and I distributed fliers
about our summer camp to be held here at the community center. That
first summer in 2007, we received 100 children. We have been hosting the
summer camp every summer since then, and we get between 100 and 105
children each summer. We hold a half-day camp from 7:30 a.m. to 12:30 p.m.
every weekday, and we charge $5 per child for the entire summer. We fund
the camp with our own money and donations from private businesses.
We plan four field trips every summer, and sometimes the mayor's office
donates the transportation, and other times we arrange and pay for
transportation ourselves. Members of the community board of directors
and volunteer parents staff the camp. We also get volunteers to offer
workshops for the children in arts and crafts, puppet making, nutrition,
values, dance, and drumming, et cetera. This summer, for the first time,
the mayor sent eight high school students to work as camp counselors.

I asked Isme why she became active in community work. She responded:

I started out helping at events twenty-five years ago, and at that time I had
my kids at home. My husband did not think I should work. We agreed
that I would stay home and offer my kids a good quality of life. And so
that's what I did. I have five children, but when they grew up and started
leaving home, I decided that I would spend my time helping the kids in
the community. There is a lot of need here and a lot of children in need.
Sometimes during the summer camps, some of the kids ask if they can
take leftover food to their house so that they can have something to eat
later, and that is hard to hear. It doesn't seem like it, but there are a lot of
people in need here.

Isme told me that, one by one, her children slowly migrated in search of
work. Four of her five children now lived in Boston. As she talked to me,
her granddaughters, one twelve and another four years old, hung around
to listen. She explained that her daughter, who lived in Lowell, Massachusetts, sent the girls to her for the summer so that they wouldn't "lose their
cultural customs and their native language."

When I asked Isme to explain what she meant when she said that she and her husband agreed she would not work outside the home, and instead would stay at home to give her children *calidad de vida* (quality of life), she said that providing quality of life for her children meant "having a parent who was fully there for them to take care of them." In many ways I can see that through her selfless community work, Isme has continued sharing her quality-of-life ethos with the children of the community at large.

THE GARDEN AT EL COQUÍ COMMUNITY CENTER

At the time of my fieldwork, another project was taking place at the community center, the Huertos Caseros Comunitarios Coquí (or Coquí's Community Garden). One of the most active gardeners was Leticia, who was married to Nelson Santos, a respected community elder. When I asked Leticia how she became involved in community volunteer work, she explained that she has been doing this kind of work alongside her husband since she was a young woman. Leticia was a strong, imposing elder woman. I had heard from others that she was a "doer," not one to sit down for too long to chat. I had seen her throughout the week as she rushed in and out, carrying trays of food for the Coquí Solar workshop. The day she sat down to speak with me, she explained that she had been busy cooking all the breakfasts and lunches for the workshop.

About the garden project, she told me that the group comprised eleven members, eight women and three men. The active members were for the most part community elders, but a few young people had begun to show interest in gardening. When I asked about funding the project, Leticia said, "We never wait for anyone to do what we have to do. We don't wait for private or government funders. We try to be a group that is completely self-sustaining. In this phase of the project, we are trying to make our own compost and collect our own seeds that neighbors donate to us. We try to recycle and be self-sufficient."

The folks from the local Agricultural Extension office had been supportive of the project. The members worked closely with Yaminette, an agronomist, community volunteer, and Agricultural Extension retiree. Leticia explained, "Yaminette works with us. She is always with us, and we meet every Monday at 6 p.m. to discuss the project." She said,

> Extensión Agricola wrote a grant to Mycogen to obtain funds to help us buy materials to develop the garden project. We also wrote a grant to

Special Communities to be able to purchase beehives so we can also harvest honey. In this phase 1, we are trying to see what crops do well and what we have to do to get better at this. So far, we have planted and harvested cilantro, basil, and other herbs to make *sofrito*. In the future, we would like to sell good soil and compost, and our harvest. Our short-term goal is to be able to sell our goods to the community. The municipality owns eleven lots that are fallow, and they told us they are willing to let us use those lots for community agriculture. In the future, we'd like to expand the gardens and use that land.

I asked how the group planned to use the money earned from the garden project. Leticia answered, "We hope to reinvest the money from our sales in other community projects. We don't expect to earn money individually, but rather we want to invest in a fund for other projects." Leticia is also part of a house-repairing project that fixes the houses of elderly and needy residents. "This work is solidarity work for the good of the community," Leticia told me before getting up to clean up after the day's workshop.

Times of crisis require thinking beyond the usual horizons. When I conducted fieldwork between 2015 and 2017, I was struck time and again by the selfless acts of the individuals I met. They shared a profound belief in the value of their work and of their communities. In their model, money was not at the center of life. Instead, they emphasized values such as solidarity, mutual help and support, self-sufficiency, empowerment, autonomy, and critical compassion. They understood that the ecosystem was their wealth, and that continued threats to their well-being must be met with informed and empowered resistance. A positive by-product of the metropolitan state's approach to hinterland communities like these is that individuals have learned to be creative and to fend for themselves. In many ways, the poor and marginalized in Puerto Rico, who have long been at the front lines of modernity, seem more adept than their middle- and upper-class counterparts to live with/in the "crisis."

These communities and their ecosystems continue to be under threat. For instance, during the early years of my research in this region, there were plans to build an underwater liquefied natural gas (LNG) pipeline in the Jobos Bay, a project known as the Aguirre Offshore Gas Port (Lloréns 2017). There are also rumors that the government plans to cut down and fill Punta Arenas, an important mangrove reserve, to build a luxury tourist development. To not only survive but also thrive, these communities will have to continue to build social and material systems that can withstand the current crisis and those yet to come.

WOMEN'S COMMUNITY WORK IN THE AFTERMATH OF HURRICANE MARÍA

Women's roles as mothers and caregivers are an important source of pride on the island. In this cultural context, the notion of ecofeminism helps to highlight the ways in which women care for their families and communities, often engaging with their natural surroundings and serving as vital environmental observers and protectors (Mies and Shiva 1993; Gaard 1993). Women act as "doers," creators, community and bridge builders, and defenders of the natural environment. The majority of the organizations that compose IDEBAJO, including Diálogo Ambiental and the El Coquí Community Board, have more women members than men.

I call the women activists of the IDEBAJO collective "eco-feminists" because their work is rooted in environmental concerns and in the struggle against contamination and injustice in their communities. But they are also eco-feminists because of their ability to make "a good life" for themselves and others outside of paid employment. For these women, the creation, reproduction, and sustainability of life is central to their vision of community and of meaningful social relations. The women have experienced firsthand the negative impacts of industrialization in terms of their environment, health outcomes, and staggering rates of unemployment and poverty. In Puerto Rico, gender norms are strongly correlated to socioeconomic class, but these working-class women challenge the cultural prescription that women should remain at home and leave civic and public duties to men. At the same time, it would be misleading to think of the "home" as an isolated household unit: they don't see the private realm of the home as the only place to make an impact because the notion of "home" extends to the community.

Before Hurricane María made landfall, Puerto Rican society already faced a humanitarian and economic crisis. But in places like the Puerto Rican town of Salinas in the southeast, a number of organized, committed, and engaged groups already worked to find solutions. In the immediate aftermath of Hurricane María, community members were some of the first to respond. Isme Figueroa, president of the El Coquí community board, told me in December 2018, "After the hurricane, the community worked many, many hours clearing roads and helping each other. There is still so much left to do. . . . I am just thankful we are alive." In the weeks after the hurricane, community "oases," such as the one Isme helped organize in Coquí, sprang up across the island to distribute supplies and to feed, clothe, and offer support to residents. The vast majority of the community volunteers working in these centers were women.

"It is mainly the women who continue to cook and deliver meals and organize community activities, especially children's events," Isme said. "It is important for us to do this work because the children were highly affected by the hurricane. . . . It is mainly we women who are in charge of taking care of the children, but we also take care of the sick and elderly." In Salinas and Guayama, Isme, along with several other local women, worked tirelessly for five months after María hit, cooking and delivering 440 meals each week to residents in need across the four communities of Las Mareas, Aguirre, San Felipe, and Coquí. Isme explained that some people ate their meals at the community center in Coquí, but community members delivered meals to those who were "bedridden, ill, or to families with children who don't have a car."

After the hurricane, the women from the Coquí community collective took advantage of their skills and connections. They cooked for large groups, built relationships with other women in their communities, delegated tasks, and trained young women to join the effort to ameliorate pressing needs. It began as an urgent, short-term effort to provide clean water and food to children and residents. In the fifteen months since the hurricane, it has turned into a community-led and community-organized clearinghouse that has continued to provide clothing, medicine, supplies, solar lamps, and child and elder care to families whose houses were destroyed. The group has also organized entertainment and cultural and sporting events since María hit.

Abandoned in many ways by the federal and local governments, individuals in "faraway" communities like those in the southeast have learned to be creative and fend for themselves. They work to solve problems, even when they live on the frontline of environmental injustice and suffer the impacts of environmental degradation. In *Paradise Built in Hell*, Rebecca Solnit writes, "Disasters are extraordinarily generative, and though disaster utopias recur again and again, there is no simple formula for what arises: it has everything to do with who or what individuals or communities were before the disaster and the circumstances they find themselves in. But those circumstances are far richer and stranger than has ever been accounted for" (Solnit 2009, 22). Solnit emphasizes the importance of what was already there to determine outcomes. Time and again, I was surprised to hear people report on positive aspects of life after the hurricane. Isme told me that the months after the storm were some of the most gratifying moments she experienced in recent times because she saw the community come to life: "The basketball court was full, like old times when the kids were not always on their phones or their tablets. It was so nice to see people in the park, outside, talking to each other like old times."

Similarly, when I looked at the photographs of the events and meetings IDEBAJO posted on Facebook, I saw people who seemed happy to be together. I talked to members of the collective about this, and they reported feeling grateful to have each other. They also commented that after the storm, many new members joined the community organizations and attended their events. Mayra, an IDEBAJO volunteer, said, "People wanted to help, and they joined our efforts, cooking, delivering meals, and attending our gatherings." One man remarked, "The hurricane brought with it work for us. I have been busy clearing out trees and debris. I had not had work in quite some time. I'd be glad if a hurricane strikes every five years, that way I can have work again." Carmen, another volunteer, remarked, "The hurricane brought us closer. We got busy helping each other, trying to put things back together, and spending a lot of time with family and neighbors. I cherish those days because now, only four months after the storm, we are slowly drifting apart again. That's the one thing I want back from the early days after the hurricane: the sense of togetherness, the feeling that we are all in this together."

While women buttress important initiatives, such as community and environmental justice work, they often do so without receiving public recognition or pay. And although this is slowly changing, men have historically served as the public faces of history or spokespeople for social and environmental justice movements, while women are busy in the background building, supporting, and maintaining those very movements. I argue that this is another facet of "matriarchal dispossession," that women's contributions to Puerto Rican society are often not elevated to their respectful place, they are discounted and devalued, and their voices are silenced or relegated to the background. Women's community work is often aimed at making change and affecting communities in real ways. Their work encompasses both the conceptual search for solutions to problems facing communities and the practical applications of those solutions.

The work of Diálogo Ambiental is one such example of this resistance. Diálogo is a nonprofit community environmental organization whose members, mainly women and girls, have organized multiple environmental awareness activities, such as the Convivencia Ambiental camp. In 2018, that camp had run for twelve consecutive years, and for ten of those years, the camp's total budget was only $300 to $600 dollars. It was not until Hurricane María, when IDEBAJO began to receive sizable donations from individuals, organizations, and granting agencies, that the camp finally, in 2018, had funds to hire a local youth as a camp coordinator. The camp is organized by a volunteer community education commission within Diálogo, composed mostly of women and girls who plan the promotional, financial, and logistical aspects of the program. The successful 2018 summer workshop was themed "To Survive We Have to Live in Community."

The camp workshops have exposed dozens of local youths to the nature reserve. Workshop activities focusing on the Jobos Bay watershed promote a holistic approach to the area's natural environment, history, and culture. Youth participants—often led by young women—have done cleanup activities and bird-watching, have created artwork and written essays about their experiences, and have participated in radio programs, photography workshops, and other activities. All the programs rely on donations and volunteers. According to Yaminette, who has volunteered with Convivencia Ambiental for the past twelve years, "It is imperative for these young people to learn to appreciate the wealth of the local ecosystem so that when they become adults, they can protect it and pass down their knowledge of the ecosystem and how to protect it to their own children."

The youths have their own reasons for participating, and Yaminette shared some of the feedback she has received from them:

"I never knew how beautiful my community was."

"I love bird-watching in the reserve."

"I get to kayak in the bay, and I always wanted to learn kayaking."

"I love spotting manatees and sea turtles when the group goes out in the bay."

"We have to defend our ecosystem and not let anyone take it away from us."

The Jobos Bay community is fundamentally dependent on the natural environment, and the natural environment is integral to the tight-knit social relationships with kin and community. In a 2015 study about well-being and the use of natural resources in the southeast, Carlos G. García-Quijano and colleagues found that people rated "spending time with family and friends," "having a good relationship with my community," and "doing work to help my community" as much more important than "the ability make a lot of money." The study also found that dependence on local environments and social interdependence are mutually reinforcing for these coastal communities (2015b).

The nature of women's initiatives in this region reflects these values. They emphasize values like solidarity, mutual help and support, self-sufficiency, empowerment, autonomy, and compassion. Women engaged in community initiatives understand that the ecosystem is their wealth and they must protect it in order to safeguard their and their children's future. And this resistance takes many forms. With this work, I have aimed to document the lives, work, and contributions of women who are in danger of being left out of the historical record. If I have learned anything from personal and official history, it is that if we let the histories of these women vanish, we might lose sight of the real source of strength and continuity in our communities.

ON NEOLIBERALISM'S INSIDIOUSNESS AND THE WILL TO FIGHT AGAINST IT

When Hurricane María made landfall in Puerto Rico in September 2017, it found a society in the throes of a sociopolitical and economic crisis. Economic downturns and recession coupled with waves of mass migration had characterized the Puerto Rican experience since the early decades of the American occupation. Vulture capitalists had circled and preyed on the colony since the second half of the twentieth century, though the facade of political and economic stability began to officially unravel in the 1990s (García-Colón and Franqui-Rivera 2015). The debt crisis and the neoliberal austerity policies that followed depleted the local state such that it cannot provide even the most basic resources to its citizens.

Currently, philanthrocapitalists interested in the island's recovery dot the post-hurricane landscape (Klein 2018).[12] In light of this, everyday women—mostly mothers but not all affiliated with local organizations such as IDEBAJO—are turning into community organizers and advocates to secure the well-being of their communities. Often, they fight against great and powerful forces, such as the Department of Education and the likes of Applied Energy Systems, Monsanto, Pioneer, Syngenta, and Dow AgroSciences, to name a few.

Glenis was one such mother and community advocate. She was one of the leaders of a small group of mothers working to stop her neighborhood's elementary school from being shut down. It was 2018, the height of the austerity cuts in public services. Public school closures had been mandated by Governor Ricky Roselló's administration, and they were being carried out by Julia Kelleher, the secretary of education. I spent time with Glenis and other mothers who were organizing at the community's small plaza to stop the school closure. She had attended that community school, Escuela Pedro Soto Rivera, and so had her aunt and her cousins and now her daughter.

The mothers tried to get a meeting with the secretary of education to argue their case. They wanted to tell her that it was a fully functional, wonderful community school where the children were thriving, the facilities were updated, and the parents volunteered to clean and help the children paint murals on the walls. But the secretary was not available. They had found out about the education department's plan on April 28, 2018. On that day they set up tents and chairs in front of the school. For the remainder of the school year, they sat there every day, careful not to leave the camp unattended at any point. Their goal was to intercept any official visitors and/or moving vans that attempted to remove furniture from the school.

They reached out to the mayor of Salinas, who expressed sympathy but could not help them stop the closure. A local attorney submitted an injunction to stop the school's closing, but it was dismissed. The secretary of education argued that there were too many elementary schools in Salinas, each with low enrollment. The school in Glenis's community serviced ninety-four children from the contiguous neighborhoods: San Felipe, Mosquito, Barriada Lopez, and La Calle del Pescao.

These neighborhoods were located in a mangrove forest. The people who lived there were working-class and low-income Afro-descendant families whose ancestors worked in the sugarcane industry, once the main industry and employer in the southeast. The cement houses were owned by the neighborhood's better-off segment, and wood-and-zinc houses were owned by the poorest neighbors. Mosquito was characteristic of the region's coastal neighborhoods. The median household annual income was $18,189 in Salinas; 49.9 percent of the 27,128 residents lived in poverty, and 38.4 percent of those who lived in the town self-identified as Black or African American.[13]

For the school to remain open, Glenis was told it had to service two hundred children. So, she and the other mothers began a campaign to get children from nearby neighborhoods to enroll. The Department of Education planned to consolidate schools with low enrollment into larger schools, and Glenis and the group of mothers were able to register only a handful of students—not nearly enough. They were frustrated but kept up hope that they would prevail. Local parents had seen correctional trucks going into the school. They told the group that the state had sent these instead of Department of Education trucks to empty the school, to throw them off their trail. Glenis received visits from Social Services workers, who claimed they were investigating her for child neglect. With tears in her eyes, as much from anger as from hurt, Glenis explained,

> We found out that Julia Kelleher was going to tour schools in Salinas, Guayama, and Arroyo in order to decide what schools to shut down, and that day we went out early to the avenue to wait for her to pass by. We had our signs ready, and when we saw a caravan of cars approaching, we tried to flag them down to ask her to stop and talk to us. There were two large SUVs with tinted windows, and when they saw us, they sped up and away. . . . The windows were so dark we could not even see who was inside. They went right by, lifting dust in their tracks, ignoring us as if we were not there, as if we don't exist, like we do not matter. . . . I will never forgive those politicians in San Juan for taking away my daughter's right to attend a school in her community. We are poor people here, but that doesn't mean we do not deserve good schools for our children.

When I asked Glenis how she had become empowered to fight against the school closure, she said, "I've been volunteering in my children's schools since my son was in Head Start fifteen years ago, and since then, teachers have always told me, as a parent you have power, you have rights and a voice, don't be afraid to use it. I am not one to sit around with my arms crossed. I decided to get active and try to stop this macabre plan." Two weeks later, Glenis said that they had received the official notice of school closure. She was sad and angry to have lost the fight. She considered it unfair, an abuse of "us, the little people" by the big politicians in San Juan.

Still, Glenis was undaunted. She would continue to fight for the well-being of her community. Along with her son, Leny, she was attending the solar panel installation workshops at the Coquí Community Center and was hoping to get off the grid soon. She was looking forward to volunteering in her daughter's new school when the school year started. But she said that when elections came around, she would not vote. She was tired of voting for people who did not work for her and her community's best interests, "because the local politicians are in the pocket of the San Juan politicians, and all they care about is themselves and getting kickbacks from corrupt dealings. No, I won't vote again. For what?"

One day Glenis said she wanted to introduce me to Evelyn, who lived two streets over in San Felipe. Evelyn had been organizing neighbors to seek redress from one of the *semilleras* (seeders), the local name given to the multinational corporations producing experimental seed and agrochemical GMOs in southeast Puerto Rico. Dow AgroSciences was located to the north of the Mosquito and San Felipe neighborhoods. To the east, they were flanked by the AES coal plant, and by the Aguirre Power Plant Complex to the west. To the south, the neighborhood turned into a thick mangrove forest leading directly to the Caribbean Sea.

Glenis and I walked over to the neighborhood school that had just been shuttered. She wanted to show me the murals the children had helped paint. Then we stopped by Evelyn's mother's house, directly across from the school. Sure enough, Evelyn was just getting off her bike to drop off food for her elderly parents. As Glenis introduced us, Evelyn looked me up and down with distrust.

Evelyn, an athletic woman in her late fifties, was an energic talker with kind eyes. Glenis told Evelyn she should talk to me about the devastating mudslides in her community. Evelyn immediately started cursing the local politicians: "They don't do anything to help, they don't back their constituency, they make promises they don't keep, and they only want votes." She also railed against local activists for being in the mayor's pocket: "There is no one that communities like ours can really trust or count on to help when we most need help." It was evening, and nighttime was setting in. She said I should come by her house during the day and gave me her phone number.

A few days later, Evelyn met me at the front gate. "C'mon," she said, "I'm going to introduce you to my neighbor across the street. She has been one of the people most affected by the mudslides." We walked hurriedly over to a two-floor cement house painted tan. I could clearly see mud marks halfway up the first floor as she called to her neighbor, "This woman is here to learn about the mudslides, and I want to show her your house." Then she told me, "Go ahead, take pictures." A woman in her early eighties emerged and explained, "Yes, we had muddy water all over the yard. It was awful, and no one has helped us, no one. We still have to paint the house. It looks dirty. When the mudslide hit, we had to run to get our dogs and chickens out of harm's way. Now we worry every time it rains that it will happen again."

Dow AgroSciences has a subsidiary to the north of the neighborhood, a block over from Evelyn's street. Before this GMO transgenic seed and agrochemical multinational set up an office and agricultural field, the land was a cow pasture planted with grasses and bush. When Dow AgroSciences leased the land, it tore up the grasses and planted its experimental seeds. In removing the grass that kept the soil from shifting, it exposed the sandy red clay soil typical of this desert coast.

A month after Hurricane María, when residents still had no electricity (even though their neighborhood is flanked by two of Puerto Rico's most significant producers of electricity), torrential rains caused a mudslide from the Dow AgroSciences land into the neighborhood. In November, more rains caused a second mudslide. Evelyn explained that the mudslides destroyed several neighbors' yards and, ever since, there has been a glossy sheen in the yards. She believed chemicals in the mud caused their yards to look as though the ground were always wet.

We walked to five different houses and, in each one, the neighbors let me look at the mud marks on their walls and the glossy sheen in their yards. They each told me that the company sent diggers to clear the mud from the streets, but it refused to compensate people for their losses. People lost furniture and appliances, their yards were ruined, and exterior house paint was damaged when the mud seeped into the yards as well as inside their houses. Evelyn has just paid to have the exterior of her house painted because she could not stand the mud stains.

The multinational had so far refused to take responsibility for the mudslide. Community members asked the mayor to help, but to no effect. They sent a notarized letter to the Dow AgroSciences headquarters and were still waiting to receive an answer. On the hot day we spent walking from house to house, Evelyn and her neighbors said no one could be counted on to help, and they were left alone to defend themselves. At each house, I was told that they would not vote again, that politicians were in the pockets of the multinationals, that they did not care about local communities. Evelyn told me that when she and her neighbors went to the mayor's office to ask for help, they were told, "You should just stay quiet. The corporations have powerful lawyers, and you will lose. They are just too powerful." Indignant, Evelyn contacted a San Juan environmental lawyer, who helped them craft the notarized letter they had sent.

Evelyn invited me to her house for a cold drink of water. She showed me her file of documents and photographs on the case. The list of neighbors backing the claim against the multinational had over thirty signatures. I then met her husband, Ramón, a tall, thin man in his early sixties. He had just retired as a driver with a local truck company. At the kitchen table, we looked at a photograph from the case file of a woman sitting inside her living room. She was looking down at her feet covered in red clay mud. Evelyn said, "This photo here is that shuttered house you saw during our walk." She explained that the woman in the photo with the modest house had lost all of her belongings, furniture, and appliances in the mudslides. This woman had been so depressed by having been hit by María, not having electricity, and then being affected by two consecutive mudslides that she had closed her house and left to visit her children in New Jersey. She had yet to return home. Evelyn explained,

> The company told us that the mudslides were not their fault or responsibility. Now who is going to help her repair her house and buy new furniture and appliances? We are poor people here. This is an abuse. We are being abused by this company. And what will happen when it rains again? They dug a trench around their property to keep the water and mud from flowing out. So, if they did this, they took action to repair the flaw. Then they know it is their responsibility. They even sent their machines to clean our streets, so that was also accepting responsibility. Yet they refuse to compensate us for our losses. We had to paint our house and make a barrier with cements blocks around our properties to try and prevent the mud from flowing into our house. You saw that several of us did this, spent our money creating a barrier—now, they should reimburse us. I talked to a guy down the street who works at Dow, and he said he can't help us because he is afraid of losing his job.

Evelyn's husband, Ramón, looked wary. In some of the photos taken just nine months before my visit, he was cleaning the mud and debris from the front of their house. He looked burly and robust—at least fifty pounds heavier. An astute observer, Evelyn noticed my shock when I asked in disbelief, "Is this you, Ramón?"

Later we walked out to their well-tended herb and vegetable garden, and Evelyn showed me the land crabs they were cleaning and fattening up for a meal. She whispered softly that Ramón had colon cancer and was very sensitive about his condition as well as his dramatic weight loss. He was embarrassed about being so skinny and looking sick and was hardly going outside anymore. The cancer had come on suddenly, but he was fighting it. He did not want anyone to know about his condition, she said, and she asked me not to mention it in front of him.

Dr. Gerson Jimenez, the director of the remaining local hospital (two other hospitals had recently closed down due to economic difficulties) shared that between 2010 and 2014, he documented 164 new cancer cases in the region, a 70 percent increase in local cancer rates. Stomach, prostate, colon, lung, and liver cancers were the most prevalent. Dr. Jimenez, who had been at that hospital for forty years, said respiratory illnesses had also increased exponentially in the region. He attributed the increase to the contaminants from the AES coal power plant, the Aguirre Power Complex, and the GMO agrochemical industry, all heavy and "dirty" industries located in the region. "The worst illness afflicting the region is poverty," he said. "Because this is a poor region, people are powerless. They have little political clout and voice with which to defend themselves against the onslaught of contaminating industries sited here." Dr. Jimenez was speaking to me in the language of environmental justice because for forty years he had been an active member of several environmental groups and initiatives that fought against pollution and contamination in the region.

At Evelyn and Ramón's house, we discussed the region's legacy of contamination and pollution, and Ramón pensively explained, "What will happen here is what happened in Vieques with the navy. All these companies are contaminating us and contaminating our water. Then they'll leave and leave all the contamination behind. They will leave us all sick, and people don't know what to, who to turn to. The politicians only come around when they want our votes, but when we need them, they are nowhere to be found." Evelyn followed, remarking, "That's true, because here we have cancers, respiratory illnesses, allergies, chest pains . . . but the problem is that people here are scared of the companies because they are rich and powerful, and they tell us, when we go to City Hall, when we go to government agencies to complain, they say, you better get a good lawyer because those people have powerful lawyers . . . and the odds are against you."

I left their house and neighborhood feeling heartbroken, grief-stricken, and angry at my inability to do little more than document their struggles.

I hoped at the very least that powerful people who cared about environmental justice would learn about what was happening in Puerto Rico's southeast. I hoped that together we could exert pressure to end these heinous acts of injustice and abuse. Time and again, throughout my time listening to and documenting the environmental injustices faced by community members, I felt anger, grief, and sometimes even despair at the multinationals' cavalier destruction of the ecosphere, enabled for decades by the local and federal governments. I was heartened again and again, though, by the willingness of community members to speak up and to continue to fight and resist injustice.

It was clear that communities like this one, and people like Glenis and Evelyn, suffer as a result of the neoliberal austerity debt policies dismantling public goods and services that are coupled with environmental deregulation and the state's near-total withdrawal from environmental governance. In light of the dysfunction and near annihilation of the liberal-democratic benefactor state, some community members, by virtue of their social and environmental activism, exercise a kind of democracy from below that is both emancipatory in its empowering dimensions and coercive because people are reacting to having almost no political voice or representation. Significantly, these communities go beyond the protest. In the process of fighting for their ecosystem, they also craft solutions to ensure the community's well-being and long-term survival. Communities such as the ones in the Jobos Bay are forging a semblance of what autonomy and liberation for the common good can be.

CHAPTER 4

LIVING WITH/IN ECOLOGICAL CATASTROPHE

Hurricane María parked on top of us. It lasted such a long time. It was a
loud, roaring monster, and we felt the earth trembling. We looked out
the windows and saw the mountains shaking. We felt the ground
shaking. It was as if a hurricane and an earthquake were happening at
the same time. It was so loud, it sounded as if everything around
us—the earth itself, the trees—were screaming. When it was all over
and we saw the mountains . . . it was like we had left one world behind
and entered another, where everything looked sad, dead. Everything
changed overnight. All these months later, I have not recovered, and I
still hear the roars, the screaming earth. I will never forget those sounds.

—DOÑA MERCEDES, JANUARY 2018

THE SCIENTIFIC COMMUNITY HAS REACHED CONSENSUS THAT
without significantly curbing greenhouse gas emissions, life on earth will
be increasingly untenable.[1] Some believe that we are dangerously close to
the tipping point of total ecosystems collapse, which would make the devastating effects of climate change irrevocable (Lenton et al. 2019; Rockström et al. 2009). The effects of the Anthropocene, "a geological era of
humanity's own making," have introduced the specter of ecological catastrophe on a global scale (Dibley 2012, 139; Crutzen and Stoermer 2000; Davis
et al. 2019). But in the Americas, catastrophe has long been unfolding as a
result of the "raciological-ecological" extractive transformation imposed
by European colonialism on Indigenous and Black populations, nonhuman animals, plants, water, and land (Davis et al. 2019, 6; Wynter 2015). In
the Anthropocene, humans' continued manipulation of and extractive
entanglements with "Nature" (conceived as distinct from "Man") have produced "monstrous hybridity" such as "climate change, soil modification,

social acidification," genetically modified organisms, and so on (Dibley 2012, 7; Dyer-Witheford 2009).

Ushered by European colonialism, the ravenous extractivism fueling the racial Capitalocene's engine is responsible for engendering the anthropogenic geological time in the Americas and in the Caribbean that some refer to as the Plantationocene (Vergès 2017, Davis et al. 2019; Haraway 2015; Tsing 2015; Aikens et al. 2019). In the American hemispheric context, this still-unfolding era is defined by the accelerating capital-intensive practices that began with Indigenous genocide and land expropriation and the trafficking of abducted, enslaved Africans to labor on the stolen land, the turning of territory as well as people into property, the enclosing of spaces and their inhabitants, mass surveillance, and the continued dehumanization, exploitation, and incarceration of necropolitical humans, nonhuman animals, and the natural world (Woods 2002, 2017; McKittrick 2011, 2013). The intensification of the catastrophic effects of anthropogenic climate change, such as hurricanes, uncontainable wildfires, heat waves, floods, and drought, evidence the delusional modern conceit of "Man's" mastery over Nature (Plumwood 1993; Latour 2004; Haraway 2007; McIntyre and Nast 2011; Dibley 2012; Wynter and McKittrick 2015; Vergès 2017, 2019; Anderson and Perrin 2018; Davis et al. 2019). But as Hurricane Katrina, the Flint water crisis, and Hurricane María illustrated, the disproportionate impacts of human-caused environmental change are greater among already economically, politically, and racially marginalized and vulnerable populations (Pulido 2018; Nixon 2017; Lloréns 2018b; Davis et al. 2019).

In this last chapter, I reflect on what I learned between December 2017 and August 2018 from women survivors of Hurricanes Irma and María. Additionally, I examine the multiple ways in which people in the island's southeast use intergenerational Black ecological knowledge to make meaningful lives within the ruins of the plantation, all the while resisting the social and ecocidal death-logics wrought by the racial Capitalocene in the Anthropocene. This chapter foregrounds the catastrophic climate change that many of the hurricane survivors, after having experienced nearly complete devastation, believe is already upon us. I offer a decolonial perspective of Puerto Rican history and theorize how the state's sociopolitical and cultural construction as patriarch, together with conceptions of the colonized motherland, contributes to the historical marginalization of Black women's lives, knowledge(s), and sociopolitical, ecological, and environmental contributions, as it supports the continued extraction and degradation of the feminized territory.

To conclude, I draw on Jared Sexton's tripartite scheme of "racial slavery," "settler colonialism," and "orientalism." Each of these illustrates a coeval mode of action and systems that European and American racial capitalism deployed in relation to Indigenous peoples and enslaved Africans, and to the regions of Asia, the Middle East, and Latin America (2016, 589). Arguably as a result of Puerto Rico's geographic location and liminal sociopolitical position in the Americas, all of these sociopolitical and economic schemes have overlapped and coexisted in the archipelago. Each created conditions—social, physical, psychological, historic, political, and economic—that resonate in and shape the present.

I interpolate Puerto Rican studies to *think beyond* the muck of the (colonial) nation-state's exceptionalism and cultural nationalist ideologies, as these continue to "limit" and "fixate" views and understandings of the archipelago and its people, their movements and flows, in relation to European, American, and Latin American whiteness. What would it look like to engage in a deprovincialized conceptual and epistemological excavation, an unfolding of the layers—Indigenous, Black, and European? To what ends were these so easily folded into the prevalent hegemonic ideology of "a harmonious racial mixture," which was then seized upon in relation to white American colonialism and distorted, marred, and arrested? What if, instead, the archipelago was understood as a node in a much larger conceptual ecology that could be examined from various vantage points, including, as I do in this book, the methods and insights of hemispheric, continental, and global Black and Indigenous thought? (Jackson 2012; T. L. King 2019; Alamo-Pastrana 2016). I aim to integrate conceptions of the Puerto Rico archipelago and the lives of Puerto Ricans into the flow of Black and Indigenous hemispheric and global thought and sociopolitical movements by explicitly delinking these conceptions from the prevalent Euro-centered coloniality of knowledge.

THE HURRICANE AFTERMATH'S EXPONENTIAL
OVERBURDEN ON WOMEN

In January 2018, I visited Doña Mercedes, a sixty-eight-year-old resident of a mountain neighborhood that straddles the border of Arecibo and Utuado in the island's northwest. She had spent her entire life in the lush tropical mountains there, but the intensity and destruction left behind by Hurricane María had frightened her so much, she was planning to move to a house nearby in the flat plain at the base of the mountain. Her modest wooden house had been nearly destroyed, and while she and her family waited for the new cement house to be ready, they were living in the tattered house with a blue tarp as a makeshift roof. Doña Mercedes and Don Manuel, her seventy-year-old husband, lived with two of their four adult children, two teenage grandchildren, and a few outdoor dogs, cats, and chickens.

As we sat on plastic chairs under a carport that doubled as a seating area, I spotted several calabazas (*Cucurbita moschata*, known as winter squash) growing in the *pastizal* (grassland) surrounding the house. I asked about the large and healthy-looking calabazas protruding from the lush grasses, and Don Manuel and Doña Mercedes invited me to walk through their property to see all the food they grew. They showed me herbs, lemons, grapefruit, bananas, soursop, and several kinds of medicinal and ornamental plants. I commented on how verdant the mountains were, on the plumpness of the calabazas and the bananas. The mountain air smelled fresh and felt clean. The trees swayed in a continuous light breeze. They said they sometimes spotted rhesus macaque monkeys in the nearby trees, and they wondered what had happened to them during the storm. I spotted five Google Internet balloons from their house, floating high above us in the sky. I had read about Google's Project Loon, an experimental project that deployed solar-powered "stratospheric balloons" to beam Internet signals to Earth in hard-hit disaster areas.[2] The post-hurricane period was marked by the intensification of experimental technologies and projects recalling the archipelago's long history as a site of exploitative military, medical, economic, political, and technological experimentation (Baver 1993; Concepción 1995; Berman Santana 1996; McCaffrey 2002; Dietrich 2013; de Onís 2017, 2018; among others).

After our walk through their yard, Don Manuel remarked, "Nature has rebounded well and much faster than us." In a hushed tone, he explained, "Mercedes has been very depressed since the hurricane. She is sad all the time. I feel fine, but seeing her this way worries me. I don't want to move from here, from this land . . . I will move with her to the cement house to make her happy, but I will probably spend a lot of time here. We are alive, and that is what matters. I tell her that we are going forward with our lives."

The electric authority told Don Manuel that it was likely they would not get electricity again until June 2018. In the meantime, they were making do with electricity gathered from two solar panels connected to a truck battery that was in turn hooked up to an inverter and a charge controller inside their house. When I complimented their resourcefulness, Doña Mercedes told me that one of their adult sons had come up with the idea. He bought the solar panels from a local man who had listed them online, then he bought the truck battery from an auto shop. Don Manuel told me that they planned to invest in more solar panels and possibly stay off the grid altogether. The grid had been unreliable for years, repeatedly damaging their home appliances. They were often left "scrambling in the dark, and plus, electricity has become basically unaffordable for us poor people."

Later Doña Mercedes told me that seeing her house destroyed was depressing. After the hurricane she was not the same person she used to be:

> I won't lie to you. I have been depressed and melancholic. I want my house back. I am doing the laundry by hand, but it is a lot of work. I am just holding on at this point. This is the worst thing that has happened to Puerto Rico, and the government has stolen the money, and they are not doing anything. It feels like we are living in the 1940s, like when I was a child. Our house was a one-room wooden shack, and we didn't have electricity. What I detest the most about not having electricity is feeling isolated and the fact that I have to wash all the clothes in buckets by hand. It is so much work, washing clothes by hand, and with two teenagers and the amount of dirty clothes they produce, I have developed blisters. Right now, it feels like life is just too much work. With hauling heavy buckets of water for every need, my body aches all over and I have no energy.

Mercedes was not alone in feeling overwhelmed, depressed, and tired. A 2018 Oxfam report called "The Weight of Water on Women" documented the differential gender impacts of post–Hurricane María life. It found that "because women are usually the managers of the household—responsible for taking care of people and domestic systems—they were the ones who shouldered most of the burdens of managing water needs (2018, 2). Additionally, the report explained, "Laundry nearly always fell to women in the household. Among the physical problems they encountered from doing laundry by hand: fatigue, pain in backs and shoulders, dry and cracked skin on hands (from contact with detergents)" (2018, 12). In Puerto Rico's patriarchal society, the domestic and the emotional spheres of caregiving for the husband, the children, and the elderly are the domain of women. Cultural judgments about what makes a "good woman" involve her ability to properly care for her family. This includes cooking; feeding; enforcing hygiene and proper presentation and comportment of children; caregiving for elderly, ill, and disabled relatives; and maintaining a clean, neat house. Consistently available water and electricity help to ease the burdens that come with the heavy cultural expectations placed on women. In the post-disaster scenario, without potable running water and electricity to power appliances, women felt an "exponential overburden," as they tried to cope and restore normalcy in their daily lives (2018, 12).

After leaving Mercedes's house, I drove down the PR-123, a winding mountain road in Utuado. I stopped to chat with a man and a woman collecting water from a spring. Carmen and Orlando, a gregarious couple in their sixties, told me that the water had not yet returned to their mountain home. Their solution had been to drink bottled water and to fetch spring water for all other household needs and for their animals. Orlando remarked, "We got our electricity two weeks ago, but not our water. But I would rather have water than electricity because water is life. I think here in Puerto Rico, we are still rich because we have water, health, family, and life." Carmen chimed in: "You know, the politicians use us poor folks to get our votes. They come around during election time. But when the disaster hit, they disappeared and left us to fend for ourselves. Even when the electricity came back, it came back first for rich people, but we poor are the last to get these basic services back." Carmen said it had been difficult to keep their house clean and to care for their three dogs with no running water, so they fetched water at this mountain spring three times a week. "The housework has multiplied. It feels like it never ends. [The] good thing is that Orlando likes to help out around the house. Without his help, it would be unbearable."

Carmen told me that together they care for one of their adult children, an Iraq veteran whose experience on the war front left him disabled. About her son's condition, she said, "In this society, you are only a person when you can contribute. The minute you can't, you are cast aside and treated as less than human." Their younger son had lived with them until after the hurricane. He had a master's degree but could not find a job, so he was working at a shoe store. But after the hurricane, it shut down, and he was unable to find another job. He was recruited to work at a wiring factory in Michigan, and although he didn't even know where Michigan was, he was so desperate that he took the job. "He says it is very cold there and he sends us pictures of himself in the snow," Carmen told me. "He says he likes it and is happy to have a job. As a mother, I worry about him and wonder if he'll ever be able to return to live with us here. It makes me sad that my son had to leave in order to make a living."

In January 2018, I was driving in Luquillo, on the island's northeast shore, when I came across a tent encampment beneath a roofed basketball court. The basketball court was located between a stretch of busy highway and the seashore. I parked nearby and walked toward the small tent community. I spotted a young, neat-looking woman washing down some dining room chairs with a hose. I asked her whether the chairs had been from her home. "No," she said. "These were donated to me recently. They are for my new house." Before I could go any further, I was greeted by another woman, who identified herself as Ana. I got the impression that Ana was the spokesperson for the encampment. I explained to Ana that I was conducting research on how people were coping in the hurricane's aftermath and asked if I could ask her a few questions about her situation. Ana, an outgoing forty-year-old Afro–Puerto Rican woman, said she was happy to chat with me: "I want to tell everyone that the government is not helping me and my kids. We have been left to fend for ourselves." Without pausing, she explained further:

> I am always here because I do not own a car, and so whenever someone comes by, I am the person who is often interviewed. The local TV news have come twice, and I told them the reason I am here. I told them the truth, that I lost everything, and that the municipal government did not help me, and I had been asking the municipal government for help with my house since 2009 because it was falling apart, and the dirt road was washing away every time it rained. Some of the others staying at the camp got annoyed with me for talking to the news, but I told them that the reason I get to tell my story is because I am stuck here without a car.

Ana showed me around the encampment. She said she had been living in two large tents with her family for the last two months. She shared the tents with her two daughters, aged seventeen and twenty, and two grandchildren, a six-month-old baby boy and a two-year-old toddler girl. I met them all during my visit. There were several other tents, and Ana explained that one was occupied by Yamil and Clarisa and their five-year-old son. In another lived an elderly couple, and a single man in his fifties lived in another. She said others had come and gone in the last eight weeks but that she was reaching a point of desperation because she had been unable to find a place to live:

I don't have a car or a phone. I have nothing. I lost it all, even my clothes.
The clothes I am wearing right now were donated. My house was on a
piece of land my father left me up in a hill far away from the road. The
house was made out of wood and zinc, and it all blew away. I used to plant
and sell plantains, yucca, and pumpkin at the traffic light, and that's how
I made a living in the last few years. I am very poor, I am sick, and I only
live off the small welfare check and the produce I used to sell.

I asked Ana if she had relatives in the area and whether there were any
family members who could help. She told me, "I am on my own with my
daughters and grandchildren. I am responsible for the five of us." She went
on, "When I was younger, I lived in Paterson, New Jersey, with my parents,
but they decided to move back to Puerto Rico. My mom died a year and a
half ago. My father was a heroin addict; he also died. They both died from
cancer."

About the situation of the tenants of the homeless camp, she said,

Everyone here at the camp has received a Section 8 voucher to rent a
house, but the problem is finding a house that will pass the inspection.
Right before the storm, I went to stay with a family member. Then after
the storm, when I went to see my house, it was destroyed. I lost my house
and everything in it. I stayed with my relative for a month, but when I
told them I could not contribute money to the household, they kicked me
out with my grandkids. Then I went to a shelter at a school, but they
closed down the shelter and asked the families to leave because they were
going to start classes. That's when I came here, to the basketball court.
I have been here two months. Because the encampment can be seen from
the highway, many people have come here to bring us tents, water, food.
We have military food, solar lamps, clothes, toys. . . . Most of the donations we have received have come from churches. A group of doctors and
veterinarians came here as well. I have asthma, and they treated me and
left me with medications, so I am all set. The stray dogs who live here have
been treated by vets as well. We have been helped by churches, doctors,
individuals who stop by with food and tents. Even some people came here
from Cuba and gave me a tent. You see that big tent? That's my tent, and I
received that from two Cubans who came here and brought it to me. I got
a gas stove from an American man. I mean, mostly individuals and
private entities like churches and chefs have helped us. They have done
way more than the government.

After spending a couple of hours at the camp, I told Ana that I would return in a few days and asked her what I could bring her. She said washing detergent and diapers. I returned in a few days with two cases of water, three boxes of diapers, and laundry detergent. When I greeted her, she cried uncontrollably, saying that she felt trapped at the camp:

> Other people here have cars, and phones. I don't have those things. So even though I have been given a Section 8 voucher, I have been unable to find a house. I wish the government gave me a list of houses and one of the free Obama phones so that I could call around. It is really difficult to get things done here without a car and a phone. I am stuck here. I have walked around here looking for houses but have not found anything. When I got here, I went to the mayor's office and demanded that they put a security guard here because this is a dangerous situation. We are living here in the open by the highway; anyone could come by and hurt us, so the mayor assigned officers who come in shifts of twelve hours to guard this place. They are my friends now. They let me borrow their phone so that I can try to find a house. Yamil and Clarisa found a house. In fact, Yamil and Clarisa have already moved into their house. The lady let them move in ahead of passing the inspection so that they no longer have to sleep here with their five-year-old son. I noticed that when people find a house, they change, and they stop helping out here. I am the only one here who cooks, cleans, and organizes the donations. Just me. It is a lot of work, and I feel overwhelmed. I am here with my underage daughter and her two children. She has mental problems. She looks normal, but she has serious mental problems. Her father raped her when she was fourteen years old.

Stunned at this revelation, I asked Ana if she reported it to the police.

> ANA: Yes, I put him in jail. I applied to Law 54 and sent him to jail. I am her mother, and I have to help her . . . and she has these little kids. That boy there is the girl's father. He comes here and spends time with his daughter and takes care of her. [I had noticed that a teenage age boy was taking care of the two-year-old girl the entire time I was there.]
>
> HLL: Why doesn't he take his daughter to his house?
>
> ANA: He doesn't have a steady place to live. He stays here and there, and that's not good for the child. In fact, when I first got

here, the department of children and family got wind that I was here with the kids, and I heard they were coming to take away the kids, so I ran away. For two days, I hid with the kids in the tent by the beach, but then I had nowhere to go, so I came back, and the social worker came here and told me, "Ana, stop hiding. We just want to give you food for you and the kids." I was so relieved. But they told me they are coming back and that I need to be in a house by early February or else they will take away the kids. I am starting to go crazy here . . . I don't know what I'm going to do. They all depend on me . . . I have to find a way to get us out of here.

Ana's situation revealed that long after the storm, the catastrophe of abject poverty remained. As of July 2018, Puerto Rico's poverty rate was 43.1 percent, but the rate among the archipelago's children was 58 percent (Mayol-García 2019). Mayol-García and Burd also found that in Puerto Rico, "single parents are more likely than married parents to have low education, low income, to be younger and to be part of an ethnic/racial minority" (2018, 1). Homeless encampments housing families with children in Puerto Rico are extremely rare. Thus, the situation in which Ana and the others at the camp found themselves is outside the norm and signals an extreme level of poverty in the context of the archipelago.

Ana mentioned feeling hindered because she did not own a car. In Puerto Rico, where public transportation is nonexistent, not having a car becomes a major hurdle in accomplishing the tasks required to sustain a family. Ana grew up poor but inherited a parcel of land from her father. Without relatives to help her, she had been able to fend for herself before the hurricanes by combining government assistance and produce selling. Now she felt adrift and desperate, and she felt her mental health declining. As a single mother experiencing matriarchal dispossession, still in charge of two daughters and two grandchildren, Ana felt it was her responsibility to improve her and her family's situation. She mentioned that a FEMA caseworker with whom she had become friendly told her to go to a hotel and that FEMA would pay for it. Ana refused the offer because she believed that going to a hotel would be isolating and that at the basketball court everyone could see the tents and their living situation. She believed that exposure was a good thing and that if she went to a hotel, her situation would be filed under "resolved" and she would never get the help needed to find a permanent place to live.

FIG 4.1 View of the homeless tent encampment where Ana and her children lived, Luquillo, Puerto Rico, January 2018.

Though she would have been more comfortable, not to mention safer in a hotel room, I believe Ana had a good point. By remaining an eyesore in the tent encampment for all to see, Ana ensured that the local and federal government could not easily ignore her plight. This was a difficult strategy, but she believed it would help her get into permanent subsidized housing much quicker than if she allowed FEMA to, in her words, "hide me away in a hotel room." Even though Ana and her family were indigent, she still enacted a measure of agency over life decisions.

Ana's refusal to move away from the "public eyesore" of the tent encampment near the highway was a kind of calculation, "a mode of doing" that Verónica Gago calls a "vitalist pragmatic" (2017, 142, 161).[3] This "vitalist pragmatic" emerges from calculation as conatus, where conatus is "the perseverance of being" (Gago 2017, 161). Gago explains, *"Calculation is conatus* means stealing, working, making neighborly bonds, and migrating to live. It does not accept dying, or seeing life reduced to a minimum of possibilities. The acceptance of the rules of calculation is intimately paired with a movement of the production of subjectivity, of 'wanting.' These are verbs: 'undertaking,' 'getting by,' 'saving yourself'" (2017, 164).

In Puerto Rico, living in public is dangerous for women and children. It is also an embarrassment to the local municipality to have families living in a homeless tent encampment in a basketball court near a busy thoroughfare. Ana's homeless encampment was actually located right beside the *kioskos* (kiosks) of Luquillo, a coastal street-food culinary tourist destination. Combined, these circumstances were precisely what gave Ana some leverage to negotiate with state representatives. In refusing the "decent" and "safe" space of the hotel room, she was also refusing to make her abandonment invisible to the public. In Ana's calculation to "disobey" and "reject" the state's offer and instead remain living in unhoused precarity, she reckoned that her current hardship would lead to the speedier achievement of her goal: suitable and stable housing. The women discussed in the next section had the same goal of securing stable, affordable housing, and they also chose apparent hardship in the short term in order to achieve their goal in the long term. These kinds of decisions do not register as clearly resistive because they rest on the individual-family's abnegation, which depends and gambles upon an "uncertain" yet desired outcome.

Ana and her children were not going hungry or thirsty. In fact, they received several plates of food from the nearby *kioskos* daily as well as from a local church. They also had two large tents filled with food, snacks, and water that would last several months. Ana told me they were storing these for their move. Their food and water needs were taken care of.

In light of this, securing housing, their ultimate goal, was something for which they could "hold out." In offering a temporary hotel room, the state did not calculate on the kind of "illegible" resistance Ana was willing to enact, one that put the long-term gain ahead of short-term comfort, safety, and gendered notions of propriety and decency. Taking risks is one of the strategic practices deployed not only by those at the very top of the neoliberal order, such as financiers and hedge fund managers, but also by those at the bottom—the sector that is believed to lack the know-how of political and economic calculation.

Yet for Ana, making a bad decision could have been catastrophic because her poverty put her much closer to disaster. To some degree, her approach also had to account for "safety first." As James Scott has explained about people who live on the margins of the state, "There is a defensive perimeter around subsistence routines within which risks are avoided as potentially catastrophic and outside of which a more bourgeois calculus of profit prevails" (Scott 1976, 24). Practicing agency, self-management, and decision-making might appear irrational for people like Ana in relation to legible neoliberal "rational calculations." Successful navigators of life at the margins or in extreme poverty, though, learn or craft the know-how to negotiate with neoliberal governance, sometimes by acquiescing and other times by challenging altogether the established order to achieve their end goals. The existence of women like Ana challenges neoliberalism's hegemony or total hold on the population (Gago 2017; Colectivo Situaciones 2009). Left with little recourse or surplus, fungible humans like Ana attempt to subvert the existing neoliberal structures, sometimes failing and sometimes reinventing their agency.

AFTER MARÍA: DEPICTING MATRIARCHAL DISPOSSESSION

Maura Toro-Morn and Ivis García Zambrana write that "Puerto Rican women have encountered a gendered, racialized inequality that has spelled disaster for their families" (2017, 12). As mothers charged with ensuring the well-being of their families, Puerto Rican women on the island and stateside face inequalities including low wages, under- and unemployment, lack of access to affordable childcare and housing, and health disparities, which contribute to their marginalization (Toro-Morn and García Zambrana 2017; Colón-Warren 1998). Toro-Morn and García Zambrana's assertion is made visually obvious in the 2019 Netflix documentary *After María*, directed by Nadia Hallgren, a Bronx-born, Afro-Diasporican filmmaker. *After María* depicts three mothers and their family members who, displaced from their homes by the storm, took part in FEMA's program Transitional Shelter Assistance for Puerto Ricans. In an interview, Hallgren explained, "We ended up deciding to focus on these women in our film because they were the most open to opening up their lives to us, telling their stories. We also loved the story of these three moms who were brave. Two of the women's husbands came with them, but it was the women who led the charge. They were the ones who came to New York for the sake of their children and their families. So many of us know this story from our own mothers."[4]

The documentary shows the travails of the three mothers as they navigate everyday life from the confines of their small hotel rooms in the Bronx. After meeting in the hotel, the three women and their families create a small community and become emotionally close and reliant on each other in a foreign and largely inhospitable environment. The documentary exposes the hardships they face, but also the caring and sustaining ways in which disadvantaged women forced to live on the capitalist margins try to provide dignified lives for their families. They celebrate birthdays, listen to music, get haircuts, make dinner, go to Orchard Beach, and sell costume jewelry and clothes to earn a modest living. They also share traumatic experiences and tears while trying without luck to find affordable housing. When the Transitional Shelter Assistance program ends, the women have no place to go. They are faced with having to enter the homeless shelter system in New York City. As a result, the families are separated, and their small but important care-based sisterhood is torn apart.

Upon its release, the short documentary received heated backlash from some in the Puerto Rican community because the women depicted, as well as their strategy of migrating to find and secure services to meet their needs, was read as an "embarrassment to the nation." Several online petitions emerged, asking Netflix to remove the documentary from its streaming service. I watched the documentary and tried to understand what offended the thousands of aggrieved Puerto Rican viewers who signed the petitions. It became apparent that what had offended many was that Puerto Rican poverty was front and center. But this poverty was experienced in the way I had experienced it growing up—with a mother who found ways to be joyful by celebrating life, who created a strong, caring solidarity and reciprocal community with other women, and who formed emotionally reliant relationships in order to survive. The mothers were depicted as hardworking and emotionally resilient even in the face of catastrophe.

One of the petitions, with a total of 48,759 signatures, explained that "'After Maria' is a documentary based on 3 Puerto Rican families and how they 'survived' after the hurricane. This documentary disrespects the honor, values and working spirit of our commonwealth by ridiculing us as poor, inconsiderate and maintained by [FEMA]. People from Puerto Rico did not like the documentary and are criticizing it in all social media, news, and papers."[5]

The documentary depicts the reality of women, of mothers living within dispossessed matriarchy. According to the petition statement, showing this reality is disrespectful because it ridicules poor Puerto Ricans. I contend that the negative reception the documentary received has to do with the still-potent antipathy felt for the diaspora, which includes the judgment of the Afro–Puerto Rican director, Nadia Hallgren, as an outsider not fit to tell an "authentic" Puerto Rican story—ironically, even though she told a story of the displacement of Puerto Rican women to the Bronx, where she was born and raised. Another criticism is that the film shows families that are *mantenidas* (taken care of, dependent on government assistance) and that this reality does not need to be shown, certainly not under a Trump presidency that already blames poor families of color, particularly Latinxs, for their own poverty, fashioning them a burden to the country. Still, it seems as if the backlash unfairly blames the victims—in this case, the mothers—for trying to make a go of life stateside with the tools at their disposal. Another petition against the documentary with 16,593 signatures explained, "In this documentary there is little to no mention of the *people who actually suffered through this hurricane who stayed on the island—people who actually suffered without water, electricity, food, or medical help.* The doc shows people who do little to help their situation therefore diminishing the struggles of the people of the island itself" (emphasis in original).[6]

Arguably, *After María* does not diminish the struggle of people who remained in Puerto Rico. It focuses exclusively on three mothers who decided to migrate. The focus on poor mothers is important, and I suspect that among the issues that produced ire in certain viewers was seeing single, independent mothers trying to make good lives for themselves and their families. The petition's statement above harks back to the "Yo no me quito" slogan about the heroism of the people who stay to face difficult living conditions on the archipelago versus those who make the "cowardly" decision to migrate. Known popularly by the hashtag-slogan #YoNoMeQuito, translated as "I will not give up on Puerto Rico," this cultural nationalist movement was in full swing in 2015–16. A rough but more direct translation is "I won't quit." If this translation is used, the slogan means "I won't quit on Puerto Rico." It seems that this latter translation represents the heart of the matter, and so not quitting really refers to not migrating, to remaining and forging a life on the island. This slogan, invoked in the name of Puerto Rican cultural nationalism, attested to the bravery of those who stayed on the island and endured the multiple crises. When the slogan first emerged, it referred to the debt crisis and the Zika epidemic. The early, pre-María rendition of this "movement" portrayed those who left the island as traitors, too cowardly to endure the mounting crises, too self-interested, and ultimately lacking commitment (and love) for Puerto Rico.

After Hurricane María, the diaspora became the island's most significant ally (Alicea and Toro-Morn 2018; Lloréns and Stanchich 2019). The "Yo no me quito" slogan/movement expanded to highlight diasporic folks who have come to Puerto Rico's aid, diminishing but not completely doing away with the shaming of those who migrate. Now the movement has morphed into a message of self-help, positivity, and resilience to Puerto Ricans to "lift themselves up by their bootstraps." The message of "resilience" also calls for Puerto Ricans to do away with a victim mentality, to work hard and never give up because their future and, indeed, their reality depend entirely on each individual's mind-set. The rhetoric animating this movement completely ignores the structural, racial, and gendered conditions that produce rampant inequality in Puerto Rico and among stateside Puerto Ricans.[7]

RACIALIZED CAPITALISM'S DISPOSSESSIVE LOGIC

It is noteworthy that in dominant political narratives, the internal Puerto Rican racial and socioeconomic hierarchy barely comes into focus, even when the financial, political, environmental, and humanitarian crises in the archipelago affect poor and Black communities with greater intensity (Lloréns 2016; Lloréns et al. 2018; Garriga-López 2018; Bonilla and LeBrón 2019; Brusi and Godreau 2019; Molinari 2019). This is because the state refuses to confront the staggering class- and race-based social inequalities that plague it. The poorest among the island's population suffer the worst impacts of the financial debt crisis. They endure the closure of neighborhood schools and hospitals. They experience the accelerated emptying caused by metropolitan disinvestment in rural towns. They suffer massive unemployment and are unable to rebuild secure homes after storms. The archipelago's present predicament has been centuries in the making. As José I. Fusté notes, "Puerto Rico's economic rut did not appear in the late twentieth century but rather is a continuation of a pattern of dependency and debt that goes further back" (2017, 108). Fusté continues, "In this recent neoliberalization of twenty-first-century US colonialism, capital accumulation has shifted from dispossessing people's lands and labor to dispossessing their individual and collective assets" (2017, 108).

Racialized capitalism's dispossessive logic reconfigured the Puerto Rican archipelago as a "debtor state." Since 2016, its finances have been handled by a federally imposed fiscal board, created by the Puerto Rico Oversight, Management, and Economic Stability Act (PROMESA), which has thus far proven ineffective in redressing the catastrophic conditions experienced by the people of Puerto Rico (Fusté 2017; Prado-Rodriguez 2019; Morales 2019c, 2019d; Bonilla and LeBrón 2019; Zambrana 2021, among others). Indeed, the austerity measures the fiscal board instituted, such as closing over three hundred public schools and hospitals and cutting the public university's budget, coupled with cutting budgets for Medicaid and FEMA assistance—coming from a Republican federal government that has constituted Puerto Rico as a financial liability and burden—have only worsened everyday living conditions for the country's large population of disadvantaged poor (Lloréns 2018b; Bonilla and LeBrón 2019; Molinari 2019). The Caribbean's significance as a site of extraction and wealth making for global capital has waned and, along with the massive expulsion of its inhabitants and the logic of "letting die," has accelerated the region's abandonment (Mullings 2019; Walcott 2015; Negrón-Muntaner 2018). Yet, the women whose lives I document here refuse to succumb to the extractive whims of a faceless global capital and instead rearticulate and realize human lives through their everyday practices and ethics of care, mutual aid, and solidarity.

After the hurricanes, the already circulating "emptying island" narrative intensified (Figueroa Rodriguez 2017; Negrón-Muntaner 2018). This trope congealed in the national zeitgeist in 2015, when the island's debt crisis became global news (Sin Comillas 2015; Negrón-Muntaner 2018). As I have argued elsewhere, global economic forces exacerbated by United States colonialism have long made migration from the archipelago to the continental United States part and parcel of people's reality (Lloréns 2018b, 159). Thus, the twenty-first-century notion that so-called native Puerto Ricans disappeared from the face of the archipelago illustrates the degree to which creolized Spanish colonial settlers naturalized, through the replacement of the Taíno inhabitants and the continued marginalization of Afro-descendants, their belonging as post-Columbian "natives." The narrative of the archipelago emptying of its rightful inhabitants emerged after over one hundred years of Puerto Rican migration to the continental United States. Most of this migration involved increasingly unemployed agricultural workers and the poor and was, to differing degrees, sponsored by the state (Pérez 2004; García-Colón and Meléndez 2013; Meléndez 2017; García-Colón 2020). Interestingly, although migration stateside spans well over a century, Puerto Rican cultural identity is alive and well wherever Puerto Ricans live. This is partly because within the context of the US, diasporic Puerto Ricans feel the need to assert that they are a people with a territory and a history.

As I wrote in *Imaging the Great Puerto Rican Family* (2014), in the mid-twentieth century, emergent mass media constructed and indoctrinated Puerto Rican identity via photographs, newspapers, television, films, art, and radio. Notions about a traditional Puerto Rican culture, best exemplified through the flag, songs, poetry, dance, art, and objects and in the tragic efforts of proindependence figures such as Puerto Rican nationalists

Pedro Albizu Campos, Lolita Lebrón, and Rafael Cancel Miranda, created the core of a symbolic "sovereign" political apparatus that resists the existing US colonial condition. Arlene Dávila has described the ways the Commonwealth political machinery and later the corporate sector "sponsored identities" in an effort to construct an "authentic" Puerto Rican culture (1997). This kind of cultural nationalism was not centered on working and valuing the land and safekeeping the environment. Instead, its focus was affective, not material—that which could be easily carried by the thousands of Puerto Ricans migrating from the island. This, in effect, allowed for a deterritorialized identity to flourish. It made Puerto Ricans "Boricua even if born on the moon," as Juan Antonio Corretjer noted in 1980 in his poem "Boricua en la luna" (Boricua on the moon). As a result, Puerto Rican identity and nationalism became separated from the idea of making a life on so-called ancestral land and protecting the environment for future generations.

It must also be acknowledged that the populations of small islands tend to be transitory. Migration to and from small islands such as Puerto Rico has historically followed the ebb and flow of climatic hazards as well as economic conditions. The movement of populations in and out of islands has been central in Caribbean habitation patterns since prehistoric times (Keegan and Hofman 2017; Rouse 1992). Perhaps it is time to revisit the idea that people born on islands such as Puerto Rico are meant to remain there for the duration of their lives (Lloréns 2019). Conceptualizing Indigenous and Black populations from the Global South as people who belong to their ecosystems as "naturally" as plant species do frames their mobility and migration as a pathological condition of uprootedness, in contrast with wealthy cosmopolitan Westerners, who are highly mobile, global citizens (Lloréns 2019; Malkki 1992; Tacoli 2009).

The early twenty-first century is marked by global neoliberal austerity measures coupled with the specter of climate catastrophe (Sheller 2018). Under the current conditions, Puerto Ricans have been cast as debtors and climate refugees (Lloréns 2019). Currently, Puerto Rico's total population of 3.2 million is the lowest it has been since 1979, and, under the current economic and political conditions, migration forecasters expect migration to continue.[8] It is predicted that by 2025, the population will be well below 3 million inhabitants, leveling at 2 million by the year 2050.[9] In terms of ecological sustainability, a population well below 3 million inhabitants would be a positive turn for the archipelago. Puerto Rico's twenty-nine landfills are beyond capacity, a problem that was exacerbated with the billions of tons of debris created by Hurricanes Irma and María (Karidis 2019). Electricity demand and consumption in the archipelago is high, and as of 2019, 98 percent of it comes from fossil fuels. The local and federal governments bemoan the lack of economic growth, a trend expected to worsen with continuous population loss and with the repayment of what many call an "unpayable debt." The late capitalist calamity gripping Puerto Rico does not bode well for future economic growth. Instead, a more sensible future is one in which the degrowth of the population, the economy, and the demand for electricity and natural resources is increasingly the norm. Ecologically, planning for a sustainable future might save the territory from additional economic, political, and environmental harm.

ENTER THE ERA OF CLIMATE APARTHEID?

Plans to revitalize the economy, such as the one designed by the Foundation for Puerto Rico called "The Visitor Economy," aim to make Puerto Rico "a premier destination for the world to visit, vacation, winter, retire, reside, and export." Such plans propose an unjust future in which Puerto Ricans migrate stateside only to make way for tourist developments and service sector jobs to cater to "the visitor economy."[10] Ecologically, this would be disastrous. In the Caribbean, hotels are major contributors to greenhouse gas emissions (Duffy-Mayers 2017). Tourists consume staggering amounts of electricity and produce large quantities of waste. Increasing flights and cruise ships into the island's airport and ports would also lead to an increase in greenhouse gas emissions and environmental pollution. Turning Puerto Rico into a full-fledged tourist economy, in which its highly educated work force is confined to minimum wage jobs in the service and retail industries, would only deepen the economic and political discontent and lead to continued migration and to the deepening pauperization of the working-class population (Cordero Guzman 2018).

Wealthy Puerto Ricans, on the other hand, have been preparing for a future in which green gentrification and climate apartheid is increasingly the norm. Theirs is an already existing world of gated communities with manicured parks and communal green areas for leisure and exercise (i.e., golf clubs) and access to private beaches. Rooftop water cisterns and water filters, as well as industrial generators that run on gasoline to deal with the usual electricity blackouts, are already common features in the homes of the wealthy (Lloréns and Stanchich 2019). Gentrification from tourist developments and wealthy individuals seeking Puerto Rican residential addresses for tax exemptions in places such as the island municipality of Vieques; the town of Rincón, on the island's west coast, famous for its surfing; or any of the luxurious gated communities in Dorado or Rio Grande has only intensified after the storms. On May 14, 2019, former governor Ricardo Rosselló signed into law the Puerto Rico Opportunity Zone Development Act of 2019, designating 98 percent of the archipelago an opportunity zone and offering hefty tax incentives and exemptions to lure investors to Puerto Rico (Cintrón Arbasetti 2019).

In a December 2019 *Mansion Global* interview, Cristina Villalón, a principal interior designer and partner of Puerto Rico's largest architectural firm, was asked what the biggest surprise in the Puerto Rico luxury real estate market has been. She responded, "In Puerto Rico, I've been really surprised to see that the new luxury homes, upward of $10 million, are selling like hotcakes. Some of the Ritz residences that are beachfront started at $2.5 million and are now going as high as $8 million, and this is in less than two years." When asked "What's the most valuable amenity to have in a home right now?" Villalón answered, "Independent power and clean water. After living through Hurricane Maria, and experiencing what it's like to have no power for months, access to energy is absolutely priceless, which is why we're designing our house off the grid and having a water cistern, and the best water filter out there. We don't want to depend on government agencies" (Cohen Blatter 2019). The interior designer also discussed the ongoing construction of her family home inland, which she said will be an important necessity in this time of rising sea levels. "We will have Tesla tiles, which are solar roof tiles that are beautiful. They're a way to have a solar roof without the big, ugly solar panels" (Cohen Blatter 2019). Villalón's comments are tinged with a techno-libertarian ethos in which the wealthy are able to afford (beautiful) technological fixes that allow them to bypass the burdensome inefficiencies of government services. In this neoliberal view, the government's subpar water and electricity services are reserved for those who cannot afford to "free" themselves from so-called dependence. Villalón's statement also points to the climate apartheid scenario that Philip Alston, the UN's special rapporteur on extreme poverty and human rights, warned about, "where the wealthy pay to escape overheating, hunger and conflict while the rest of the world is left to suffer" (2019).

"WE ARE EVEN MORE ORGANIZED": COMMUNITY WORK AFTER THE HURRICANES

In December 2017, I visited Isme in Salinas. Isme was the president of the El Coquí neighborhood association. She was in charge of managing the community center, coordinating volunteer help, and planning and running the community's annual summer camp, her brainchild. Like all the community members who volunteer and collaborate at the center, most of whom work at home to care for children or elderly relatives or are retired or unemployed, Isme volunteers her time for "the good of the community." The community center is part of the IDEBAJO collective, whose goal is "the defense of sustainable and endogenous community development."

Isme showed me around the center. The space was nearly empty compared to a month ago, she said, when so much aid had arrived that it entirely filled up the ample one-room structure. Now, supplies remained in only one corner, where boxes of bottled water, diapers, cleaning supplies, and canned food were stacked from floor to ceiling. Isme explained,

> I think about María as a monster because it was so strong and destroyed everything in its path. After the storm, I started to work at the community center right away. I started cooking for the community because we set up an oasis here. We cook, we are still cooking, and we filter water, and people come pick it up here. I lost my house in Hurricane Hugo, but this hurricane was much stronger. I believe that the hurricane is the earth asking for help. The earth needs help because we are destroying it. People don't want to plant food. They eat from cans. They don't want to cook fresh food. Children here are suffering, and many are traumatized. I spent $1,800 on gas and oil for electricity. This is a lot of spending. People are so busy now, fixing, still clearing, filling out paperwork, going to offices. . . . Three months after the storm and we are busier than ever. I lost my refrigerator and washer. I thank God we are alive; glory be to God.
>
> I feel proud that we were so well organized here at the community center and IDEBAJO before the storm, because when the storm hit, we went straight to work. We have received donations from the diaspora, from Sierra Club, and from other organizations, such as PECES in Humacao. After this experience, we are even more organized, and we will continue to aid the community.

The organizations that compose IDEBAJO run on the work of volunteers. Because they were well organized prior to the storm, they were in a position to begin assisting the community with food and water almost immediately after it (Lloréns and Santiago 2018b). Writers and scholars have called attention to the ways in which communities that are well organized prior to a catastrophic event are often able to respond to the needs of their community much quicker than their governments (Solnit 2009; Beckles 2018). It is well-known and documented that Puerto Rico community members became first responders after the hurricanes, while it appeared that the local and federal governments were mostly missing in action (Lloréns and Santiago 2018b; Bonilla and LeBrón 2019). The period of post-hurricane recovery in Puerto Rico has been marked by a lack of transparency, scandals surrounding contracts, and a general lack of coordination between the federal and local governments (Bonilla 2019; Morales 2019d, 2019a). Because by 2017 IDEBAJO was nationally known and respected as a community-led *autogestión* (self-management) organization, in the aftermath of the hurricane it quickly became a point of contact for external donors and a clearinghouse for the region.

In 2010, IDEBAJO began when members of various nonprofit community and environmental organizations in the Jobos Bay region formed a coalition. Their goal was to support the social and economic well-being of their communities. Communities in this region have been organizing to protect the Jobos Bay ecosystem against contamination and pollution since the early 1970s, long before they formed IDEBAJO (Berman Santana 1996; García-Quijano 2006; de Onís, Lloréns, and Santiago 2020b). Among the early organizations are the Asociación de Pescadores; Punta Pozuelo de Guayama; and the Corporación de Bahía de Jobos and Sur Contra la Contaminación (SURCO) (Berman Santana 1996; García-Quijano 2006).

In 2015, when I began conducting ethnographic work on environmental injustice and environmental racism in the southeast and documenting the environmental justice work of IDEBAJO's Diálogo Ambiental and the Coquí Community Board, members complained they lacked funds and access to grants to carry out their many socio-productive projects. In pre-hurricane times, IDEBAJO worked on a shoestring budget, which often meant very slow progress on projects and almost exclusive reliance on the generosity of small local businesses and member donations. Though their resolve to forge ahead was admirable, I worried that without accessing major grants or generating income from their projects, they would continue to languish in the island's southeast, which from San Juan stands as a remote and largely forgotten, inconsequential place.

LIVING GOOD LIVES AMONG THE RUINS OF THE PRESENT

Here I briefly discuss two findings that offer a fuller understanding of the values held by many of the women I interviewed, who manage to forge good lives on the margins of society. First, not everyone in the Puerto Rican archipelago or in the diaspora values or wants the same kind of life. That is, not everyone desires or values progress, ascending the so-called economic ladder, economic growth, and access to spheres of power (García-Quijano et al. 2015b; Gómez-Barris 2017; García-Quijano and Poggie 2019; García-Quijano and Lloréns 2017; García-Quijano and Lloréns 2018; Lloréns 2019). Second, because they have lived marginal lives, they have long been aware that the state is not a benevolent entity invested in safeguarding and ensuring the well-being and rights of its citizenry (García-Quijano and Lloréns 2016). Recent scholarly narratives have focused on the inability of the local and federal state to ameliorate the social and economic conditions of island residents. While these powerful actors are central to concerns about Puerto Rico's future, fixating on the "top" and the "center" sociopolitical spheres, in my view, runs the danger of glossing over the myriad ways in which social sectors on the "bottom" or at the "margins" have been navigating the multiple economic, social, and political crises that have historically plagued them. With these assertions, I am not suggesting that those who live on the margins of society are somehow exempt from suffering and hardship; rather, in this book, I aim to illuminate how Afro–Puerto Rican women exercise their agency by crafting life-affirming strategies that resist long-term oppressive systems, such as the racial capitalism with which Caribbean people have long grappled.

In Puerto Rico, this is evidenced by the way the local Puerto Rican and US federal governments have historically administered the island and its people. But the Puerto Ricans' situation vis-à-vis the state is not exceptional. This is clear in the patterns of state response to Hurricane Katrina in 2005, and more recently in Puerto Rico and the US Virgin Islands. The catastrophes reveal that the state does not have the best interests of its citizens in mind. The local island government's history of using migration as an "escape valve," experimentation on both land and people, and instances of neglect offer cracks through which to peer into the falsity of taken-for-granted notions about the state's benevolence (García-Quijano and Lloréns

2016, 2017, 2018). However, by looking at the daily lives of less powerful people such as the rural poor, we can see that the climate catastrophes are but a temporally intensified version of the continued neglect, abandonment, and even active harm that the modern state subjects its less powerful subjects to at all times, what Rob Nixon calls "slow violence" (2011; Lloréns 2016; García-Quijano and Lloréns 2017, 2018). Moreover, for too long, the lives and voices of Afro–Puerto Rican women have been drowned out by the centrality and loudness of the world of men; by our complicit patriarchal obsession with canonizing, upholding, and nurturing the voices of men at the peril of those of women; and in the telling and retelling of our stories from men's points of view.

Current conversations about the Puerto Rico government's failure to bring relief to the people of the island have overlooked the history of oppression and neglect of the vast majority of Puerto Ricans by the local island and federal state. Moreover, the rise of neoliberal, libertarian tendencies within governments, as is currently the trend in the United States and in Puerto Rico, has resulted in the promotion of corporate interests, privatization, and deregulation at the expense of the well-being of the vast majority of the population. In Puerto Rico, rural coastal resource users have long understood the limitations of the state in considering their ways of life and needs. As a result, they have carved meaningful lives on the margins (García-Quijano 2006, 2015a, 2019; Lloréns 2019). These folks' ancestors might have started out by marooning themselves from state oppression, but I contend that for the Caribbean's rural population, living away from the centers of power and strategically choosing, as needed, when to participate in the formal economic and political spheres, has given them certain freedoms that middle- and upper-class people living in cities and burdened by debt do not have (Griffith and Valdés Pizzini 2002; García-Quijano et al. 2015b, 2019; Lloréns 2019). Arguably, hinterland Caribbean populations, such as those of Puerto Rico's southeast, depend on their rugged sense of independence and a certain degree of rogueness to make a go of life and to even thrive in capitalist modernity, a system that has continuously excluded them.

In the two decades I have been carrying out ethnographic research and life history interviews with women and men in Puerto Rico's hinterland, it has become clear that they do not expect the state to understand their problems, much less fix them (Lloréns 2005; García-Quijano 2006; García-Quijano and Lloréns 2016, 2017; Lloréns and Santiago 2018b). In fact, rather than feeling abandoned or victimized by San Juan's government, they see their rugged independence as a point of pride (Lloréns 2005; García-Quijano 2006). They are people who craft their own solutions to pressing problems affecting them and their communities. People on the rural coast tend to view San Juan's political class largely with distrust (García-Quijano 2006; García-Quijano et al. 2015b). The racial composition of Puerto Rico's coasts, specifically the prevalence of Afro-descended communities, might account for this (Lloréns 2005, 2018a). Forced to live within the confines of racialized capitalism, Blacks in Puerto Rico and in the Americas have consistently experienced the state as a source of tyranny and oppression. In other words, the state has been a source of control, exclusion, discipline, and punishment. Similarly, the modernizing state—with its industrialization plans that actively degraded and harmed the environment—turned increasingly hostile to the lifeways of farmers, fishers, foragers, and ecosystems (Griffith and Valdés Pizzini 2002; García-Quijano et al. 2015b; García-Quijano and Lloréns 2017; Lloréns et al. 2018; Lloréns 2019). Afro-descendants escaped the disciplinary purview of the state by establishing communities in the coastal rural hinterland, deep in mangrove forests or in dense, steep mountainsides (Lloréns 2005, 2018a; García-Quijano et al. 2015). In these communities, women have created intergenerational sisterhoods of care that transcend the archipelago and sustain life in the diasporic Afro–Puerto Rican experience. Time and again, the women I spent time with prioritized safeguarding their families' and friends' well-being, as well as that of their communities and environment. They were invested in care, compassion, solidarity, and mutual aid as ways of living in a time they perceived as largely hostile to their lives, to their communities, and to the natural world. They also believed that women are powerful and resourceful enough to make positive contributions to their communities. Isme, a tireless community worker whose life-affirming efforts are an example for future generations to continue protecting our fragile biosphere while living good, sustainable lives, offers hope that a more just world is indeed on the horizon:

> While I am alive, I will do my part to care for this piece of earth. I have to try to help the kids in my community. If I don't give love to my home, we risk living in a sad, terrible world where we are disconnected from each other. . . . For me, not having money and being poor is not a terrible thing, because I have wealth in the form of family, friends, my community, and this beautiful place I live in. As long as I have people I care for and who care for me and we help each other and we help keep the earth alive by

protecting it and caring for it, we will have good lives. That is the work we are doing here in El Coquí. We are working to make good lives for our grandchildren, and for their children. . . . That is why we work hard. We will continue to make this a good place to live and a place where we have clean air, clean water, where we can plant and harvest food, and a clean ocean to fish in, where we can live in solidarity with each other and with the earth who sustains us.

"WHAT IS IT THAT ALL OF THESE OUTSIDERS WANT FROM US?": ON THE EXTRACTIVISM OF SUFFERING

After the hurricane, IDEBAJO's persistence paid off. It received donated funds and was awarded several large grants from diasporic, private, and nonprofit organizations. The Coquí community center received a solar array and Tesla batteries and now operates completely off the grid. Subsequently, two local environmental leaders were awarded environmental justice prizes for their work. Ruth Santiago from Diálogo Ambiental has been fighting for environmental justice in the Jobos Bay for three decades. The Sierra Club honored her with the 2018 Dr. Robert Bullard Environmental Justice Award. In 2019, Mabette Colón, a youth leader from Comunidad Guayamesa Unidos por tu Salud, was awarded the Nsedu Obot Witherspoon (NOW) Youth Leadership Award from the Children's Environmental Health Network for activism work against toxic coal ash contamination.

In the aftermath of the storm, IDEBAJO's achievements as first responders helped build its national and international reputation. As a result, IDEBAJO also received an avalanche of journalists, filmmakers, and academics wanting to conduct disaster research on them and the communities they served, a rush of interest that has yet to diminish. Nelson and Roberto, two IDEBAJO leaders, asked me in July 2018 about the attention: "What is it that all of these outsiders want from us? What are they looking for?" I explained as best I could that, for the most part, I believed that post-disaster newcomers felt they could assist Puerto Rican communities by getting their stories out to the world, while at the same time advancing their careers. But Roberto and Nelson were wary of being mined, wary of what they saw as people who had never been there before, who did not understand the local culture and context. They came in for a few days and took their photos and stories but did not give anything back to the communities. And then they told their stories as if they were authoritative sources. Roberto and Nelson were also concerned about how they might be represented. It was important to them that outsiders understood community members as a people who persevere in the face of hardship, who had worked hard to gain respect and build a sense of community autonomy. They were not passive victims of a neglectful state with which they had long ago dispensed. They wanted outsiders to know that their community work was based on solidarity, mutual aid and reciprocity, and love for their neighbors, community, and ecosystem. They wanted outsiders to know that they had been doing this work long before they were in the spotlight and would continue to do it long after the shining lights from the disaster dimmed.

I shared with them that since the disaster, a number of academics, filmmakers, and journalists had also asked me to put them in contact with the people I knew from my fieldwork in Puerto Rico. In many ways, the disaster had the effect of turning me, a so-called native anthropologist, into a mediator whose access was assumed to be able to open doors for stateside folks now interested in documenting the communities with whom I worked. The perception of my own position "as an insider" vis-à-vis the communities with whom I worked in the Jobos Bay was oblivious of the ways in which I, too, as a member of the diaspora, as a university-educated woman located in the North, was also an outsider in the eyes of community members (albeit an outsider who had been born in the region, had migrated stateside in midchildhood, had come back as an adult, and for the last two decades had conducted research in the region).

In the island's cultural imagination, the southeast region is notoriously hard to get to know. A rural coast, its communities tend to be remote, often located within dense coastal forest and vegetation. In this region, people are kind and welcoming to outsiders but also quietly distrustful and wary until they get to know people well. To gain access to the communities and individuals with whom I worked, I spent years building relationships based on trust, solidarity, and reciprocity (de Onís, Lloréns, and Santiago 2020). In the aftermath of Hurricane María, I was overwhelmed by a stream of e-mail messages with requests, many of which I felt were extractive of my work. I often pointed people in the direction of my publications about Puerto Rico, which span fifteen of the twenty years I have been doing "home-work" in the southeast. Still, some just took ideas, culturally contextual insights, and words from my published scholarship without ever bothering to cite it. It has been emotionally difficult to witness post-disaster newcomers taking advantage of the suffering and generosity of the people of Puerto Rico.

As has been previously documented, representations of the human suffering that results from cataclysmic events are magnets for photojournalists, photographers, media, and researchers. These narrative and visual tales lend themselves particularly well to an interest in the dramatic and the extraordinary (Farbotko and Lazrus 2012). Imagery and narratives depicting the suffering of others from a distance have, in our era, become part of a broader, thriving market that Arthur Kleinman and Joan Kleinman have called the "globalization of suffering" (1997, 2). In the West, the iconography of suffering has a long history (Sontag 2002). In Susan Sontag's words, "The suffering most often deemed worthy of representation is that which is understood to be the product of wrath, divine or human" (2002). To this I add that the iconography of the suffering of Black and Brown bodies has long been a source of fascination and is now an eminent photographic trope in the West (Lloréns 2019). Sontag describes the power of the photograph to shock viewers: "The ante keeps getting raised—partly through the proliferation of such images of horror" (1990, 19).

Writing about the ways in which individuals who experience catastrophic disasters use culturally appropriate frames to make sense of the emotional and visual upheaval in the aftermath, Susanna M. Hoffman notes that "no matter what place in the world it occurs, what form it might take, whether singular or chronic, peoples' explanations of disaster tend to rely on creative, often mythological imagination" (2002, 113). In Puerto Rico, I heard many hurricane survivors depict María in various symbolic terms. The strength of the hurricane and its catastrophic impacts were far from what people believed to be within the "normal" range for a hurricane. Mercedes called it a "roaring monster," the "earth screaming"; Isme said "the hurricane was earth asking for help, because we are hurting it, killing it"; Evelyn said it was "a demon"; Julia told me that it was a "warning sign, and if we don't change our ways, the next one will be stronger"; Roxana believed that the "hurricane was a cleansing of all that is negative, giving us a chance to start fresh." Repeatedly, informants thanked God for their still being alive, noting that many had not been so lucky. They told me stories of people who died during the storm or shortly thereafter. Some, they said, committed suicide because they could not withstand the new reality. Isabel, a family physician, told me in December 2017 that people in Puerto Rico were "living and walking around in a daze since the hurricanes; some are euphoric, but many are depressed. This is a natural reaction in the face of the enormous calamity through which we are living, and sadly, I believe that our national mental health has gone from bad to worse."

ILLUMINATING THE SCALES OF THE COLONIALITY OF POWER: SETTLER COLONIALISM, RACIAL SLAVERY, AND ORIENTALISM

In *The Intimacy of Four Continents*, Lisa Lowe wrote, "A history of the present refuses a simple recovery of the past and troubles the giveness of the present formation. It is not a historical reconstruction that explains or justifies our present, but a critical project that would both expose the constructedness of the past and release the present from the dictates of that former construction" (2015, 136). In what follows, I attempt a critical application of Lowe's provocative assertion, to trouble the "giveness" of this narrative formation by exposing the "constructedness" of the past, and the present, which will soon, too, become past.

I am a "new world" half-breed born of a monstrous lineage of not-quite-human, not-quite-woman beings. I am one of the damned Frantz Fanon wrote about. We have no memory of the time before. The remaining shreds of memory are uncertainties, conjectures about who our people might have been, where they might have come from. Maybe our ancestors were African. Maybe they were Taíno, or Spanish, or Corsican, or Lebanese. Maybe they were free; maybe they were enslaved; maybe they were indentured. Maybe they were healers. Or itinerant merchants. Or prostitutes. Maybe they were raped.

Once a *babalao* in Cuba tossed his cowrie shells on a table across from me and, from their alignment, divined, "You come from a lineage of herbalists, healers, people who came from the East. There is an Arab man standing beside you." Long ago an *espiritista* (medium) in Puerto Rico told my mother, "You are a Gitana, a Gypsy, destined to never find a home in this world." Using the language of percentages, a DNA ancestry test quantified my brother's ancestry as French, Spanish, African, and Amerindian, in that exact order of prominence. We have been left to devise a lineage, an ancestry, from the tattered scraps left behind in the wake of colonialism(s), a history glued together from the broken pieces of continents, people, love, repulsion, heartbreak, anger, intimacy, and the sexual desires that birthed us.

My mixed-race, ambiguous phenotype often marks me as belonging to many of the places where I have traveled in the Global South. Ambiguity confers the mixed-race person a kind of shape-shifting power *and vision.*

Along with racial ambiguity comes the possibility of viewing and regarding the world from several identity vantage points. But no matter the lens or angle, my views are never from the white privilege that travels effortlessly across borders with its privileges unquestioned, intact, sometimes even heightened. My views of the world emerge from the perspective(s) of a "wretched" woman. Explaining the hegemonic workings of the coloniality of power and knowledge from a Fanonian perspective, Nelson Maldonado-Torres writes, "The modern world is constituted out of the fabrication of multiple lenses of damnation that anchor apartheid and dehumanization as forms of being-in-the-world" (2019, 338; Fanon 2004). The ambiguity I carry is born of the kind of race mixture unique to the New World. My brown skin carries the mark of intimacy between colonizers and colonized, of powerful and powerless, of my mother's line without a motherland, making me a "cosmic hobo."[11]

The large island, then known as Borikén, was first colonized by Spain in 1493, and in 1898, the Puerto Rican archipelago was colonized by the United States. The Spanish colonial settlers committed genocide against the Taíno inhabitants and imported enslaved Africans as their property to labor in the protoindustrial plantations (Horne 2018). Eve Tuck and Wayne K. Yang explain, "In order for the settlers to make a place their home, they must destroy and disappear the Indigenous peoples that live there" (2012, 6). The disappearing of the Taíno, who the Spanish settlers then narrativized as the source of the archipelago's mythical and noble heart and soul, provided the settlers a blank canvas on which to create the colonial nation-state known today as Puerto Rico. Patrick Wolfe writes that "settler colonialism destroys to replace" (2006, 388; Tuck and Gaztambide-Fernández 2013, 77). The Puerto Rican national "creation" story, taught in the primary school curriculum, tells of the vanishing of the Taínos. They were noble, childlike savages ravaged by European diseases, and though they became physically extinct, the story goes, Spanish men had mated with Taíno women, leading to surviving Taíno genes in the Puerto Rican DNA (Martínez-Cruzado et al. 2001; López 2008). Thus, many modern Puerto Ricans have Taíno ancestry in their DNA, but the official narrative states that Taíno individuals and their culture largely disappeared within the first century of Spanish colonization. "In their study about mitochondrial DNA, Martínez-Cruzado and colleagues found that ... because inheritance is only through the mother, the mtDNA only traces the migrations of women. These results imply that there have been few migrations of women to Puerto Rico in post-Columbian times relative to the quantity of local women in the country, and that the cumulative effect of all those migrations after 500 years of colonial history has been to reduce the percentage of Indigenous mtDNA from 100% to 61%" (Martínez-Cruzado 2002, 3).

These findings support the state-sanctioned miscegenation, a kind of Indigenous "replacement" strategy widely practiced by Spanish colonizers throughout its Latin American colonies (Wolfe 2006; González 2011; Tuck and Yang 2012). In the early post-conquest years, Indigenous and, later, African women, whose mtDNA was passed down through their mother's female line, became the vessel through which the colonizer would reproduce himself. In effect, these not-quite-human female entities were tasked with birthing the hybrid new nations of the "new world." The European colonial patriarch seeded the new world's animal-mother as a way to reproduce not sons or daughters but laborers to work on extracting resources in the name of capital accumulation. Yet, as Tiffany Lethabo King asserts, "The spatial capacity of Black femaleness exceeds its use value as a laborer (plower, tiller, planter) on the land" (2016, 1027). In the context of the "New World socio-political order of conquest," Black femaleness is prefigured in the landscape and geophysical and spatial territory itself (Spillers 1987, 67; King 2016, 1026–27; McKittrick 2006; Morgan 2004). In line with national constructions of "insider" or authentic Puerto Ricanness versus "peripheral," "transient," or "contingent" Puerto Ricanness, the Puerto Rican archipelago, including land and sea, has been imagined in the shape of two premodern, fungible females. The interior of the island has been conceived as the heart of the Taíno mother, the essential and authentic birthplace of the modern Creole Puerto Rican, and the coastal plains and moody seas as the tempestuous, dangerous, but alluring Black mother. Thus, the territory itself, as site of extraction onto which conceptions of the European colonial outpost, turned colonial nation-state, was gendered as feminine, as sites (land and sea) to be penetrated and produced, by Spanish conquistadors, settlers, and white Creoles.

The proposition that modern Puerto Ricans contain Taíno DNA in their genetic pool is widely accepted, but the idea that some Taíno people survived colonization has been outright rejected (Martínez-San Miguel 2011; Haslip-Viera 2001, 2006; López 2008; Forte 2005). Yet individuals who identify as Taíno persist, though they remain on the fringes (and understood as a fringe identity) on Puerto Rican society and culture. Studying the archipelago's "Taíno revival" at the beginning of the twenty-first century, Sherina Feliciano Santos found informants who self-identified as Taíno and claimed a living Taíno cultural identity (Feliciano Santos 2021). But their erasure from the archipelago's historical postcolonial conception has been so total- izing that Feliciano Santos remarks that these contemporary Taínos lived an "impossible identity" (2011, 2021). Writing about the Taíno revival in the second decade of the twenty-first century, Christina González explained,

> Beyond material legacies and identity assertions, Taíno resurgence revolves around living in the world in a Native Caribbean way. Many in the movement call upon embodied memories of traditions and values disseminated across generations, often by family matriarchs, which espoused mindful relations in a world where all things have life, from plants, stones, rivers, forests, caves, sun and moon, to deceased relatives and disincarnate beings inhabiting their islands. Marilyn Balana'ni Díaz, Puerto Rican Taíno and principal *abuela* (grandmother) of the Taíno community Concilio Taíno Guatu-ma-cu a Borikén, emphasizes this relational sense of belonging: "You are part of nature. You're not outside of it. . . . We are part of the plants. We are part of the cosmos." (2018)

In neo-Taíno world making, "being in relation" extends beyond the human, to encompass all living as well as dead entities, whose spirits form part of our fragile biosphere (Glissant 1990). Living in relation and in tune with place, space, and its more-than-human inhabitants is essential to this cosmological vision. This is a way of life that advocates attentiveness, care, respect, and the maintenance of a thoughtful balance between the human and the more-than-human world. Still, Puerto Rican individuals who claim a Taíno cultural identity are often subjected to ridicule or are told that using this Indigenous identity is a strategy to subsume their African heritage and thus enacts anti-Black racism (Feliciano Santos 2021; Duany 2001; Jiménez Román 2001; Cruz-Janzen 2003). But there are a number of individuals who claim an Afro-Boricua identity, who combine and uplift their Black and Indigenous cultural heritage while rejecting the Spanish colonial settler ideology and master narrative that erases the historical and present existence, relevance, and lifeways of these minoritized popula- tions. As Eve Tuck and Rubén Gaztambide-Fernández remark, "The settler-state is always already in a precarious position because Indigenous peoples and descendants of chattel slaves won't do what they are supposed to do, fade away into history by either disappearing or becoming more like the settler, the true description of the human" (2013, 77).

Puerto Rico's Creole neoliberal elites have yet to reckon with their history of Indigenous genocide and the enslavement of Africans who, through unpaid labor, built wealth for the metropole and for a small white Creole land-owning class, while pauperizing the great majority of poor, rural settler colonials through outright neglect. Along with the masses of proletarianized Creoles, dispossessed Blacks and Afro-descendants were mainly left to fend for themselves on the margins of Puerto Rican society. But while white Creoles and light-skinned, mixed-race people have to contend with class-based stigmas, they do not pay the color line's heavy toll. To this day, the Puerto Rican color line works in tandem with a pigmentocracy to favor the social ascendancy of light-skinned, mixed-race individuals and White Creoles. In Puerto Rico, anti-Black racism is widespread. It is experienced most violently by persons whose skin color and/or visibly African phenotype marks them unequivocally as Afro-descendant, rather than as ambiguously mixed-race persons (Lloréns, García-Quijano, and Godreau 2017).

When the United States entered the scene, the archipelago's racial and socioeconomic class divisions were deeply entrenched. In other words, a racial hierarchy was firmly in place, in which descendants of the Spanish, island-born whites, known as Creoles, held naturalized racial dominion over the totality of the island's social, political, and economic spheres. It is this white Creole elite who create and mediate official accounts of Puerto Rican history. Enslaved Africans, free Blacks, and their descendants occupied the lowest social and spatial rungs of Puerto Rican society, mostly confined and enclosed in urbanized barrios or coastal, wetland, and mangrove settlements and largely barred from ascending the ladder of public sociopolitical life. But in Puerto Rico, as was common throughout the Spanish colonial world, Creoles rarely entered into legal marriage with their concubines. Intermating between Spanish men and Taíno and African women, not marriage, produced a large population of mixed-race Puerto Ricans. Such was the socio-racial world that existed upon US colonial intervention in the archipelago.

Ramón Grosfoguel calls Puerto Rico under US possession an economic "exploitation colony" because, unlike Hawaii, for example, the United States did not wish to establish a settler population of white US citizens in the archipelago (2003, 7; Lloréns 2014). Instead, in an Orientalist move, the United States constituted the archipelago as a society of childlike mixed-race "people of color" (Lloréns 2014). Its land provided a strategic location in the Caribbean for military bases, for the testing of military weaponry and medicines, for the recruitment of soldiers to fight American wars, and as a consumer market for American goods, and in more recent years, as a tax haven for wealthy Americans.[12] The United States classifies Puerto Ricans as Hispanics, a label tinged with Spain's Mediterranean whiteness but still racialized as a Latin Americanized Spanish-speaking mestizo Other within the continental US context. But in its determination to only understand and uphold as authentic "Nordic whiteness," the United States has failed to grasp the internal racial logics of the white and light-skin supremacy that already existed in Puerto Rico and that remains nearly intact in the twenty-first century. In other words, as is classic of imperial colonial practices, the United States does not know or even see Puerto Rico in its own terms, glossing over internal dynamics and all the while enacting top-down, uninformed decisions that impact the ongoing social dynamics in the archipelago. It can also be argued that to some degree San Juan's neoliberal, Euro–Puerto Rican elites also function and make decisions without truly knowing or taking into account the large number of proletarianized and impoverished masses.

The task of thinking about Puerto Rico and Puerto Ricans first as a Spanish colonial settler society that was then colonized by the United States is complicated. As Shona N. Jackson, writing about Guyana, has explained, "It requires the difficult assessing of Creoles as themselves settlers because of the ways in which they maintain power within a post-colonial state" (2012, 3). With the disappearance and total erasure of the Taíno, the white (Spanish) Creole intelligentsia created a discourse that the large majority of Puerto Ricans are racially mixed, with only a small, marginal, and socioeconomically and politically dispossessed Black population and a small but socially and politically powerful group of Euro–Puerto Rican elites. But the prevailing national myth that all Puerto Ricans are mixed race conceals several other identities, cultural and political realities, and ways of existing in and outside the archipelago. First, some people now claim a fully Taíno cultural identity (Feliciano Santos 2021; González 2018). Second, the practice of guarding European (mainly Spanish) "blood purity" is alive and well among some of the island's Creole elite families (Kinsbruner 1996; López 2008; Lloréns 2014, 2018d). Third, some people claim full African ancestry (Lloréns 2018a). Fourth, some uplift their Afro-Taíno heritage and reject Spanish colonial ancestry. Fifth, generations of migrants to the continental United States have produced a category of people who consider themselves Diasporican and/or Puerto Rican–American. Sixth, various other identities emerge as a result of national intermixing, such as the Domini-Rican or Mexi-Rican. It is obvious that there are multiple ways, then, to be a Puerto Rican person.

Still, the prevailing and totalizing structure of white supremacy in the archipelago makes it so that privilege accrues to Creole whites. White and light-skin privilege confers access, benefits, and the possibility of social, political, and economic ascension. Minoritized individuals in the archipelago, mainly Black and Afro-descendant (because it is believed that Taínos are extinct), remain left out of the national imaginary's center, and their marginal lives condemn them to damnation. For Frantz Fanon, the "damned of the earth" are those who have been dehumanized and ascribed perpetual "backwardness" in Europe's conception of man-as-human (Gordon 2015; Walcott 2015). Today, the dominant class of white Puerto Ricans, or the "Criollo bloc," holds social, economic, cultural, and political power (Villanueva, Cobián, and Rodríguez 2018). I think of them as colonial settlers, and this is particularly obvious when looking at this class from the perspective of the island's southeast region, which was until recently parceled into contiguous sugar plantations, later sugar mills, owned and managed by a small number of Euro–Puerto Rican families. The post-plantation reality looks different from nonplantation regions and is lived differently in this region deeply marked by more than three centuries of social, political, and economic life as a plantation. Euro–Puerto Ricans reap the full benefits of white privilege, and many still claim Spain as the archipelago's *madre patria* (mother fatherland). As colonial mother, Spain unequivocally traces her descent and confers authority to the paterfamilias. As a colonial plantation outpost, Puerto Rico was constructed as fertile and lush female land/territory, an estate, the property of the Spanish patriarchal colonizer and his male descendants. In other words, the Criollo (the o marking him as male) bloc's hold on power is conferred by a lineage and allegiance to Europe's masculine project of colonial modernity, which excludes pre-Columbian Americans and Africans from its definitions of the human. This construction persists in the continued physical and symbolic annihilation of the Indigenous and African man and the erasure and subjugation of the Indigenous and African woman.

With this perspective, I call into question the assertion that the Hispanic Caribbean's creolization—which marks the region as a quintessentially modern American space-place peopled by individuals from Europe, Africa, and Asia—dissolved the powerful colonial settler class into its ranks, and in the process made the colonial settler distinction difficult to untangle within the present-day context. It is precisely through its practices of violent erasure, rejection, denial, ridiculing, its claims of "impossibility" and/or extinction, its so-called alternative narratives of identity, of humanness, and of belonging, and its conceptions of place and responsibilities to the human and the more-than-human worlds that the settler class installs its totalizing, extractive, and dominant vision of a Euro-centric human world. Throughout this book I have shown how Afro–Puerto Rican women are produced and how, at the same time, they use their agency to produce "modes of human life." Some of them have long rejected the dominant structure of colonial settler narratives about how to be human in this world.

Thinking about dominant narratives of creolization and of being human with and through the work of Caribbean intellectuals such as Sylvia Wynter, Edward Kamau Brathwaite, Stuart Hall, Edouard Glissant, and David Scott, Rinaldo Walcott suggests "that we live in brutal times, reminiscent of the colonization of the Americas and plantation slavery, and that the making of the modern nation-state, as we now live it, accentuates an 'unknown creolization' that we cannot name but must struggle to recognize. I am inferring that the brutalities which produce the Caribbean, and by extension the Americas, also generate the production of new modes of hu-man life, even today" (2015, 188).

Critical Black scholars reject the "settler grammar" that singularly casts the enslaved African as labor and land as property (T. L. King 2019, 22; Rifkin 2019; Sexton 2016; Jackson 2012; Hartman 1997; Wilderson 2010; Spillers 1987). Labor, they contend, was not the principal metaphysics or organizing principle of Black life on American hemispheric plantations. Rather, "Black fungibility defines and organizes Black value within relations of conquest" (T. L. King 2019, 22). Writing in relation to Saidiya Hartman and Hortence Spiller's insights about Black fungibility, Tiffany Lethabo King explains, "Black fungibility is an expression of the gratuitous violence of conquest and slavery whose repertoire has no limits or bounds. It operates both materially on the body and produces Blackness (as idea and symbol) as a discursive space of open possibility" (2019, 23).

In the context of Puerto Rico, Black fungibility has meant the erasure of Black people from conceptions of who and what practices built the archipelago's national ethos and the nation itself. Other well-documented egregious scripts and master tropes have been *crafted onto* Black bodies and lives (Godreau et al. 2008; Godreau 2015). The Creole intelligentsia folklorized Black Puerto Ricans, turning them into contemporary relics of pre-modern times, forever "backward" and "not of the present time" (Godreau

2015; Lloréns 2014). Folklorization has also meant that only the "historical cultural contributions" that emerged in the context of their enslavement are valued, such as music, food, and dance—all believed to be frozen in time.

But actual Black Puerto Ricans are denied, along with their ecological, scientific, linguistic, and present-day stylistic contributions. It is believed that they compose a small fraction of Puerto Rican society living mainly on the coast, and that they will cease to exist altogether with the passing of time due to intermarriage and race mixing (Lloréns 2014). They are deemed dangerous, criminal, outside of normativity, and requiring discipline (Dinzey Flores, 2013; LeBrón 2019a).

As a result, in Puerto Rico, as in other parts of the American hemisphere, Black people suffer at the hands of state-sanctioned racial terror and violence. They are contained and enclosed in marginalized communities, both urban and rural, and these communities tend to also be national sacrifice zones in which residents experience environmental injustice and racism, as is the case of Puerto Rico's southeast (Lloréns 2016). Still, they are not passive victims of racial violence and terror. Rather, they actively continue to resist their erasure, marginalization, and obliteration.

The May 25, 2020, assassination of Mr. George Floyd by Minneapolis Police, a state-sanctioned killing, is the kind of anti-Black violence that Afro-pessimist theorist Frank Wilderson claims works as a "health tonic for global civil society. Anti-Black violence is an ensemble of necessary rituals that are performed so that the human race can know itself as Human and not as a slave, meaning not as Black" (2020, 39).[13] This killing, along with a too-numerous-to-mention list of Black men, women, and children killed both in the United States and in the rest of the American hemisphere (the murder of politician Marielle Franco in Brazil immediately comes to mind) has reinvigorated the Black Lives Matter clarion call. As I have discussed in this book and in my previous scholarship (2020, 2018a, 2014), it is common to hear Puerto Ricans say that "there is no racism among us because we are all mixed." This statement marks as "eccentric," "mentally unbalanced," or "outsiders" Puerto Ricans who call out anti-Black racism in the archipelago or across the diaspora.

This occurs despite a long history of antiracist activism in Puerto Rico, which began in the mid-1800s with the movement to abolish enslavement in the archipelago. The recent police murders in the continental United States resonated so deeply in the archipelago that antiracist activists from Colectivo Ilé and Revista Etnica decided to hold a Black Lives

Matter commemoration for the victims of anti-Black violence at the hands of the state. This historic gathering took place in Loíza on June 1, 2020. Related events happened simultaneously in the towns of Vieques and Arroyo. The remembrance was also dedicated to Adolfina Villanueva, a Black woman from Loíza and mother of six who perished at the hands of Puerto Rico's police on February 6, 1980, when she protested her own forceful eviction (Abadía-Rexach 2021). No one was ever prosecuted for her death. On June 2, 2020, La Colectiva Feminista, an antiracist and Black feminist collective, held an antiracism rally in Old San Juan in solidarity with the now global Black Lives Matter Movement. These events are historic and portend an emergent era when Puerto Rican anti-Black racism will no longer be secret, silenced, marginalized, erased, or chucked off as felt by only a few mentally unstable, problematic, or eccentric Blacks. It is encouraging to see a young generation of feminists, antiracists, and advocates for LGBTQI and gender rights and environmental and climate justice hard at work shaping a more just, livable, inclusive, and sustainable archipelago.

EPILOGUE

A Word about Black Puerto Rican Ecological Knowledge

> El otro día me dio vértigo tan terrible que estaba caminando recostada de las paredes del apartamento. Entonces me acorde que tengo una matita de yerba bruja en un tiesto en la ventana, fui cogí unas hojitas y las machuque encima de la hornilla y me eche varias gotitas en cada oído y sentí un alivio inmediato. ¡Yo tengo mi medicina sembrada en los tiestos de mi apartamento!
>
> —ANA HILDA

THERE IS A SCENE IN DAHLMA LLANOS-FIGUEROA'S NOVEL *Daughters of the Stone* in which Mati and her husband, Cheo, exchange tense words about their opposing feelings on sending their daughter Concha to school in a fast-changing Puerto Rico. Because schooling had not been a possibility for earlier generations of this Black Puerto Rican family, Cheo is adamant that Concha must go to school as a way to improve her lot in life. For Mati, an herbalist and healer, school and book learning were suspect; after all, she reasoned that school books were/are written by, about, and for *blanquitos* (whites), and will only teach her daughter Concha "to be what they want her to be" (2009, 136). In Mati's indignation she asks, "Those books you love so much—what lives in there and who put it there? The only knowledge we need is all around us. The trees and the plants . . . there lies the truth. Where is the sun and the wind in your books? Where are the plants to heal and cure? Whose way of knowing is in there? For what purpose?" (135–36).

In this passage, Mati centers local Afro-ecological knowledge passed down intergenerationally as a source of indispensable knowledge for survival and for living a good life. In her view, the books and schools of the *blanquitos* are dangerous because they do not teach Black students about themselves, about valuing their ways of knowing, understanding, and seeing the world and about the significance of the local ecology to their well-being. Today, it is often mistakenly assumed that in the Puerto Rico archipelago, Black ecological or Afro-ecological local knowledge is a thing of the past. In this epilogue, centering the sustainable practices and life-ways of Black Puerto Ricans, I conclude with a brief word about these "otherwise" but traditionally Black ways of living and of making sustainable lives that are still well and alive in the archipelago. Indeed, the Black Puerto Rican ecological knowledge and practices I briefly detail here attest to a deep history of resistance in the service of supporting their, their family's, and their community's socio-ecological well-being.

THE PRACTICES OF PRESENT-DAY MAROONS

I met Milagros, Doña Idalina, and her husband, Don Rafa, as well as Don Paco and his girlfriend, Doña Maria, in late December 2017, three months after Hurricane María ravaged their beachfront community. I met them by chance after an American FEMA worker I had befriended at the Luquillo tent community where Ana lived directed me to their hidden seaside community several towns away. I made my way first by car and then by foot because there was no car access to their mangrove-adjacent homes, which was the case even before the storm. There were about sixteen homes on this stretch of beachfront, whose location they asked me not to disclose because it was an informal community. This meant that even though these parcels of land had been continuously inhabited since at least the nineteenth century, according to the residents, they had no land titles, and the government considered them "illegal squatters." The beachfront homes varied in size. A few were no more than a one-room wooden shack. Others, like Milagros's and Idalina's, had been modest but beautiful rustic homes before the storm. A few looked more opulent both in size and construction style. But today, three months after the storm, it looked like a bomb had been dropped in the middle of the community. The houses were in various states of disrepair. Some of the large cement houses were intact; others, mainly the wooden shacks, were completely destroyed.

When I first met Milagros, who I came to know as a determined and self-sufficient Black Puerto Rican woman in her fifties, she was on her roof fixing the television antenna. I noticed there were three solar panels on her roof. She climbed down and explained that before the storm, she had six solar panels and a small windmill to produce electricity for her house, but the storm's wind had destroyed three panels and the windmill. She showed me the destroyed pieces of solar panel and windmill amid the debris strewn in her yard. The entire community, in fact, was littered with the broken pieces of their homes. Milagros explained that the community had potable water, but it lacked a connection to the public electricity system. This was why shortly after moving in fourteen years ago, she took a technical course on electricity and solar panel installation. She installed her home's solar panels and battery system herself and installed additional systems for several neighbors, too, including for Idalina and Rafa, her close friends.

Milagros invited me inside and showed me photos of what her house looked like before the storm. It had been a beautiful mint green, airy beachside cottage with a tropical ornamental garden in front. She had first moved there looking for peace of mind after her daughter, at twenty-six years old, was shot to death in what she described as a "massacre" in her hometown. There were large framed photos of her only child throughout the house. One of them depicted her graduation from nursing school, shortly before her untimely death.

Her daughter had been riding in a car with two friends when armed men pulled up and shot them to death. This tragedy had broken her, and she moved to get away from it all. The sea was the only thing that calmed her, the only balm in what she described as an otherwise "unlivable world out there" on the island. This community was as far as one could get from the hustle and bustle of urban life and as close as one could get to the sea without living in a boat. We walked around Milagros's sandy yard, and I noticed a tank to hold land crabs in her yard. She said that during the season for it, she hunts crabs in the mangrove forest behind her house and sometimes makes a little money selling them, but mostly she cooks them for herself, family, and friends.

A few houses down, I met Doña Idalina and Don Rafa, a welcoming Black Puerto Rican couple in their early seventies. When I came upon them, they were busy building a seawall in front of their house using cement blocks they had foraged from the debris. They had also foraged and piled up wooden planks and nails, which they were planning to reuse to rebuild their battered wooden house. I noticed their land crab traps and tanks, and when I asked about these, Doña Milagros was impressed that I knew what the items were for. I told her that I grew up in a family of gardeners, crabbers, and foragers, and she gave me a hug and invited me in to see her house.

Doña Idalina told me they had owned this beachfront cottage for over twenty years, and although they owned a modest cement house in town, a house they had acquired with FEMA money after Hurricane Georges had destroyed their previous house, they now spent most of their time here, at the beach, a calm place where they could get away from their troubles. Don Rafa had recently had open-heart surgery, and they both felt this was the best place for him to recover. She asked Don Rafa to show me the scar from the surgery. He unbuttoned his shirt and showed me an impressively wide and large scar in the upper part of his chest.

I was struck by its similarity to Don Paco's scar, but I did not say anything. I had met Don Paco, another one of the neighbors, earlier. A strong Black man in his early eighties, he had been busy rebuilding a wall in his wooden house. He was shirtless when we met, and I could see the big, wide scar on his chest. I sat with his girlfriend, Maria, on the balcony of their modest wooden cottage, and she told me that Don Paco had had open-heart surgery not too long ago.

Of the people I met in the neighborhood, Don Paco had owned his cottage the longest. He explained that he was born and raised in Santurce and had first come to this community as a young man, running away from the police in the 1950s. He decided then that he would never leave because "this place was as close to paradise as I would ever get." He made a living fishing and crabbing and working odd construction jobs.

The first time he had been to the neighborhood, other Black men and women were living in shacks along the beach, but as people died and outsiders discovered the place, there had been an influx of people with money building up large, fancy cottages. It didn't help that a fancy boat marina, where the very wealthy kept their yachts and sailboats, had set up shop adjacent to the community. This made the community visible to outsiders, and their privacy was slowly eroding. Don Paco also worried that the marina was eyeing their community in the hopes of expanding, and that it was pressuring the municipality to expel them. All of them, Don Paco, Doña Milagros, Doña Idalina, Don Rafa, and Doña Maria, mentioned their hope that as a result of Hurricane María and the close bond they had developed with the FEMA worker (who first told me about this community and who asked to not be identified in my work), that they might be able to finally get help getting legal titles to their land parcels.

As I looked around this beautiful seaside community of present-day maroons, I, too, felt the allure of the hidden place. The cool breeze of the

Atlantic swayed the palm trees, and the blue ocean was open wide and vast in front of us. But I also understood the hardship of making a life on "illegal" land where the municipality constantly threatened to expel them, and the marina owners complained that the community was an eyesore. Storms coming off of the Atlantic hit this place particularly hard, destroying their houses time and again. When there were strong winds and high waves, the sea came all the way up to some of the houses, and with sea level rise, this was happening more often. Over the years, Doña Idalina had witnessed the shoreline creeping ever closer to her home. They had no electricity and no road access to their homes, so together, the community members had built and maintained a walkway made of wooden planks in the sand, which made tugging in carts full of belongings much easier.

This was not an easy place to live and was certainly not a place for the fainthearted. To live and thrive day to day in this off-the-grid coastal environment, people needed ecological knowledge about how to survive. They needed to know, for instance, how to avoid the swarm of mosquitoes that descended at dusk, where to hunt for crabs, what fish were plentiful and how to fish them, what plants and fruits were available to forage and when, how to stay dry during the rainy season, how to keep the sand from

FIG E.1 Seaside community where residents do not have electricity unless they install their own solar panels; the community was devastated by Hurricanes Irma and María, December 2017.

your home's interior, and how to avoid the authorities who wanted to expel you. The people I met there were rugged individuals who prided themselves on being self-sufficient. Both Don Paco and Don Rafa, with chest scars as proof of recently mended hearts, hoped to live out their remaining days in that peaceful place where the sea served as a cure to life's problems and worries, where the sea was medicine.

Black Puerto Ricans have crafted fugitive practices that have allowed them to survive, and even thrive, at the margins of the state. Geographic and spatial segregation gave way to the creation, preservation, and reproduction of Black Puerto Rican cultural traditions, ways of life, and local ecological knowledge (García-Quijano 2006; Lloréns 2018a). This vast reservoir of Black ecological knowledge is based on over three hundred years of reliance on gardening, fishing, and coastal resource foraging (García-Quijano 2006; García-Quijano et al. 2015a).

The histories of hemispheric American maroons and their communities have long captured the academic imagination, but accounts of their counterhegemonic practices often overlook how the cultural values and practices that developed in these rural-coastal refuges persist today among many of the descendants (Bledsoe 2017; Lloréns and García-Quijano 2020). These include cultivating subsistence agricultural plots; fishing and foraging; using plants and herbs for medicinal purposes; cooking; maintaining familial and community networks of sharing, exchange, reciprocity, and mutual aid as defense strategy and as alternative livelihoods from wage-labor peonage and debt; stewarding nonhuman animals and the environment while still eating and drinking from them; and rejecting and/or being skeptics of metropolitan ways of life, politics, and values.[1] All of these systems were built and passed down intergenerationally (Griffith, García-Quijano, and Valdes Pizzini 2013; Lloréns and García-Quijano 2020).

In the southeast, many inhabitants do not aspire to what they see as capitalist and hurried ways of life in the San Juan metropolis, for instance. Instead, they define success in life and well-being by community solidarity and livelihood independence (García-Quijano and Poggie 2019). These "maroon" cultural values are not relics of the past. They are vital today in Black and Afro-descendant coastal and mountain communities throughout Puerto Rico (Lloréns and García-Quijano 2020).

Black and majority Afro-descendant communities in the archipelago tend to be among the most socioeconomically disadvantaged and, as result, tend to engage in much more sustainable consumption practices. For instance, Puerto Rico has one of the highest electricity rates in the

United States, and as I have documented elsewhere, Black communities in the Jobos Bay tend to use less electricity. They rely on fans rather than air-conditioning, unplug appliances that are not in use, and do not turn on lights during daylight hours (Lloréns 2018c). Black communities use less electricity partly because of the prohibitive cost of electricity. This, of course, leads to more deliberate and sustainable practices of electricity consumption. In these communities, adults and children often sit outside on balconies or under shady trees in their yards for part of the day. They observe the neighborhood's comings and goings, a practice that also serves as a low-tech surveillance mechanism.

Middle- and upper-class metropolitan folks, in contrast, tend to live in suburban cement houses in gated communities. They rely on air-conditioning, use lights during the day, and control gates electrically with high-tech surveillance safety systems. After Hurricanes Irma and María, many low-income communities received solar lamps, solar phone and tablet chargers, and in some cases, entire solar household arrays to power homes. As a result, many folks in the southeast use their solar phone chargers instead of the wall plugs, even when they are at home and electricity is available. Certainly, the general population has a better understanding of where electricity comes from since the hurricanes, and a keener awareness of the kinds of environmental harm fossil fuel–powered electricity entails. Interest in establishing community solar electricity cooperatives has grown across communities, a pursuit once seen as marginal (Santiago, de Onís, and Lloréns 2020; de Onís, Lloréns, and Santiago 2020b; de Onís 2018, 2021).

In Black Puerto Rican coastal neighborhoods and towns, bike riding is another visible sustainable practice. People own cars, but bikes are prevalent, and for many they are a preferred mode of transportation that spans across generations. It is not rare to see older men and women riding around town to visit family members or to run errands. This practice is not only good exercise, it also saves money on gasoline, particularly because people use bikes to traverse short distances in the neighborhood or town. Bike riding around town also allows for easy socializing.

Sociality, solidarity, and mutuality are themselves resilient systems; that is, these "grassroots" practices persist even in the face of the whims of modern capitalist and neoliberal governance. Fugitive practices that reject individualism and center the ethics of relational care are prevalent in Black families and communities. These practices are built upon trust and solidarity. In fact, social support is a powerful protection against the crushing stresses and traumas of the anti-Black racism, violence, and terror that are central to the Black experience in the Americas. Beyond being in the presence of others, social support requires reciprocity. This is at the heart of Black relational care practices, which come with the feeling that one is cared for and truly seen and heard in another person's mind and heart. These practices are so central to Black Puerto Rican culture that they are passed down intergenerationally and persist even in the diaspora. These are the kinds of sustainable practices the "urbanized and modernized" can learn from to make good, healthier, and livable futures.

Local Black/Afro ecological knowledge is central to Black Puerto Rican cultural practices and lifeways, so it is no wonder that Black Puerto Ricans, particularly women, have long been at the forefront of demanding that the ecosphere they depend on for sustenance and cultural integrity is protected. If the archipelagic ecosystem is to survive the devastation of climate change, it is time to learn from Black Puerto Ricans. They have been stewarding the ancestral land and sea and passing down cultural lifeways and fugitive practices for generations, bringing them along wherever they go in the archipelago and in the diaspora.

NOTES

1 *Pasteles* are a Puerto Rican tamale-like food, made of bananas and root vegetables and wrapped in a banana leaf, that women make mainly during the Christmas season. Whenever possible, family groups or groups of women get together to make this labor-intensive food. My mother, a *cocinera*/cook by trade, has made and sold *pasteles* since her youth.

2 See NOAA's *National Hurricane Center Tropical Cyclone Report*, NOAA, February 14, 2019, www.nhc.noaa.gov/data/tcr/AL152017_Maria.pdf; see *Ascertainment of the Excess Estimated Mortality from Hurricane María in Puerto Rico*, Milken Institute of Public Health, George Washington University, August 29, 2018, www.washingtonblade.com/content/files/2018/09 /PuertoRicoReport.pdf

3 The longest blackout recorded to date occurred in 2013 after Typhoon Haiyan struck the island, leaving over seven thousand dead.

4 See "President Donald J. Trump Approves Major Disaster Declaration for Puerto Rico," FEMA, September 21, 2017, www.fema.gov/news-release/2017/09 /21/president-donald-j-trump-approves-major-disaster-declaration-puerto -rico.

5 See "Trump Contrasts Puerto Rico Death Toll to 'a Real Catastrophe Like Katrina,'" CNN Politics, October 3, 2017, www.cnn.com/2017/10/03/politics /trump-puerto-rico-katrina-deaths/index.html.

6 See Puerto Rico's Department of Health COVID-19 data, www.salud.gov.pr /Pages/coronavirus.aspx.

7 My ethnographic methodology is an exercise in "narrative reparation" that engages with and illustrates care, affection, love, anger, respect, admiration, and sometimes even resignation, all of which are palpable in the text. This method is informed by Eve Kosofsky Sedgwick's notion of "reparative reading."

CHAPTER 1. SURVIVING MATRIARCHAL DISPOSSESSION

1 Fred Moten cites this phrase from poet/scholar Nathaniel Mackey at 1:07: 42: "Fred Moten & Saidiya Hartman at Duke University: The Black Outdoors," Franklin Humanities Institute, October 5, 2016, www.youtube.com/watch?v=t _tUZ6dybrc. Here I extend Moten's use of Mackey's phrase to describe a way

of being that falls beyond what is considered the social norm, as well as a
social perception of how the "dispossessed" seemingly lead disorderly and
unplanned lives.

2   See the online resource "Matriarchy as a Sociocultural Form: An Old Debate
in a New Light," paper presented at the 16th Congress of the Indo-Pacific
Prehistory Association, Melaka, Malaysia, July 1–7, 1998, https://web.sas
.upenn.edu/psanday/articles/selected-articles/matriarchy-as-a-sociocultural
-form-an-old-debate-in-a-new-light/.

3   This citation comes from the open-access online book, which does not offer page
numbers. See *A Billion Black Anthropocenes or None*, Kathryn Yusoff, 2018,
https://manifold.umn.edu/projects/a-billion-black-anthropocenes-or-none.

4   I use "enslavement" to denaturalize this life circumstance. When "slavery"
appears in this text I am quoting directly from other authors.

5   Patricia Hill Collins defines issues of "survival, power, and identity" as central
to "motherwork" but cautions that women of color might be doing more than
their fair share of community development work (2000).

6   See, for example, Nathan Glazer and Daniel Patrick Moynihan's *Beyond the
Melting Pot* (1963) and many other "sociological problems" studies since then.

7   Interview with Carmen in Arroyo, PR, in July 1998.

CHAPTER 2. DOING HOME-WORK IN THE MOTHERLAND

1   Rapid Response Research Grant: "The Political and Moral Economies of
Recovery from Hurricanes Irma and Maria in Puerto Rico and the U.S. Virgin
Islands," Grant #1806303, National Science Foundation, www.nsf.gov
/awardsearch/showAward?AWD_ID=1806303.

2   Though, as a child, I first migrated to New York City, I moved around to Texas
and Boston before settling in Hartford, Connecticut (see Lloréns 2006), but in
Puerto Rico, "Nuyorican" (New York Puerto Rican) is often used as a generic
label to identify individuals who were born in or who grew up stateside,
despite geographic location. Recently, a conscious shift in the diaspora marks
our stateside locations; for instance, I identify myself as a Hartford-Rican, but
I am part of the greater whole that is the New England–Ricans. Folks who
grew up in Florida are Florida-Ricans, and so forth. This is a way to highlight
that each state has its particular political, cultural, and environmental history
that affects our particular subjectivities.

3   Here I mean to call attention to Jamaica Kincaid's assertions about the
sociocultural, political, and everyday life in *A Small Place* (1988).

4   I'd like to thank one of the anonymous reviewers for suggesting I think
further about undisciplining and what decolonizing ethnography actually
looks like.

5   For confidentiality purposes, all names used here are pseudonyms.

6   See "Malcolm Describes the Difference between the 'House Negro' and the
'Field Negro,'" Michigan State University, January 23, 1963, http://ccnmtl
.columbia.edu/projects/mmt/mxp/speeches/mxa17.html.

7 See "Fred Moten & Saidiya Hartman at Duke University: The Black Outdoors," Franklin Humanities Institute, October 5, 2016, www.youtube.com/watch?v=t_tUZ6dybrc.

8 See "About," Rematriating Borikén, accessed January 17, 2019, https://rematriatingboriken.com/about.

9 See "About," Rematriating Borikén, accessed January 17, 2019, https://rematriatingboriken.com/about.

10 See "PERSPECTIVES: Healing, Restoration, and Rematriation," *News & Notes* (Spring/Summer 1995), p. 3, Indigenous Law Institute, http://ili.nativeweb.org/perspect.html; see "Rematriation," Rematriating Borikén, accessed 17 January, 2019, https://rematriatingboriken.com/rematriation.

11 See "Haudenosaunee Women and Equality," Oneida Indian Nation, accessed January 17, 2019, www.oneidaindiannation.com/haudenosaunee-women-and-equality.

12 For 2000 census data, see Table 3: Race and Hispanic or Latino Origin: 2000, p. 65, available at www.census.gov/prod/cen2000/phc-1-53-ENG.pdf. For 2010 census data, see Table 3: Race and Hispanic or Latino: 2010, p. 90.

CHAPTER 3. LIFE-AFFIRMING PRACTICES

Interview with Leticia Ramos, IDEBAJO, 2016.

1 Though the Initiative for the Eco-development of the Jobos Bay, Inc. (in Spanish, IDEBAJO) was formalized in 2010, the Jobos Bay community has organized coalitions and initiatives since the 1970s to protect the environment and prevent contamination. Important examples are the Punta Pozuelo Fishers Association in Guayama, Puerto Rico, the Corporation of the Jobos Bay, and South Against Contamination (SURCO) (Berman Santana 1996).

2 See Arundhati Roy, "The Greater Common Good," *Outlook*, May 24, 1999, https://magazine.outlookindia.com/story/the-greater-common-good/207509.

3 To protect their privacy, the names of interviewees are pseudonyms.

4 Casa Pueblo was previously named el Taller Comunitario de Arte y Cultura de Adjuntas.

5 See Theresa Horvath, "The Health Initiatives of the Young Lords Party: How a Group of 1960s Radicals Made Health a Revolutionary Concern" (n.d.), Hofstra University, accessed June 27, 2019, www.hofstra.edu/pdf/community/culctr/culctr_events_healthcare0310_%20horvath_abstract.pdf.

6 See "98.7% Latino or Hispanic," Quick Facts Puerto Rico, US Census Bureau, accessed January 8, 2021, www.census.gov/quickfacts/table/BZA010212/72/embed/accessible.

7 See "Persons in Poverty, percent," Quick Facts Puerto Rico, US Census Bureau, accessed January 8, 2021, www.census.gov/quickfacts/fact/table/PR/IPE120218.

8 In Puerto Rico, the US-imposed sterilization policies on women in the 1950s and 1960s, the testing of experimental reproductive medicines and procedures, and the testing of agents (such as Agent Orange) and other hazardous chemicals on the island favor its inclusion as an environmental justice community.

9 See "EPA Laws & Regulations," Exec. Order 12,898, Section 1-1, 59 Fed. Reg. 7629 (February 14, 1994), www.epa.gov/laws-regulations/summary-executive -order-12898-federal-actions-address-environmental-justice.

10 See "Puerto Rico's Population Decline Has Become Widespread in Recent Years," Pew Research Center, March 24, 2016, www.pewresearch.org/fact-tank /2016/03/24/historic-population-losses-continue-across-puerto-rico/ft_16-03 -24_puertorico_pop.

11 See "Salinas es el más pobre," El Nuevo Día, November 12, 2015, www.indicepr .com/suroeste/noticias/2015/11/12/52013/salinas-es-el-mas-pobre/.

12 See "Hub of Philanthropic Engagement-Puerto Rico," FEMA, www.fema.gov /disaster/4339/philanthropy-puerto-rico.

13 See "Salinas Municipio," Quick Facts Puerto Rico, US Census Bureau, accessed January 8, 2021, www.census.gov/quickfacts/fact/table /salinasmunicipiopuertorico/SEX255218#SEX255218.

CHAPTER 4. LIVING WITH/IN ECOLOGICAL CATASTROPHE

Epigraph: Interview with Doña Mercedes, January 2018. I conducted this interview with Mercedes, a lifelong resident of Calichosa, a neighborhood in the mountains between the towns of Arecibo and Utuado on Puerto Rico's west coast.

1 See "The Intergovernmental Panel on Climate Change," accessed May 8, 2020, www.ipcc.ch.

2 See Steve Kobach, "Alphabet Quietly Made Its Experimental Balloon Project a Full-Fledged Corporation—a First Step to a New Google Spinout," Business Insider, October 12, 2017, www.businessinsider.com/googles-parent-company -quietly-made-project-loon-a-corporation-2017-10.

3 I am indebted to one of the anonymous book reviewers for directing me to Gago's work.

4 See "Petitions Emerge Demanding Post-Hurricane 'After Maria' Documentary Be Removed from Netflix," NBC New York, May 28, 2019, www.nbcnewyork .com/news/local/petitions-emerge-demanding-after-maria-documentary -removal-netflix/1751092/.

5 See "Remove 'After Maria' from Netflix Streaming Platform," Change.org, accessed November 10, 2019, www.change.org/p/netflix-remove-after-maria -from-netflix-streaming-platform.

6 See "Immediate Removal of the Netflix Documentary After Maria!!!," Care2, accessed November 10, 2019, www.thepetitionsite.com/771/518/838/immediate -removal-of-the-netflix-documentary-after-maria/.

7 See Jacquellena Carrero, "#YoNoMeQuito Movement Aims to Inspire, Uplift Puerto Ricans," NBC News website, May 12, 2016, www.nbcnews.com/news /latino/yonomequito- movement-aims-inspire-uplift-puerto-ricans-n573016. See also the movement organizers' website, accessed September 6, 2017, www.yonomequitopr.com/. The premiere of a documentary about the

#YoNoMeQuito movement and marketing of the #YoNoMeQuito Foundation aired on local Puerto Rican television on June 17, 2018.

8 See Antonio Flores and Jens Manuel Krogstad, "Puerto Rico's Population Declined Sharply after Hurricanes Maria and Irma," Pew Research Center, July 26, 2019, www.pewresearch.org/fact-tank/2019/07/26/puerto-rico -population-2018/.

9 See "U.S. Census Bureau proyecta población en Puerto Rico estará por debajo de tres millones de habitantes en tan solo 8 años (2025)," Red State Data Center de Puerto Rico (SDC-PR), September 9, 2017, https://censo.estadisticas .pr/Comunicado-de-prensa/2017-09-17t125335; and Eva Lloréns Veléz, "Puerto Rico Population in 2050: 2 Million, Fiscal Board Demographer Says," *Caribbean Business*, August 20, 2017, https://caribbeanbusiness.com/puerto -rico-population-in-2050-2-million-fiscal-board-demographer-says.

10 See "A Way Forward for Puerto Rico—The Visitor Economy," Foundation for Puerto Rico, accessed January 10, 2021, www.finance.senate.gov/imo/media /doc/Foundation%20for%20Puerto%20Rico.pdf.

11 This is a phrase I heard Fred Moten use at "The Black Outdoors: Saidiya Hartman and Fred Moten," Franklin Humanities Institute, October 5, 2016, www.youtube.com/watch?v=t_tUZ6dybrc.

12 See The 20/22 Act Society, accessed January 9, 2021, www.the2022actsociety .org/#tax-incentives.

13 See Zamansele Nsele, "Part I: 'Afropessimism' and the Rituals of Anti-Black Violence," *Mail & Guardian*, June 24, 2020, https://mg.co.za/article/2020-06 -24-frank-b-wilderson-afropessimism-memoir-structural-violence/.

EPILOGUE

Personal communication from Ana Hilda. Ana Hilda, my mother, shared, "The other day I had vertigo and it was so bad that I was walking holding on to my apartment's walls. But then I remembered I have *yerba bruja* [*Kalanchoe pinnata*] planted in a pot by the window. I harvested a few leaves and bruised them over the stove's burner and squeezed a few drops into each ear and felt immediate relief. I have my medicine planted in pots throughout my apartment!"

1 This theme is developed at length in Dr. Carlos G. García-Quijano's unpublished book manuscript "How to Resist Extinction in a Post-capitalist World: Coastal Foraging, Ecological Knowledge, and Well-Being in Coastal Puerto Rico."

REFERENCES

Abadía-Rexach, Barbara I. 2009. "(Re) Pensando la negritud en la música popular Puertorriqueña." *Revista de Ciencias Sociales* 21 (8): 8–43.

———. 2021. "Adolfina Villanueva Osorio, Presente." *NACLA Report on the Americas* 53 (2): 174–80.

Acosta Belén, Edna. 1986. "Puerto Rican Women in Culture, History and Society." In *The Puerto Rican Woman: Perspectives on Culture, History, and Society*, edited by Edna Acosta Belén, 1–29. New York: Praeger.

Adams, Michelene. 2006. "Jamaica Kincaid's *The Autobiography of My Mother*: Allegory and Self-Writing as Counter Discourse." *Anthurium: A Caribbean Studies Journal* 4 (1). https://scholarlyrepository.miami.edu/anthurium/vol4/iss1/1.

Aikens, Natalie, Amy Clukey, Amy K. King, and Isadora Wagner. 2019. "South to the Plantation." *ASAP Journal*. http://asapjournal.com/south-to-the-plantationocene-natalie-aikens-amy-clukey-amy-k-king-and-isadora-wagner/#easy-footnote-bottom-1-4530.

Alamo-Pastrana, Carlos. 2016. *Seams of Empire: Race and Radicalism in Puerto Rico and the United States*. Gainesville: University of Florida Press.

Alegría Ortega, Idsa E. 2007. "Ejes temáticos del pensamiento racial en Puerto Rico: Una aproximación." *Revista de Ciencias Sociales* 17: 154–87.

Alegría Ortega, Idsa E., and Palmira Ríos González, eds. 2005. *Contrapunto de género y raza en Puerto Ric*. San Juan: Centro de Investigaciones Sociales, Universidad de Puerto Rico.

Alexander, Simone A. James. 2001. *Mother Imagery in the Novels of Afro-Caribbean Women*. Columbia: University of Missouri Press.

Alfonso, Omar. 2018. "Toxins from AES's Ashes are Contaminating Groundwater in Puerto Rico." *Centro de Periodismo Investigativo*. https://periodismoinvestigativo.com/2018/03/toxins-from-aess-ashes-are-contaminating-groundwater-in-puerto-rico.

———. 2019. "Damage by Coal Ash to the Southern Aquifer Cannot be Undone." *Centro de Periodismo Investigativo*. https://periodismoinvestigativo.com/2019/03/damage-by-coal-ash-to-the-southern-aquifer-cannot-be-undone.

Alicea, Marisa, and Maura Toro-Morn. 2018. "Reflections on the Community Responses to Hurricane Maria in Chicago: Preliminary Notes and Observations." *Latino Studies Journal* 16 (4): 548–58.

Alston, Philip. 2019. "World faces 'climate apartheid' risk, 120 more million in poverty." *UN News*. https://news.un.org/en/story/2019/06/1041261.

Anderson, Kay, and Colin Perrin. 2018. "'Removed from Nature': The Modern Idea of Human Exceptionality. *Environmental Humanities* 10 (2): 447–72.

Antrobus, Peggy. 1995. "Women in the Caribbean: The Quadruple Burden of Gender, Race, Class and Imperialism." In *Connecting Across Cultures and Continents: Black Women Speak Out on Identity, Race and Development*, edited by Achola O. Pala, 53–60. New York: United Nations Development Fund for Women.

Aratani, Lauren. 2019. "Lin-Manuel Miranda Joins Diaspora Protests against Puerto Rico Governor." *Guardian*, July 17, 2019. https://www.theguardian.com /world/2019/jul/17/us-puerto-rico-protests-lin-manuel-miranda.

Atiles Osoria, José M. 2013. "Colonialismo ambiental, criminalización y resistencias: Las movilizaciones puertorriqueñas por la justicia ambiental en el siglo XXI." *Revista Crítica de Ciências Sociais* 100: 131–52.

———. 2019. *Profanaciones del verano 2019: Corrupción, frentes comunes y justicia decolonial.* Cabo Rojo, PR: Editora Educación Emergente.

Ayala, Edmy, and Patricia Mazzei. 2020. "Puerto Rico Orders Coronavirus Lockdown. Violators Could Be Fined." *New York Times*, March 15, 2020. https:// www.nytimes.com/2020/03/15/us/coronavirus-puerto-rico.html.

Baptista, Ana I. 2008. "Just Policies? A Multiple Case Study of State Environmental Justice Policies." PhD diss., Rutgers University. https://rucore.libraries.rutgers .edu/rutgers-lib/24087/PDF/1/play.

Baralt, Guillermo A. 2007. *Slave Revolts in Puerto Rico: Conspiracies and Uprisings, 1795–1873.* Princeton, NJ: Markus Wiener.

Baver, Sherrie L. 1993. *The Political Economy of Colonialism: The State and Industrialization in Puerto Rico.* Westport, CT: Praeger.

———. 2012. "Environmental Struggles in Paradise: Puerto Rican Cases, Caribbean Lessons." *Caribbean Studies* 1: 15–35.

Beck, Ulrich. 2015. "Emancipatory Catastrophism: What Does It Mean to Climate Change and Risk Society?" *Current Sociology* 63 (1): 75–88.

Behar, Ruth. 1995. "Introduction: Out of Exile." In *Women Writing Culture*, edited by Ruth Behar and Deborah A. Gordon, 1–32. Berkeley: University of California Press.

Bell, Beverly. 2013. *FaultLines: Views Across Haiti's Divide.* Ithaca: Cornell University Press.

Berman Santana, Déborah. 1996. *Kicking off the Bootstraps: Environment, Development, and Community Power in Puerto Rico.* Tucson: University of Arizona Press.

Bledsoe, Adam. 2017. "Marronage as a Past and Present Geography in the Americas." *Southeastern Geographer* 57 (1): 30–50.

Bonilla, Yarimar. 2019. "The Leaked Texts at the Heart of Puerto Rico's Massive Protests." *Nation.* www.thenation.com/article/puerto-rico-rossello-protests -scandal/.

Bonilla, Yarimar, and Marisol LeBrón. 2019. "Introduction: Aftershocks of Disaster." In *Aftershocks of Disaster: Puerto Rico Before and After the Storm*, edited by Yarimar Bonilla and Marisol LeBrón, 1–17. Chicago: Haymarket Books.

Bram, Jason, Francisco E. Martínez, and Charles Steindel. 2008. "Trends and Developments in the Economy of Puerto Rico." *Current Issues in Economics and Finance* 14 (2): 1–7.

Brand, Dionne. 2001. *A Map to the Door of No Return: Notes to Belonging.* Toronto: Vintage Canada.

Briggs, Laura. 2003. *Reproducing Empire: Race, Sex, Science, and U.S. Imperialism in Puerto Rico.* Berkeley: University of California Press.

Brunnée, Jutta. 2009. "Climate Change, Global Environmental Justice and International Environmental Law." In *Environmental Law and Justice in Context*, edited by Jonas Ebbesson and Phoebe Okowa, 316–32. Cambridge: Cambridge University Press.

Brusi, Rima, and Isar Godreau. 2007. "¿Somos Indígenas?" *Diálogo* 10 (1): 10–11.

———. 2019. "Dismantling Public Education." In *Aftershocks of Disaster: Puerto Rico before and after the Storm*, edited by Yarimar Bonilla and Marisol LeBrón, 234–49. Chicago: Haymarket Books.

Brusi, Rima, Yarimar Bonilla, and Isar Godreau. 2018. "When Disaster Capitalism Comes for the University of Puerto Rico." *Nation.* www.thenation.com/article/when-disaster-capitalism-comes-for-the-university-of-puerto-rico/.

Bullard, Robert. 1990. *Dumping in Dixie: Race, Class and Environmental Quality.* Boulder, CO: Westview.

———. 2008. "Environmental Justice in the 21st Century." https://uwosh.edu/sirt/wp-content/uploads/sites/86/2017/08/Bullard_Environmental-Justice-in-the-21st-Century.pdf.

Carnegie, Charles V. 2002. *Postnationalism Prefigured: Caribbean Borderlands.* New Brunswick, NJ: Rutgers University Press.

Carneiro, Sueli. 2010. "Ennegrecer al feminismo. La situación de la mujer negra en América Latina, desde una perspectiva de género." *Afrocubanas.* https://afrocubanas.wordpress.com/2010/02/27/ennegrecer-al-feminismo-la-situacion-de-la-mujer-negra-en-america-latina-desde-una-perspectiva-de-genero/.

Carrasquillo, Rosa E. 2008. *Our Landless Patria: Marginal Citizenship and Race in Caguas, Puerto Rico, 1880–1910.* Lincoln: University of Nebraska Press.

Carter, T. R., X. Lu, S. Bhadwal, C. Conde, L. O. Mearns, et al. 2007. "New Assessment Methods and the Characterization of Future Conditions." In *Climate Change 2007: Impacts, Adaptation and Vulnerability; Contribution of Working Group II to the Fourth Assessment Report of the Intergovernmental Panel on Climate Change*, edited by Martin L. Parry, Osvaldo Canziani, Jean Palutikof, Paul van der Linden, and Clair Hanson, 133–71. Cambridge: Cambridge University Press.

Cervantes-Soon, Claudia. 2014. "The U.S.-Mexico Border-Crossing Chicana Researcher: Theory in the Flesh and the Politics of Identity in Critical Ethnography." *Journal of Latino/Latin American Studies* 6 (2): 97–112.

Chandler, David. 2014. "Beyond Neoliberalism: Resilience, the New Art of Governing Complexity." *Resilience* 2 (1): 47–63.

———. 2019. "Resilience and the End(s) of the Politics of Adaptation." *Resilience: International Policies, Practices and Discourses* 7 (3): 304–13.

Chandler, Nahum Dimitri. 2014. *X—The Problem of the Negro as a Problem for Thought*. New York: Fordham University Press.

Chawla, Devika. 2006. "Subjectivity and the 'Native' Ethnographer: Researcher Eligibility in an Ethnographic Study of Urban Indian Women in Hindu Arranged Marriages." *International Journal of Qualitative Methods* 5 (4): 13–29.

Cintrón Arbasetti, Joel. 2019. "Puerto Rico with a Big 'Menu' for Opportunity Zones." *Caribbean Business*. https://caribbeanbusiness.com/puerto-rico-with-a -big-menu-for-opportunity-zones/.

Claudio, Luz. 2007. "Standing on Principle: The Global Push for Environmental Justice." *Environmental Health Perspectives* 115 (10): 501–503.

Cliff, Michelle, David Dabydeen, and Opal Palmer Adisa. 1998. *Postcolonialism & Autobiography*. Atlanta: Rodopi.

Cohen Blatter, Lucy. 2019. "Safety Is 'the Ultimate Luxury,' Says Puerto Rico–Based Interior Designer." *Mansion Global*. www.mansionglobal.com/articles/safety-is -the-ultimate-luxury-says-puerto-rico-based-interior-designer-210398.

Colectivo Situaciones. 2009. *Conversaciones en el impasse: Dilemas políticos del presente*. Buenos Aires: Tinta Limón.

Collins, Patricia Hill. 2000. *Black Feminist Thought*. New York: Routledge.

Colón-Rivera, Jorge, Félix Córdova-Iturregui, and José Córdova-Iturregui. 2014. *El proyecto de explotación minera en Puerto Rico (1962–1968): Nacimiento de la conciencia ambiental moderna*. San Juan, PR: Ediciones Huracán.

Colón-Warren, Alice. 1998. "The Feminization of Poverty among Women in Puerto Rico and Puerto Rican Women in the Middle Atlantic Region of the United States." *Brown Journal of World Affairs* 5 (2): 263–81.

———. 2003. "Puerto Rico: Feminism and Feminist Studies." *Gender and Society* 17 (5): 664–90.

Concepción, Carmen Milagros. 1988. "El conflicto ambiental y su potencial hacia un desarrollo alternativo: el caso de Puerto Rico." *Ambiente y Desarrollo* 4 (1–2): 125–35.

———. 1990. "Environmental Policy and Industrialization: The Politics of Regulation in Puerto Rico. PhD diss., University of California, Berkeley.

———. 1995. "The Origins of Modern Environmental Activism in Puerto Rico in the 1960s." *International Journal of Urban and Regional Research* 19 (1): 112–28.

———. 2000. "Justicia ambiental, luchas comunitarias y política pública." *Revista de Administración Pública* 31–32: 89–113.

Cooper, Melinda. 2010. "Turbulent Worlds: Financial Markets and Environmental Crisis." *Theory, Culture & Society* 27 (2–3): 167–90.

Cordero Giusti, Juan A. 1996. "Labour, Ecology and History in a Puerto Rican Plantation Region: 'Classic' Rural Proletarians Revisited." *International Review of Social History* 41 (4): 53–82.

Cordero Guzman, Hector R. 2018. "Puerto Rico's Crisis and Poverty: Background, Challenges and Prospects." Paper presented at A Call to Action: Future Challenges for a New Puerto Rico, Rutgers-Camden, October 15, 2018. https:// clc.camden.rutgers.edu/files/PR-Cordero-Guzman-RUTGERS-educed.pdf.

Coto, Danica. 2020. "Storm Isaias Unleashes Flooding, Landslides in Puerto Rico." *Associated Press*. https://apnews.com/article/dominican-republic-puerto-rico -floods-storms-international-news-68369d35bb10e8cf49dc74337ced7175.

Crespo-Kebler, Elizabeth. 1996. "Domestic Work and Racial Division in Women's Employment in Puerto Rico, 1899–1930." *Centro* 8 (1–2): 30–41.

Crutzen, Paul, and Eugene Stoermer. 2000. "The 'Anthropocene.'" *International Geosphere-Biosphere Programme Newsletter* 41: 17–18.

Cruz, Isabelo Zenón. 1974. *Narciso descubre su trasero: El negro en la cultura puertorriqueña*. Humacao, PR: Editorial Furidi.

Cruz-Janzen, Marta I. 2003. "Out of the Closet: Racial Amnesia, Avoidance, and Denial among Puerto Ricans." *Race, Gender and Class* 10 (3): 64–81.

Dávila, Arlene M. 1997. *Sponsored Identities: Cultural Politics in Puerto Rico*. Philadelphia, PA: Temple University Press.

———. 2008. *Latino Spin: Public Image and the Whitewashing of Race*. New York: New York University Press.

Davis, Jane M., Alex A. Moulton, Levi Van Sant, Brian William. 2019. "Anthropocene, Capitalocene, . . . Plantationocene?: A Manifesto for Ecological Justice in an Age of Global Crises." *Geography Compass*. https://doi.org/10.1111/gec3.12438.

de Onís, Catalina M. 2017. "For Many in Puerto Rico, 'Energy Dominance' Is Just a New Name for US Colonialism." *The Conversation*. https://theconversation.com /for-many-in-puerto-rico-energy-dominance-is-just-a-new-name-for-us -colonialism-80243.

———. 2018. "Fueling and Delinking from Energy Coloniality in Puerto Rico." *Journal of Applied Communication Research* 46 (5): 535–60.

———. 2021. *Energy Islands: Metaphors of Power, Extractivism, and Justice in Puerto Rico*. Oakland: University of California Press.

de Onís, Catalina M., Hilda Lloréns, and Ruth Santiago. 2020a. "Puerto Rico Seismic Shocks." *NACLA, Report on the Americas* (blog). https://nacla.org/news /2020/01/14/puerto-rico-earthquakes-renewable-energy.

———. 2020b. *¡Ustedes tienen que limpiar las cenizas e irse de Puerto Rico para siempre!': La lucha por la justicia ambiental, climática y energética como trasfondo del verano de Revolución Boricua 2019*. Cabo Rojo, PR: Editora Educación Emergente.

Díaz-Quiñones, Arcadio. 1993. *La memoria rota*. Rio Piedras, PR: Huracán.

Dibley, Ben. 2012. "'The Shape of Things to Come': Seven Theses on the Anthropocene and Attachment." *Australian Humanities Review* 52: 139–53.

Diegues, Antonio Carlos. 1995. "Os pescadores artesanais e a questão ambiental." In *Povos e mares: Leituras em sócio-antropologia marítima*, edited by Antonio Carlos Diegues, 131–39. Universidade de São Paulo: NUPAUB-USB.

Dietrich, Alexa S. 2013. *The Drug Company Next Door: Pollution, Jobs, and Community Health in Puerto Rico*. New York: NYU Press.

Dietz, James. 1986. *Economic History of Puerto Rico*. Princeton: Princeton University Press.

Dinzey Flores, Zaire Zenit. 2013. *Locked In, Locked Out: Gated Communities in a Puerto Rican City*. Philadelphia: University of Pennsylvania Press.

Dinzey Flores, Zaire Zenit, Hilda Lloréns, Nancy López, and Maritza Quiñones on behalf of the Black Latinas Know Collective. 2019. "Black Latina Womanhood: From Latinx Fragility to Empowerment and Social Justice Praxis." *Women's Studies Quarterly* 47 (3–4): 321–27.

Dolce, Chris. 2020. Severe Drought in Puerto Rico Prompts State of Emergency, Water Rationing. *The Weather Channel Online*. https://weather.com/safety/news /2020-06-30-severe-drought-puerto-rico-state-of-emergency.

Domenech Cruz, Roxanna D. 2015. "Las mujeres, la justicia socioambiental y el cambio climático: Un homenaje a Haydée Cardona." *Perspectivas en Asuntos Ambientales* 4: 14–24.

Doucet-Battle, James. 2016. "Bioethical Matriarchy: Race, Gender, and the Gift in Genomic Research." *Catalyst: Feminism, Theory, Technoscience* 2 (2): 1–28.

Duany, Jorge. 2001. "Making Indians Out of Blacks: The Revitalization of Taíno Identity in Contemporary Puerto Rico." In *Taíno Revival: Critical Perspectives on Puerto Rican Identity and Cultural Politics*, edited by Gabriel Haslip-Viera, 55–82. Princeton: Marcus Wiener.

———. 2002. *Nation on the Move: The Construction of Cultural Identities in Puerto Rico and the Diaspora*. Chapel Hill: University of North Carolina Press.

Duffy-Mayers, Loretto. 2017. "Case Study 4.4: Caribbean Hotel Energy Efficiency and Renewable Energy Action (CHENACT)." In *Coastal Tourism and Climate Change in the Caribbean*, vol. 1, edited by Martha Honey and Samantha Hogenson. New York: CREST.

Dyer-Witheford, Nick. 2009. "Twenty-First Century Species-Being." Paper presented at the Sixth Annual Marx and Philosophy Conference, London, June 6, 2009.

Espiritu, Yen Le. 1997. "Race, Gender, Class in the Lives of Asian Americans." *Race, Gender & Class*, 4 (3): 12–19.

Evans, Brad, and Julian Reid. 2014. *Resilient Life: The Art of Living Dangerously*. Cambridge: Polity.

Farbotko, Carol, and Heather Lazrus. 2012. "The First Climate Refugees? Contesting Global Narratives of Climate Change in Tuvalu." *Global Environmental Change* 22 (2): 382–90.

Fanon, Frantz. 2004. *The Wretched of the Earth*. New York: Grove.

Federici, Silvia. 2012. *Revolution at Point Zero: Housework, Reproduction and Feminist Struggle*. Oakland, CA: PM Press.

Feliciano Santos, Sherina. 2011. "An Inconceivable Indigeneity: The Historical, Cultural, and Interactional Dimensions of Puerto Rican Taíno Activism." PhD diss., University of Michigan.

———. 2021. *A Contested Caribbean Indigeneity: Language, Social Practice, and Identity within Puerto Rican Taíno Activism*. New Brunswick: Rutgers University Press.

Figueroa, Luis A. 2005. *Sugar, Slavery, and Freedom in Nineteenth-Century Puerto Rico*. Chapel Hill: University of North Carolina Press.

Figueroa Rodriguez, Raúl. 2017. "La isla que se vacía." *El Nuevo Día*. www .elnuevodia.com/opinion/columnas/laislasevacia-columna-2306210/.

Figueroa Vásquez, Yomaira C. 2020a. "Your Lips: Mapping Afro-Boricua Feminist Becomings." *Frontiers: A Journal of Women Studies* 41 (1): 1–11.

———. 2020b. *Decolonizing Diasporas: Radical Mappings of Afro-Atlantic Literature*. Evanston, IL: Northwestern University Press.

Findlay, Eileen J. Suárez. 1999. *Imposing Decency: The Politics of Sexuality and Race in Puerto Rico, 1870–1920*. Durham, NC: Duke University Press.

———. 2014. *We Are Left without a Father Here: Masculinity, Domesticity, and Migration in Postwar Puerto Rico*. Durham, NC: Duke University Press.

Fitzpatrick, Joseph P. 1971. *Puerto Rican Americans: The Meaning of Migration to the Mainland*. Englewood Cliffs, NJ: Prentice-Hall.

Flores, Juan. 2009. *The Diaspora Strikes Back: Caribeño Tales of Learning and Turning*. New York: Routledge.

Forte, Maximilian C. 2004–5. "Extinction: The Historical Trope of Anti-indigeneity in the Caribbean." *Issues in Caribbean Amerindian Studies* 6 (4): 1–24.

Franco Ortiz, Mariluz, Hilda Lloréns, Maria I. Reinat-Pumarejo, Bárbara I. Abadía-Rexach, Gloriann Sacha Antonetty Lebrón. 2019. "Hacia una conversación justa sobre el racismo y los privilegios de raza y géreno en Puerto Rico." *8ogrados* (blog). www.8ogrados.net/conversacion-justa-sobre-racismo-y-privilegios-de-raza-y-genero-en-puerto-rico/.

Frazier, Franklin E. 1939. *The Negro Family in the United States*. Chicago: University of Chicago Press.

Fuentes, Marisa J. 2016. *Dispossessed Lives: Enslaved Women, Violence, and the Archive*. Philadelphia: University of Pennsylvania Press.

Fusté, José I. 2017. "Repeating Islands of Debt: Historicizing the Transcolonial Relationality of Puerto Rico's Economic Crisis." *Radical History Review* 128: 91–119.

Gaard, Greta C. 1993. *Ecofeminism: Women, Animals, Nature*. Philadelphia: Temple University Press.

Gago, Verónica. 2017. *Neoliberalism from Below: Popular Pragmatics & Baroque Economies*. Durham, NC: Duke University Press.

Gandy, Matthew. 2002. Between Borinquen and the *Barrio*: Environmental Justice and New York City's Puerto Rican Community, 1969–1972. *Antipode* 34: 730–61. doi:10.1111/1467-8330.00267.

García, Ana María, dir. 1982. *La Operación*. Latin American Film Project. Film.

García-Colón, Ismael. 2020. Colonial Migrants at the Heart of Empire: Puerto Rican Workers on U.S. Farms. Oakland: University of California Press.

García-Colón, Ismael, and Harry Franqui-Rivera. 2015. "Puerto Rico Is NOT Greece: Notes on the Role of Debt in US Colonialism." *CUNY, The Graduate Center*. www.focaalblog.com/2015/08/26/puerto-rico-is-not-greece-the-role-of-debt-in-us-colonialism/.

García-Colón, Ismael, and Edwin Meléndez. 2013. "Enduring Migration: Puerto Rican Workers on U.S. Farms." *Centro Journal* 25 (2): 96–119.

García López, Gustavo A. 2015. "Recuperar los comunes para un país vivo: Perspectivas desde la lucha contra el despojo y por la autogestión comunitaria en Casa Pueblo, Puerto Rico." *Ecología Política* 49: 51–60.

———. 2018. The Multiple Layers of Environmental Injustice in Contexts of (Un)natural Disasters: The Case of Puerto Rico Post–Hurricane Maria. *Environmental Justice* 11 (3): 101–8.

———. 2020. "Environmental Justice Movements in Puerto Rico: Life-and-Death Struggles and Decolonizing Horizons." *Society & Space*, February 25, 2020, www.societyandspace.org/articles/environmental-justice-movements-in-puerto-rico-life-and-death-struggles-and-decolonizing-horizons.

García López, Gustavo, Carmen Milagros Concepción, and Alejandro A. Torres Abreu. 2018. *Ambiente y democracia.* San Juan: Editorial de la Universidad de Puerto Rico.

Garcia Preto, Nydia. 2005. "Puerto Rican Families." In *Ethnicity and Family Therapy*, edited by Monica McGoldrick, Jose Giordano, and Nydia Garcia-Preto, 242–55. New York: Guilford.

García-Quijano, Carlos. 2006. "Resisting Extinction: The Value of Local Knowledge for Small-Scale Fisheries in Southeastern Puerto Rico." PhD diss., University of Georgia.

García-Quijano, Carlos, and Hilda Lloréns. 2016. "The Myth of the Benevolent State and Everyday Acts of Resilience among Puerto Ricans." Paper presented at Puerto Rico, The Debt Crisis and Self-Determination: Exploring Paths to Decolonization Conference, New York, April 13–15.

———. 2017. "What Rural, Coastal Puerto Ricans Can Teach Us about Thriving in Times of Crisis." *The Conversation.* https://theconversation.com/what-rural-coastal-puerto-ricans-can-teach-us-about-thriving-in-times-of-crisis-76119.

———. 2018. "Many Puerto Ricans Fear Recovery Plan Could Be Greedy Land Grab." *NYDailyNews.* www.nydailynews.com/news/ny-oped-hurricane-maria-land-grab-too-costly-20180918-story.html.

———. 2019. "Using the Anthropological Concept of 'Core Cultural Values' to Understand the Puerto Rican 2019 Summer Protests." *American Anthropologist* (blog). www.americananthropologist.org/2019/10/29/understanding-the-puerto-rican-2019-summer-protests/.

García-Quijano, Carlos, and John Poggie. 2019. "Coastal Resource Foraging, the Culture of Coastal Livelihoods, and Human Well-Being in Southeastern Puerto Rico: Consensus, Consonance, and Some Implications for Coastal Policy." *Maritime Studies* 9: 53–65.

García-Quijano, Carlos, John Poggie, and Miguel H. Del Pozo. 2015a. "'En el monte también se pesca': 'Pesca de monte,' ambiente, subsistencia y comunidad en los bosques costeros del sureste de Puerto Rico." *Caribbean Studies* 43 (2): 115–44.

García-Quijano, Carlos, John Poggie, Ana Pitchon, and Miguel H. Del Pozo. 2015b. "Coastal Resource Foraging, Life Satisfaction, and Well-Being in Southeastern Puerto Rico." *Journal of Anthropological Research* 71 (2): 145–67.

Garriga-López, Adriana María. 2018. "The Other Puerto Rico." *SocialText Online.* https://socialtextjournal.org/periscope_article/the-other-puerto-rico/.

Gelabert, Pedro A. 2013. *Historia del movimiento ambiental en Puerto Rico.* San Juan, PR: Nook Books.

Gergen, Kenneth J. 1991. *The Saturated Self: Dilemmas of Identity in Contemporary Life*. New York: Basic Books.

Glaser, Mario. 2003. "Interrelations between Mangrove Ecosystem, Local Economy and Social Sustainability in Caeté Estuary, North Brazil." *Wetlands Ecology and Management* 11 (4): 265–72.

Glazer, Nathan, and Daniel Patrick Moynihan. 1963. *Beyond the Melting Pot: The Negroes, Puerto Ricans, Jews, Italians, and Irish of New York City*. Cambridge, MA: MIT Press.

Glissant, Édouard. 1997. *Poetics of Relation*. Ann Arbor: University of Michigan Press.

Godreau, Isar P. 2008. "Slippery Semantics: Race Talk and Everyday Uses of Racial Terminology in Puerto Rico." *Centro Journal* 20 (2): 5–33.

———. 2015. *Scripts of Blackness: Race, Cultural Nationalism, and U.S. Colonialism in Puerto Rico*. Urbana: University of Illinois Press.

Godreau, Isar P., Mariolga Reyes Cruz, Mariluz Franco Ortiz, Sherrie Cuadrado. 2008. The Lessons of Slavery: Discourses of Slavery, *Mestizaje*, and *Blanqueamiento* in an Elementary School in Puerto Rico. *American Ethnologist* 35, 1: 115–35.

Gómez-Barris, Macarena. 2017. *The Extractive Zone: Social Ecologies and Decolonial Perspectives*. Durham, NC: Duke University Press.

González, Christina M. 2018. "Abuelas, Ancestors and Atabey: The Spirit of Taíno Resurgence." *American Indian* 19 (3): www.americanindianmagazine.org/story /abuelas-ancestors-and-atabey-spirit-taino-resurgence.

González, José Luis. 1993 [1980]. *País de cuatro pisos y otros ensayos*. Princeton, NJ: M. Wiener.

González, Juan. 2011. *Harvest of Empire: A History of Latinos in America*. New York: Penguin Books.

Gordon, Lewis. 2015. *What Fanon Said: A Philosophical Introduction to His Life and Thought*. New York: Fordham University Press.

Gordon, Robert. 1999. "Poisons in the Fields: The United Farm Workers, Pesticides, and Environmental Politics." *Pacific Historical Review* 68 (1): 51–77.

Griffith, David, Carlos G. García-Quijano, and Manuel Valdés Pizzini. 2013. "A Fresh Defense: A Cultural Biography of Quality in Puerto Rican Fishing." *American Anthropologist* 115 (1): 17–28.

Griffith, David, and Manuel Valdés Pizzini. 2002. *Fishers at Work, Workers at Sea: Puerto Rican Journey thru Labor & Refuge*. Philadelphia: Temple University Press.

Grosfoguel, Ramón. 2003. *Colonial Subjects: Puerto Ricans in a Global Perspective*. Berkeley: University of California Press.

Guerra, Lillian. 1998. *Popular Expression and National Identity in Puerto Rico: The Struggle for Self, Community, and Nation*. Jacksonville: University Press of Florida.

Haraway, Donna. 1988. "Situated Knowledges: The Science Question in Feminism and the Privilege of Partial Perspective." *Feminist Studies* 14 (3): 575–99.

———. 2007. *When Species Meet*. Minneapolis: Minnesota University Press.

———. 2015. "Anthropocene, Capitalocene, Plantationocene, Chthulucene: Making Kin." *Environmental Humanities* 6 (1): 159–65.

Harney, Stefano, and Fred Moten. 2013. *The Undercommons: Fugitive Planning & Black Study*. New York: Minor Compositions.

Harris, Wilson. 1999. "Creoleness: The Crossroads of a Civilization?" In *Selected Essays of Wilson Harris: The Unfinished Genesis of the Imagination*, edited by A. J. M. Bundy, 327–347. London: Routledge.

Harrison, Faye V. 1997. *Decolonizing Anthropology: Moving Further toward an Anthropology of Liberation*. Washington, DC: Association of Black Anthropologists, American Anthropological Association.

———. 2008. *Outsider Within: Reworking Anthropology in the Global Age*. Urbana: University of Illinois Press.

Hartman, Saidiya V. 1997. *Scenes of Subjection: Terror, Slavery, and Self-making in Nineteenth-Century America*. Oxford: Oxford University Press.

———. 2008. *Lose Your Mother: A Journey along the Atlantic Slave Route*. New York: Farrar, Straus and Giroux.

———. 2016. "The Belly of the World: A Note on Black Women's Labors." *Souls: A Critical Journal of Black Politics, Culture and Society* 1 (18): 166–73.

———. 2019. *Wayward Lives, Beautiful Experiments: Intimate Histories of Social Upheaval*. New York: W. W. Norton.

Haslip-Viera, Gabriel. 2001. "Introduction. Competing Identities: Taíno Revivalism and other Ethno-racial Identity Movements among Puerto Ricans and other Caribbean Latinos in the United States, 1980–Present." In *Taíno Revival: Critical Perspectives on Puerto Rican Identity and Cultural Politics*, edited by Gabriel Haslip-Viera, 1–30. Princeton: Marcus Wiener.

———. 2006. "The Politics of Taíno Revivalism: The Insignificance of Amerindian mtDNA in the Population History of Puerto Ricans. A Comment on Recent Research." *CENTRO Journal* 1: 260–75.

Hernández Cabiya, Yanira. 2020. "Puerto Rico Gov Gives No Explanation Why Inexperienced Companies Were Sourcing COVID-19 Tests." *Caribbean Business*. https://caribbeanbusiness.com/puerto-rico-gov-avoids-explaining -why-inexperienced-companies-were-chosen-to-source-covid-19-tests/.

Hernández, Tanya Katerí. 2021. *On Latino Anti-Black Bias: "Racial Innocence" and the Struggle for Equality*. Boston: Beacon.

Hernández Quirindongo, Yasmín. 2019. "Hurri-Quake." *Rematriating Borikén* (blog). https://rematriatingboriken.com/2019/09/26/hurri-quake/.

———. 2019. "Rematriation Manifesto." *Rematriating Borikén* (blog). https:// rematriatingboriken.com/2019/05/15/rematriation-migration-manifesto-5-years -in-boriken/.

———. n.d. "About." *Rematriating Borikén* (blog). Accessed on March 25, 2019. https://rematriatingboriken.com/about/.

Hinojosa, Jennifer, Nashia Román, and Edwin Meléndez. 2018. "Puerto Rican Post-Maria Relocation by States." *Centro Research Brief*.

Hoffman, Susana M. 2002. "The Monster and the Mother: The Symbolism of Disaster." In *Catastrophe & Culture: The Anthropology of Disaster*, edited by

Susana M. Hoffman and Anthony Oliver-Smith, 113–42. Santa Fe, NM: School of American Research Press.

Holland, Sharon Patricia. 2000. *Raising the Dead: Readings of Death and (Black) Subjectivity*. Durham, NC: Duke University Press.

Holling, Crawford Stanley. 1973. "Resilience and Stability of Ecological Systems." *Annual Review of Ecology and Systematics* 4: 1–23.

hooks, bell. 1986. "Sisterhood: Political Solidarity between Women." *Feminist Review* 23: 125–38.

———. 1990. *Yearning: Race, Gender, and Cultural Politics*. Boston: South End Press.

Horne, Gerald. 2018. *The Apocalypse of Settler Colonialism: The Roots of Slavery, White Supremacy, and Capitalism in 17th Century North America and the Caribbean*. New York: NYU Press.

Horvath, Theresa. n.d. "The Health Initiatives of the Young Lords Party: How a Group of 1960s Radicals Made Health a Revolutionary Concern." Hofstra University. Accessed August 1, 2018. www.hofstra.edu/pdf/community/culctr/culctr_events_healthcare0310_%20horvath_paper.pdf.

Hunter, Andrea G. 2006. "Teaching Classics in Family Studies: E. Franklin Frazier's *The Negro Family in the United States*." *Family Relations* 55 (1): 80–92.

Jackson, Shona N. 2012. *Creole Indigeneity: Between Myth and Nation in the Caribbean*. Minneapolis: University of Minnesota Press.

Jaipuriar, Rashida. 2019. "Stateside Puerto Ricans, Who Responded to Island Protests, Are Still Vigilant." *CBSnews* (blog). www.nbcnews.com/news/latino/stateside-puerto-ricans-who-responded-island-protests-are-still-vigilant-n1040536.

Jiménez-Muñoz, Gladys. 1998. "Literacy, Class, and Sexuality in the Debate on Women's Suffrage in Puerto Rico during the 1920s." In *Puerto Rican Women's History: New Perspectives*, edited by Félix V. Matos Rodríguez and Linda C. Delgado, 143–70. New York: M. E. Sharpe.

———. 2003. "Carmen María Colón Pellot: On 'Womanhood' and 'Race' in Puerto Rico during the Interwar Period." *CR: The New Centennial Review* 3 (3): 71–91.

Jiménez Román, Miriam. 2001. "The Indians Are Coming! The Indians Are Coming! The Taíno and Puerto Rican Identity." In *Taíno Revival: Critical Perspectives on Puerto Rican Identity and Cultural Politics*, edited by Gabriel Haslip-Viera, 101–38. Princeton, NJ: Marcus Wiener.

Johnson, Jessica Marie. 2020. *Wicked Flesh: Black Women, Intimacy, and Freedom in the Atlantic World*. Philadelphia: University of Pennsylvania Press.

Joseph, Jonathan. 2013. "Resilience as Embedded Neoliberalism: A Governmentality Approach. *Resilience: International Policies, Practices and Discourses* 1 (1): 38–52.

Karidis, Arlene. 2019. "Puerto Rico Landfills: Is the Problem Around Capacity or Noncompliance?" *Waste 360*. www.waste360.com/landfill-operations/puerto-rico-landfills-problem-around-capacity-or-noncompliance.

Keegan, William F., and Corine L. Hofman. 2017. *The Caribbean before Columbus*. Oxford: Oxford University Press.

Kincaid, Jamaica. 1988. *A Small Place*. New York: Farrar, Straus and Giroux.

King, Lovalerie. 2007. *Race, Theft, and Ethics: Property Matters in African American Literature*. Baton Rouge: Louisiana State University Press.

King, Tiffany Lethabo. 2016. "The Labor of (Re) Reading Plantation Landscapes Fungible(ly)." *Antipode* 48 (4): 1022–39.

———. 2019. *The Black Shoals: Offshore Formations of Black and Native Studies*. Durham, NC: Duke University Press.

Kinsbruner, Jay. 1996. *Not of Pure Blood: The Free People of Color and Racial Prejudice in Nineteenth-Century Puerto Rico*. Durham, NC: Duke University Press.

Klein, Naomi. 2018. "The Battle for Paradise." *The Intercept*. https://theintercept.com/2018/03/20/puerto-rico-hurricane-maria-recovery/.

Kleinman, Arthur, and Joan Kleinman. 1997. "The Appeal of Experience; The Dismay of Images: Cultural Appropriations of Suffering in Our Times." In *Social Suffering*, edited by Arthur Kleinman, Veena Das, and Margaret Lock, 1–24. Berkeley: University of California Press.

Kuehn, Robert R. 2000. "A Taxonomy of Environmental Justice." *Environmental Law Reporter* 30: 10681.

Kunkel, Cathy. 2018. "IEEFA Puerto Rico: Massive Liquefied Natural Gas Project Dead." *Institute for Energy Economic and Financial Analysis*. https://ieefa.org/ieefa-puerto-rico-massive-liquefied-natural-gas-project-dead/.

La Fountain-Stokes, Lawrence. 2002. "Dancing La Vida Loca: The Queer Nuyorican Performances of Arthur Avilés and Elizabeth Marrero." In *Queer Globalizations: Citizenship and the Afterlife of Colonialism*, edited by Arnaldo Cruz-Malavé and Martin F. Manalansan, 162–75. New York: New York University Press.

Lassén, Ana Irma Rivera. 2016. "Afrodescendant Women: A Race and Gender Intersectional Spiderweb." *Meridians* 14 (2): 56–70.

Lassén, Ana Irma Rivera, and Elizabeth Crespo-Kebler, eds. 2001. *Documentos del feminism en Puerto Rico: Fascímiles de la historia, Vol. 1, 1970–1979*. San Juan: Editorial Universidad de Puerto Rico.

Latour, Bruno. 2004. *Politics of Nature: How to Bring Sciences into Democracy*. Cambridge, MA: Harvard University Press.

LeBrón, Marisol. 2019a. *Policing Life and Death: Race, Violence, and Resistance in Puerto Rico*. Oakland: University of California Press.

———. 2019b. "The Protests in Puerto Rico Are about Life and Death." *NACLA Report on the Americas* (blog). https://nacla.org/news/2019/07/18/protests-puerto-rico-are-about-life-and-death.

Lee, Charles. 1987. *Toxic Wastes and Race in the United States: A National Report on the Racial and Socio-economic Characteristics of Communities with Hazardous Waste Sites*. New York: United Church of Christ, Commission for Racial Justice.

———. 1992. *Proceedings: The First National People of Color Environmental Leadership Summit*. New York: United Church of Christ, Commission for Racial Justice.

———. 2021. "Confronting Disproportionate Impacts and Systemic Racism in Environmental Policy." *Environmental Law Reporter* 51 (3). https://elr.info/news

-analysis/51/10207/confronting-disproportionate-impacts-and-systemic-racism
-environmental-policy.

Lenton, Timothy, Johan Rockström, Owen Gaffney, Stefan Rahmstorf, Katherine Richardson, Will Steffen, and Joachim Hans Schellnhuber. 2019. "Climate Tipping Points—Too Risky to Bet Against." *Nature* 575: 592–95.

Lerner, Gerda. 1972. *Black Women in White America: A Documentary History*. New York: Pantheon Books.

Lerner, Steve. *Sacrifice Zones: The Front Lines of Toxic Chemical Exposure in the United States*. 2010. Cambridge, MA: MIT Press.

Levy, Teresita A. 2015. *Puerto Ricans in the Empire: Tobacco Growers and U.S. Colonialism*. New Brunswick, NJ: Rutgers University Press.

Lewis, Oscar. 1966. *La Vida: A Puerto Rican Family in the Culture of Poverty—San Juan and New York*. New York: Random House.

Lewis, Simon L., and Mark A. Maslin. 2018. *The Human Planet: How We Created the Anthropocene*. New Haven: Yale University Press.

Llanos-Figueroa, Dahlma. 2009. *Daughters of the Stone*. New York: Thomas Dunne Books.

Lloréns, Hilda. 2005. "Fugitive Blackness: Representations of Race, Art and Memory in Arroyo, Puerto Rico." PhD diss., University of Connecticut.

———. 2006. "Dislocated Geographies: A Story of Border Crossings. *Small Axe* 10: 74–93.

———. 2008. "Brothels, Hell and Puerto Rican Bodies: Sex, Race, and Other Cultural Politics in 21st Century Artistic Representations." *CENTRO: Journal of the Center for Puerto Rican Studies* 20 (1): 192–217.

———. 2014. *Imaging the Great Puerto Rican Family: Framing Nation, Race, and Gender during the American Century*. Lanham, MD: Lexington Books.

———. 2016. "Puerto Rico, Environmental Injustice and Racism Inflame Protests over Coal Ash." *The Conversation*. https://theconversation.com/in-puerto-rico-environmental-injustice-and-racism-inflame-protests-over-coal-ash-69763.

———. 2017. The Making of a Community Activist. *Sapiens*. www.sapiens.org/culture/jobos-bay-community-activist/.

———. 2018a. "Beyond *Blanqueamiento*: Black Affirmation in Contemporary Puerto Rico." *Latin American and Caribbean Ethnic Studies* 13 (2): 157–78.

———. 2018b. "Ruin Nation." *NACLA Report on the Americas* 50 (2): 154–59.

———. 2018c. "Imaging Disaster: Puerto Rico through the Eye of Hurricane María." *Transforming Anthropology* 26 (2): 136–56.

———. 2018d. "Identity Practices: Racial Passing, Gender, and Racial Purity in Puerto Rico." *Afro-Hispanic Review* 37 (1): 29–47.

———. 2019. "The Race of Disaster: Black Communities and the Crisis in Puerto Rico." *Black Perspectives* (blog). www.aaihs.org/the-race-of-disaster-black-communities-and-the-crisis-in-puerto-rico/.

Lloréns, Hilda, and Carlos García-Quijano. 2020. "From Extractive Agriculture to Industrial Waste Periphery: Life in a Black Puerto Rican Ecology." *Black Perspectives*. www.aaihs.org/from-extractive-agriculture-to-industrial-waste-periphery-life-in-a-black-puerto-rican-ecology/.

Lloréns, Hilda, Carlos García-Quijano, and Isar Godreau. 2017. "Racismo en Puerto Rico: Surveying Perceptions of Race." *CENTRO: Journal of the Center for Puerto Rican Studies* 29 (3): 154–83.

Lloréns, Hilda, and Ruth Santiago. 2018a. "Coal's Open Wounds." *NACLA Report on the Americas* (blog). https://nacla.org/news/2018/09/28/coal%E2%80%99s-open-wounds-las-heridas-abiertas-del-carb%C3%B3n.

———. 2018b. "Women Lead Puerto Rico's Recovery: In Puerto Rico's Southeast, Women Are at the Forefront of the Struggle against Environmental Degradation and Catastrophe." *NACLA Report on the Americas* 50 (4): 398–403.

Lloréns, Hilda, Ruth Santiago, Carlos G. García-Quijano, and Catalina de Onís. 2018. "Hurricane Maria: Puerto Rico's Unnatural Disaster." *Social Justice* (blog). www.socialjusticejournal.org/hurricane-maria-puerto-ricos-unnatural-disaster/.

Lloréns, Hilda, and Maritza Stanchich. 2019. "Water Is Life, but the Colony Is a Necropolis: Environmental Terrains of Struggle in Puerto Rico." *Cultural Dynamics* 31 (1–2): 81–101.

López, Adalberto, and James F. Petras. 1974. *Puerto Rico and Puerto Ricans: Studies in History and Society.* New York: Halsed.

López, Irene. 2008. "Puerto Rican Phenotype: Understanding Its Historical Underpinnings and Psychological Associations." *Hispanic Journal of Behavioral Sciences* 30 (2): 161–80.

López, Iris. 2008. *Matters of Choice: Puerto Rican Women's Struggle for Reproductive Freedom.* New Brunswick, NJ: Rutgers University Press.

Lowe, Lisa. 2015. *The Intimacies of Four Continents.* Durham, NC: Duke University Press.

Lugones, María. 2007. "Heterosexualism and the Colonial/Modern Gender System." *Hypatia* 22 (1): 186–209.

Lutz, Catherine. 1995. "The Gender of Theory." In *Women Writing Culture*, edited by Ruth Behar and Deborah A. Gordon, 249–66. Berkeley: University of California Press.

Maldonado-Torres, Nelson. 2019. "Afterword: Critique and Decoloniality in the Face of Crisis, Disaster and Catastrophe." In *Aftershocks of Disaster: Puerto Rico before and after the Storm*, edited by Yarimar Bonilla and Marisol LeBrón, 332–42. Chicago: Haymarket Books.

Malkki, Lisa. 1992. "National Geographic: The Rooting of Peoples and the Territorialization of National Identity among Scholars and Refugees." *Cultural Anthropology* 7 (1): 24–44.

Maracle, Lee. 2006. "Decolonizing Native Women." In *Daughters of Mother Earth: The Wisdom of Native American Women*, edited by Barbara Alice Mann and Winona La Duke, 29–52. Westport, CT: Praeger.

Martin, Adrian, M. Teresa Armijos, Brendan Coolsaet, Neil Dawson, Gareth A. S. Edwards, Roger Few, Nicole Gross-Camp, Iokiñe Rodriguez, Heike Schroeder, Mark G. L. Tebboth, and Carole S. White. 2020. "Environmental Justice and Transformations to Sustainability." *Environment: Science and Policy for Sustainable Development* 62 (6): 19–30.

Martínez-Cruzado, Juan C. 2002. "The Use of Mitochondrial DNA to Discover Pre-Columbian Migrations to the Caribbean: Results for Puerto Rico and Expectations for the Dominican Republic." *KACIKE: Journal of Caribbean Amerindian History and Anthropology*: 1–11.

Martínez-Cruzado, Juan C., G. Toro-Labrador, V. Ho-Fung, M. A. Estévez-Montero, A. Lobaina-Manzanet, D. A. Padovani-Claudio, H. Sánchez-Cruz, P. Ortiz-Bermúdez, and A. Sánchez-Crespo. 2001. "Mitochondrial DNA Analysis Reveals Substantial Native American Ancestry in Puerto Rico." *Human Biology* 73: 491–511.

Martínez-San Miguel, Yolanda. 2011. "Taíno Warriors?: Strategies for Recovering Indigenous Voices in Colonial and Contemporary Hispanic Caribbean Discourses." *Centro Journal* 23 (1): 197–215.

Mason, Sherri A., Victoria G. Welch, and Joseph Neratko. 2018. "Synthetic Polymer Contamination in Bottle Water." *Frontiers in Chemistry* 6: 407. doi:10.3389/fchem.2018.00407.

Massol Deyá, Arturo. 2018. *Amores que luchan: Relato de la victoria contra el gasoducto en tiempos de crisis energetica*. San Juan, PR: Ediciones Callejón.

Massol González, Alexis, Avril Andromache Johnnidis, and Arturo Massol Deyá. 2008. *The Evolution of Casa Pueblo, Puerto Rico: From Mining Opposition to Community Revolution*. London: International Institute for Environment and Development.

Matos Rodrígez, Félix V. 1998. "Women's History in Puerto Rican Historiography: The Last Thirty Years." In *Puerto Rican Women's History: New Perspectives*, edited by Félix V. Matos Rodríguez and Linda C. Delgado, 3–37. New York: M. E. Sharpe.

Mayol-García, Yerís H. 2019. "Migration, Living Arrangements and Poverty among Puerto Rican–Origin Children: Puerto Rico and the United States." Paper presented at the Population Association of America Annual Meeting. https://census.gov/content/dam/Census/library/working-papers/2019/demo/sehsd-wp2019-14-presentation.pdf.

Mayol-García, Y. H., and Burd, C. 2018. "A Binational Perspective of Puerto Rican-Origin Children's Living Arrangements: A Decade of Change and Migration in Puerto Rico and the United States, 2006 and 2015." US Census Bureau. SEHSD working paper presented at PAA 2018. www.census.gov/content/dam/Census/library/working-papers/2018/demo/SEHSD-WP2018-08.pdf.

Mayo Santana, Raul, Mariano Negrón Portillo, and Manuel Mayo López. 1991. "La familia esclava en San Juan en el siglo XIX." *Revista de Ciencias sociales* 30 (1–2): 163–98.

McCaffrey, Katherine T. 2002. *Military Power and Popular Protest: The U.S. Navy in Vieques, Puerto Rico*. New Brunswick, NJ: Rutgers University Press.

McClaurin, Irma. 2001. "Introduction: Forging a Theory, Politics, Praxis, and Poetics of Black Feminist Anthropology." In *Black Feminist Anthropology: Theory, Politics, Praxis, and Poetics*. New Brunswick, NJ: Rutgers University Press.

McClintock, Anne. 1995. *Imperial Leather: Race, Gender, and Sexuality in the Colonial Contest*. New York: Routledge.

McGee, John, and Richard L. Warms. 1999. *Anthropological Theory: An Introduction History*. New York: McGraw-Hill.

McIntyre, Michael, and Heidi J. Nast. 2011. "Bio(necro)polis: Marx, Surplus Populations, and the Spatial Dialectics of Reproduction and 'Race.'" *Antipode* 4 (5): 1464–88.

McKittrick, Katherine. 2006. *Demonic Grounds: Black Women and the Cartographies of Struggle*. Minneapolis: University of Minnesota Press.

———. 2011. "On Plantations, Prisons, and a Black Sense of Place." *Social & Cultural Geography* 12 (8): 947–63.

———. 2013. "Plantation Futures." *Small Axe: A Caribbean Journal of Criticism* 17 (3): 1–15.

Meléndez, Edgardo. 2017. *Sponsored Migration: The State and Puerto Rican Postwar Migration to the United States*. Columbus: Ohio State University Press.

Meléndez, Edwin, and Jennifer Hinojosa. 2017. "Estimates of Hurricane María Exodus from Puerto Rico." *Centro* Research Brief.

Menjívar, Cecilia. 2000. *Fragmented Ties: Salvadoran Immigrant Networks in America*. Berkeley: University of California Press.

Merino Falú, Aixa. 2004. *Raza, género y clase social: El discrimen contra las mujeres Afropuertorriqueñas*. San Juan, PR: Oficina de la Procudora de las Mujeres.

Mies, Maria, and Vandana Shiva. 1993. *Ecofeminism*. Halifax, NS: Fernwood.

Mignolo, Walter D. 2009. "Epistemic Disobedience, Independent Thought and De-colonial Freedom." *Theory, Culture & Society* 26 (7–8): 1–23.

Mihesuah, Devon A. 2000. *Repatriation Reader: Who Owns American Indian Remains?* Lincoln: University of Nebraska Press.

Mintz, Sydney W. 1974. *Worker in the Cane: A Puerto Rican Life History*. New York: W. W. Norton.

Mohammed, Patricia. 2010. *Imaging the Caribbean: Culture and Visual Translation*. Oxford: MacMillan.

Molinari, Sarah. 2019. "Authenticating Loss and Contesting Recovery: FEMA and the Politics of Colonial Disaster Management." In *Aftershocks of Disaster: Puerto Rico Before and After the Storm*, edited by Yarimar Bonilla and Marisol LeBrón, 285–97. Chicago: Haymarket Books.

Moraga, Cherríe, and Gloria Anzaldúa. 1981. *This Bridge Called My Back: Writings by Radical Women of Color*. Watertown, MA: Persephone.

Morales, Ed. 2019a. "Why Half a Million Puerto Ricans Are Protesting in the Streets." *Nation*. www.thenation.com/article/puerto-rico-protests-scandal -rossello/.

———. 2019b. "Feminists and LGBTQ Activists Are Leading the Insurrection in Puerto Rico." *Nation*. www.thenation.com/article/puerto-rico-insurrection -feminists-lgbtq/.

———. 2019c. "Puerto Rico's Unjust Debt." In *Aftershocks of Disaster: Puerto Rico before and after the Storm*, edited by Yarimar Bonilla and Marisol LeBrón, 211–23. Chicago: Haymarket Books.

———. 2019d. *Fantasy Island: Colonialism, Exploitation, and the Betrayal of Puerto Rico*. New York: Hachette and Blackstone.

Moreno, Marisel C. 2012. *Family Matters: Puerto Rican Women Authors on the Island and the Mainland*. Charlottesville: University of Virginia Press.

Morgan, Jennifer L. 2004. *Laboring Women: Reproduction of Gender in New World Slavery*. Philadelphia: University of Pennsylvania Press.

Morris, Anne R., and Margaret M. Dunn. 1992. "'The Bloodstream of Our Inheritance': Female Identity and the Caribbean Mothers'-Land." In *Motherlands: Black Women's Writing from Africa, the Caribbean and South Asia*, edited by Susheila Nasta, 219–37. London: Women's Press.

Moya, Paula L. M. 2002. *Learning from Experience: Minority Identities, Multicultural Struggles*. Berkeley: University of California Press.

Moynihan, Daniel Patrick. 1965. *The Negro Family: The Case for National Action*. Washington, DC: Office of Policy Planning and Research United States Department of Labor.

Mullings, Beverley. 2019. "Caribbean Futures in the Offshore Anthropocene: Debt, Disaster, and Duration." *Society & Space* (blog). http://societyandspace.org/2019/01/09/caribbean-futures-in-the-offshore-anthropocene-debt-disaster-and-duration/.

Muñiz-Mas, Félix O. 1998. "Gender, Work, and Institutional Change in the Early Stage of Industrialization: The Case of the Women's Bureau and the Home Needlework Industry in Puerto Rico, 1940–1952." In *Puerto Rican Women's History: New Perspectives*, edited by Félix V. Matos Rodríguez and Linda C. Delgado, 171–80. New York: M. E. Sharpe.

Muñoz Vázquez, Mayra. 2000. "Aportaciones de la psicología de comunidad en Puerto Rico a un marco teórico alterno sobre el potencial de apoderamiento de las comunidades." *Interamerican Journal of Psychology* 34 (1): 151–72.

Nasta, Susheila. 1992. *Motherlands: Black Women's Writing from Africa, the Caribbean, and South Asia*. New Brunswick, NJ: Rutgers University Press.

Narayan, Kirin. 1993. "How Native Is a 'Native' Anthropologist?" *American Anthropologist* 95 (3): 671–86.

Navarro, Tami, Bianca Williams, and Attiya Ahmad. 2013. "Sitting at the Kitchen Table: Fieldnotes from Women of Color in Anthropology." *Cultural Anthropology* 28 (3): 443–63.

Nazario Velasco, Rubén. 2014. *El paisaje y el poder: la tierra en el tiempo de Luis Muñoz Marín*. San Juan, PR: Ediciones Callejón.

Negrón-Muntaner, Frances. 2018. "The Emptying Island: Puerto Rican Expulsion in Post-Maria Time." *Emisférica* 14 (1). https://hemisphericinstitute.org/en/emisferica-14-1-expulsion/14-1-essays/the-emptying-island-puerto-rican-expulsion-in-post-maria-time.html.

Negrón-Muntaner, Frances, and Ramón Grosfoguel. 1997. *Puerto Rican Jam: Rethinking Colonialism and Nationalism*. Minneapolis: University of Minnesota Press.

Newcomb, Steven. 1995. "Perspectives: Healing, Restoration, and Rematriation." *News & Notes*: 3.

Nixon, Rob. 2011. *Slow Violence and the Environmentalism of the Poor.* Cambridge, MA: Harvard University Press.

———. 2017. "The Unequal Anthropocene." In *Living in the Anthropocene: Earth in the Age of Humans*, edited by W. John Kres and Jeffrey K. Stine, 149–52. Washington, DC: Smithsonian Books.

Oxfam Report. 2018. "The Weight of Water on Women: The Long Wake of Hurricane María in Puerto Rico." *Oxfam America*. www.oxfamamerica.org /explore/research-publications/research-backgrounder-wash-gender-report -puerto-rico/.

Pabón, Carlos. 1995. "De Albizu a Madonna: Para armar y desarmar la nacionalidad." *bordes* 2: 22–40.

Pandian, Anand. 2019. *A Possible Anthropology: Methods for Uneasy Times.* Durham, NC: Duke University Press.

Parrot, Andrea, and Nina Cummings. 2006. *Forsaken Females: The Global Brutalization of Women.* Lanham, MD: Rowman & Littlefield.

Patterson, Orlando. 1978. "Migration and Caribbean Societies: Socioeconomic and Symbolic Resources." In *Human Migration: Patterns and Policies*, edited by W. McNeill and R. Adams, 106–45. Bloomington: Indiana University Press.

Pellow, David. 2000. "Environmental Inequality Formation: Toward a Theory of Environmental Justice." *American Behavioral Scientist* 43 (4): 581–601.

———. 2018. *What Is Critical Environmental Justice.* Medford, MA: Polity.

Pellow, David, and Robert Brulle, eds. 2005. *Power, Justice, and the Environment: A Critical Appraisal of the Environmental Justice Movement.* Cambridge, MA: MIT Press.

Peña, Devon G. 2003. "The Scope of Latino/a Environmental Studies." *Latino Studies* 1: 47–78.

Pérez, Emma. 1999. *The Decolonial Imaginary: Writing Chicanas into History.* Bloomington: Indiana University Press.

Pérez, Gina. 2004. *Near Northwest Side Story: Migration, Displacement, Puerto Rican Families.* Berkeley, CA: University of California Press.

Phillips, Amber. 2019. "Why Puerto Rico's Governor Is Resigning." *Washington Post.* www.washingtonpost.com/politics/2019/07/19/why-puerto-rico-is-crisis/.

Platt, Anthony M. 1991. *E. Franklin Frazier Reconsidered.* New Brunswick, NJ: Rutgers University Press.

Plumwood, Val. 1993. *Feminism and the Mastery of Nature.* London: Routledge.

Porrata, Jose Luis. 1997. "Child Psychology and Juvenile Delinquency in Puerto Rican Society." In *Individual Differences in Children and Adolescents*, edited by Donald H. Saklofske and Sybil B. G. Eysenck, 173–81. New Brunswick, NJ: Transaction.

Prados-Rodriguez, Eva L. 2019. "Puerto Rico's Fight for a Citizen Debt Audit: A Strategy for Public Mobilization and a Fair Reconstruction." In *Aftershocks of Disaster: Puerto Rico before and after the Storm*, edited by Yarimar Bonilla and Marisol LeBrón, 250–56. Chicago: Haymarket Books.

Principles of Environmental Justice. 1991. www.ejnet.org/ej/principles.html.

Pulido, Laura. 1996. *Environmentalism and Economic Justice: Two Chicano Struggles in the Southwest*. Tucson: University of Arizona Press.

———. 2000. "Rethinking Environmental Racism: White Privilege and Urban Development in Southern California." *Annals of the Association of American Geographers* 90 (1): 12–40.

———. 2016. "Flint, Environmental Racism, and Racial Capitalism." *Capitalism, Nature and Socialism* 27: 1–16.

———. 2018. "Racism and the Anthropocene." In *Future Remains: A Cabinet of Curiosities for the Anthropocene*, edited by Greg Mitman, Marco Armiero, and Robert S. Emmett, 116–28). Chicago: University of Chicago Press.

Ramírez, Rafael L. 1999. *What It Means to Be a Man: Reflections on Puerto Rican Masculinity*. New Brunswick, NJ: Rutgers University Press.

Ramos-Mattei, Andrés. 1988. *La Sociedad del Azúcar en Puerto Rico, 1870–1910*. Rio Piedras: Universidad de Puerto Rico.

Ramos Zayas, Ana Y. 2003. *National Performances: The Politics of Class, Race, and Space in Puerto Rican Chicago*. Chicago: University of Chicago Press.

———. 2012. *Street Therapists: Race, Affect, and Neoliberal Personhood in Latino Newark*. Chicago: University of Chicago Press.

Reddock, Rhoda E. 1985. "Women and Slavery in the Caribbean: A Feminist Perspective." *Latin America's Colonial History* 12 (1): 63–80.

Reyes Cruz, Mariolga. 2008. "What if I Just Cite Graciela?: Working toward Decolonizing Knowledge through a Critical Ethnography." *Qualitative Inquiry* 14 (4): 651–58.

Rifkin, Mark. 2019. *Fictions of Land and Flesh: Blackness, Indigeneity, Speculation*. Durham, NC: Duke University Press.

Rist, Lucy, A. Felton, M. Nyström, M. Troell, R. A. Sponseller, J. Bengtsson, H. Osterblom, R. Lindborg, P. Tidåker, D. G. Angeler, R. Milestad, and J. Moen. 2014. "Applying Resilience Thinking to Production Ecosystems." *Ecosphere* 5 (6): http://dx.doi.org/10.1890/ES13-00330.1.

Rivera Casellas, Zaira. 2011. "La poética de la esclavitud (silenciada) en la literatura Puertorriqueña: Carmen Colón Pellot, Beatriz Berrocal, Yolanda Arroyo Pizarro y Mayra Santos Febres." *Cincinnati Romance Review* 30: 99–116.

Roberts, Dorothy. 2014 [1997]. *Killing the Black Body: Race, Reproduction, and the Meaning of Liberty*. New York: Vintage Books.

Robinson, Cedric J. 1983. *Black Marxism: The Making of the Black Radical Tradition*. London: Zed Books.

Robinson, Dean E. 2003. "'The Black Family' and US Social Policy: Moynihan's Unintended Legacy?" *Revue Française d'Études Américaines* 97 (3): 118–28.

Rockström, Johan, et al. 2009. "A Safe Operating Space for Humanity." *Nature* 461: 472–475. doi:10.1038/461472a.

Rodin, Judith. 2015. *The Resilience Dividend: Managing Disruption, Avoiding Disaster, and Growing Stronger in an Unpredictable World*. London: Profile Books.

Rodríguez, Clara E. 1989. *Puerto Ricans Born in the U.S.A.* Boulder, CO: Westview.

Rodríguez-Silva, Ileana. 2012. *Silencing Race: Disentangling Blackness, Colonialism, and National Identities in Puerto Rico.* New York: Palgrave Macmillan.

Rosaldo, Renato. 1989. *Culture & Truth: The Remaking of Social Analysis.* Boston: Beacon.

Rouse, Irving. 1992. *The Tainos: Rise and Decline of the People Who Greeted Columbus.* New Haven, CT: Yale University Press.

Roy-Féquière, Magali. 2004. *Women, Creole Identity, and Intellectual Life in Early Twentieth Century Puerto Rico.* Philadelphia: Temple University Press.

Sanday, Peggy Reeves. 1998. "Matriarchy as a Sociocultural Form: An Old Debate in a New Light." Paper presented at the 16th Congress of The Indo-Pacific Prehistory Association, Melaka, Malaysia, 1–7 July, 1998.

Sandoval Sánchez, Alberto. 1997. "Puerto Rican Identity Up in the Air: Air Migration, Its Cultural Representations, and Me 'Cruzando el Charco.'" In *Puerto Rican Jam*, edited by Frances Negrón-Muntaner and Ramón Grosfoguel, 189–208. Philadelphia: Temple University Press.

Santiago, Ruth. 2012. "Imminent and Substantial Endangerment to Human Health and the Environment from Use of Coal Ash as Fill Material at Construction Sites in Puerto Rico: A Case Study." *Procedia—Social and Behavioral Sciences* 37: 389–96. doi: 10.1016/j.sbspro.2012.03.304.

Santiago, Ruth, Catalina de Onís, and Hilda Lloréns. 2020. "Powering Life in Puerto Rico." *NACLA Report on the Americas* 52 (2): 178–85.

Saunders, Patricia J. 2008. "Fugitive Dreams of Diaspora: Conversations with Saidiya Hartman." *Anthurium: A Caribbean Studies Journal* 6 (1): http://scholarlyrepository.miami.edu/anthurium/vol6/iss1/7.

Schama, Simon. 1995. *Landscape and Memory.* New York: A. A. Knopf.

Schlosberg, David. 2007. *Defining Environmental Justice: Theories, Movements and Nature.* New York: Oxford University Press.

Schwartz, Mattathias, and Matt Black. 2017. "Maria's Bodies." *New York Magazine.* https://nymag.com/intelligencer/2017/12/hurricane-maria-man-made-disaster.html.

Scott, James C. 1976. *The Moral Economy of the Peasant: Rebellion and Subsistence in Southeast Asia.* New Haven, CT: Yale University Press.

———. 1985. *Weapons of the Weak: Everyday Forms of Peasant Resistance.* New Haven, CT: Yale University Press.

Seara, Tarsila, Richard Pollnac, John J. Poggie, Carlos García-Quijano, Iris Monnereau, and Victor Ruiz. 2017. "Fishing as Therapy: Impacts on Job Satisfaction and Implications for Fishery Management." *Ocean & Coastal Management* 141: 1–9. https://digitalcommons.newhaven.edu/biology-facpubs/65.

Sedgwick, Eve Kosofsky. 1997. "Paranoid Reading and Reparative Reading; or, You're So Paranoid, You Probably Think This Introduction Is about You." In

Novel Gazing: Queer Readings in Fictions, edited by Eve Kosofsky Sedgwick, 1–37. Durham, NC: Duke University Press.

Semmes, Clovis E. 2001. "E. Franklin Frazier's Theory of the Black Family: Vindication and Sociological Insight." *Journal of Sociology & Social Welfare* 28 (2): 3–21.

Sexton, Jared. 2016. "The Vel of Slavery: Tracking the Figure of the Unsovereign." *Critical Sociology* 42 (4–5): 583–97.

Sharpe, Christina. 2016. *In the Wake: On Blackness and Being.* Durham, NC: Duke University Press.

Sheller, Mimi. 2018. "Caribbean Futures in the Offshore Anthropocene: Debt, Disaster, and Duration." *Environment and Planning D: Society and Space* 36 (6): 971–86.

Shotter, John. 2012. "Gergen, Confluence, and His Turbulent, Relational Ontology: The Constitution of Our Forms of Life within Ceaseless, Unrepeatable, Intermingling Movements." *Psychological Studies* 57 (2): 134–41.

Sin Comillas. 2015. "Cada día se van 122 Puertorriqueños. ¿Cómo se afectan los negocios?" *sincomillas.com.* https://sincomillas.com/cada-dia-se-van-122 -puertorriquenos/.

Smallwood, Stephanie. 2008. *Saltwater Slavery: A Middle Passage from Africa to American Diaspora.* Cambridge, MA: Harvard University Press.

Smolicz, Jerzy. 1981. "Core Values and Cultural Identity." *Ethnic and Racial Studies* 4 (1): 75–90.

Solnit, Rebecca. 2009. *A Paradise Built in Hell: The Extraordinary Communities That Arise in Disaster.* New York: Penguin Books.

Sontag, Susan. 1963. "A Hero of Our Time." *New York Review* website. www .nybooks.com/articles/1963/11/28/a-hero-of-our-time/.

———. 1990. *On Photography.* New York: Penguin Books.

———. 2002. "Looking at War." *New Yorker* website. www.newyorker.com /magazine/2002/12/09/looking-at-war.

Spillers, Hortense J. 1987. "Mama's Baby, Papa's Maybe: An American Grammar Book." *Diacritics* 17 (2): 64–81.

Spivak, Gayatri Chakravorty. 1993. "Echo." *New Literary History* 24, 17–43.

Tacoli, Cecilia. 2009. "Crisis or Adaptation? Migration and Climate Change in a Context of High Mobility." *Environment and Urbanization* 21 (2): 513–25.

Taussig, Michael. 2018. *Palma Africana.* Chicago: University of Chicago Press.

Taylor, Ronald B. 1975. *Chavez and the Farm Workers.* Boston: Beacon.

Thomas, Lorrin. 2010. *Puerto Rican Citizenship: History and Political Identity in Twentieth Century New York City.* Chicago: University of Chicago Press.

Thornton Dill, Bonnie. 1994. "Fictive Kin, Paper Sons, and Compadrazgo: Women of Color and the Struggle for Family Survival." In *Women of Color in U.S. Society,* edited by Maxine Baca Zinn and Bonnie Thorton Dill, 149–70. Philadelphia: Temple University Press.

Tierney, Kathleen. 2015. "Resilience and the Neoliberal Project: Discourses, Critiques, Practices—And Katrina." *American Behavioral Scientist* 59 (10): 1–16.

Toro-Morn, Maura, and Ivis García Zambrana. 2017. "Gendered Fault Lines: A Demographic Profile of Puerto Rican Women in the United States." *Centro Journal* 29 (3): 10–37.

Torres, Arlene. 1998. "La gran familia Puertorriqueña 'Ej Prieta de Beldá.'" In *Blackness in Latin America and the Caribbean*, vol. 2, edited by Arlene Torres and Norman E. Whitten Jr., 285–306. Bloomington: Indiana University Press.

Torres Abreu, Alejandro. 2016. "Justicia Ambiental, participación ciudadana y política pública en Puerto Rico." *8ogrados* (blog). www.8ogrados.net/justicia -ambiental-participacion-ciudadana-y-politica-publica-en-puerto-rico-recuento -noticioso-del-2015/.

Trouillot, Michel-Rolph. 1995. *Silencing the Past: Power and the Production of History*. Boston: Beacon.

Tsing, Anna L. 2015. *The Mushroom at the End of the World: On the Possibility of Life in Capitalist Ruins*. Princeton: Princeton University Press.

Tuck, Eve. 2011. "Rematriating Curriculum Studies." *Journal of Curriculum Pedagogy* 8 (1): 34–37.

Tuck, Eve, and Rubén A. Gaztambide-Fernández. 2013. "Curriculum, Replacement, and Settler Futurity." *Journal of Curriculum Theorizing* 29 (1): 72–89.

Tuck, Eve, and K. Wayne Yang. 2012. "Decolonization Not a Metaphor." *Decolonization: Indigeneity, Education & Society* 1 (1): 1–40.

Tuhiwai Smith, Linda. 1999. *Decolonizing Methodologies: Research and Indigenous People*. London: Zed Books.

Valdés, Vanessa K. 2014. *Oshun's Daughters: The Search for Womanhood in the Americas*. Albany: State University of New York Press.

Valdés Pizzini, Manuel. 2006. "Historical Contentions: The Environmental Movement in the Coastal Zone in Puerto Rico." In *Beyond Sand and Sand: The Environmental Movement in Latin America*, edited by Sherrie Baver and Barbara Lynch, 44–64. New Brunswick, NJ: Rutgers University Press.

Vargas Ramos, Carlos. 2005. "Black, Trigueño, White . . . ? Shifting Racial Identification among Puerto Ricans." *Du Bois Review: Social Science Research on Race* 2 (2): 267–85.

———. 2014. "Migrating Race: Migration and Racial Identification among Puerto Ricans." *Ethnic and Racial Studies* 37 (3): 383–404.

Velazquez Vargas, Yarma. 2008. "Marco Said I Look Like Charcoal: A Puerto Rican's Exploration of Her Ethnic Identity." *Qualitative Inquiry* 14 (6): 949–54.

Vergès, Françoise. 2017. "Racial Capitalocene: Is the Anthropocene Racial?" *Verso* (August 30, 2017). www.versobooks.com/blogs/3376-racial-capitalocene.

———. 2019. "Capitalocene, Waste, Race, and Gender." *E-flux* (May). www.e-flux .com/journal/100/269165/capitalocene-waste-race-and-gender/.

Villanueva, Joaquín, Martín Cobían, and Félix Rodríguez. 2018. "San Juan, the Fragile City: Finance Capital, Class, and the Making of Puerto Rico's Economic Crisis." *Antipode: A Radical Journal of Geography* 50 (5): 1415–37.

Villarrubia-Mendoza, Jacqueline, and Roberto Vélez-Vélez. 2019. "Puerto Rican People's Assemblies Shift from Protest to Proposal." *NACLA Report on the*

Americas (blog). https://nacla.org/news/2019/08/22/puerto-rican
-people%E2%80%99s-assemblies-shift-protest-proposal.

Visweswaran, Kamala. 1994. *Fictions of Feminist Ethnography.* Minneapolis:
University of Minnesota Press.

Walcott, Rinaldo. 2015. "Genres of the Human: Multiculturalism, Cosmo-politics,
and the Caribbean Basin." In *Sylvia Wynter: On Being Human as Praxis,* edited
by Katherine McKittrick, 183–202. Durham, NC: Duke University Press.

Walker, Alice. 1983. *In Search of Our Mothers' Gardens: Womanist Prose.* San
Diego, CA: Harcourt Brace Jovanovich.

Walker, Brian, and David Salt. 2006. *Resilience Thinking: Sustaining Ecosystems and
People in a Changing World.* Washington, DC: Island Press.

Walker, Jeremy, and Melinda Cooper. 2011. "Genealogies of Resilience: From
Systems Ecology to Political Economy of Crisis Adaptation." *Security Dialogue*
42 (2): 143–60.

Whalen, Carmen Teresa. 2001. *From Puerto Rico to Philadelphia: Puerto Rican
Workers and Postwar Economies.* Philadelphia: Temple University Press.

———. 2005. "Colonialism, Citizenship, and the Making of the Puerto Rican
Diaspora: An Introduction." In *The Puerto Rican Diaspora: Historical Perspec-
tives,* edited by Carmen Teresa Whalen and Víctor Vázquez-Hernández, 1–42.
Philadelphia: Temple University Press.

Wilderson, Frank B., III. 2010. *Red, White and Black: Cinema and Structure of U.S.
Antagonisms.* Durham, NC: Duke University Press.

———. 2020. *Afropessimism.* New York: W. W. Norton.

Wolfe, Patrick. 2006. "Settler Colonialism and the Elimination of the Native."
Journal of Genocide Research 8 (4): 387–409.

Woods, Clyde. 2002. "Life after Death." *The Professional Geographer* 54 (1): 62–66.

———. 2017. In *Development Drowned and Reborn: The Blues and Bourbon
Restorations in Post-Katrina New Orleans,* edited by L. Pulido and J. Camp.
Athens: University of Georgia Press.

Wynter, Sylvia. 2003. "Unsettling the Coloniality of Being/Power/Truth/Freedom:
Towards the Human, After Man, Its Overrepresentation—An Argument." *CR:
The New Centennial Review* 3 (3): 257–337.

Wynter, Sylvia, and Katherine McKittrick. 2015. "Unparalled Catastrophe for Our
Species? Or, to Give Humanness a Different Future: Conversations." In *Sylvia
Wynter: On Being Human as Praxis,* edited by Katherine McKittrick, 9–89.
Durham, NC: Duke University Press.

Yusoff, Kathryn. 2018. *A Billion Black Anthropocenes or None.* Minneapolis:
University of Minnesota Press.

Zambrana, Rocío. 2021. *Colonial Debts: The Case of Puerto Rico.* Durham, NC:
Duke University Press.

Zenón, Carlos. 2018. *Memorías de un pueblo en lucha, 1978–1998.* San Juan, PR:
El Editorial el Antillano.

Zentella, Ana Celia. 2000. "Puerto Ricans in the United States: Confronting the
Linguistic Repercussions of Colonialism." In *New Immigrants in the United*

States: Readings for Second Language Educators, edited by Sandra Lee McKay and Sau-ling Cynthia Wong, 137–64. Cambridge: Cambridge University Press.

Zerner, Charles. 2000. *People, Plants and Justice: The Politics of Nature Conservation*. New York: Columbia University Press.

INDEX

DECOLONIZING FEMINISMS
Piya Chatterjee, *Series Editor*

Humanizing the Sacred: Sisters in Islam and the Struggle for Gender Justice in Malaysia, by Azza Basarudin

Power Interrupted: Antiracist and Feminist Activism inside the United Nations, by Sylvanna Falcón

Transnational Testimonios: The Politics of Collective Knowledge Production, by Patricia DeRocher

Asian American Feminisms and Women of Color Politics, edited by Lynn Fujiwara and Shireen Roshanravan

Unruly Figures: Queerness, Sex Work, and the Politics of Sexuality in Kerala, by Navaneetha Mokkil

Resisting Disappearance: Military Occupation and Women's Activism in Kashmir, by Ather Zia

Tea and Solidarity: Tamil Women and Work in Postwar Sri Lanka, by Mythri Jegathesan

Axis of Hope: Iranian Women's Rights Activism across Borders, by Catherine Sameh

The Borders of AIDS: Race, Quarantine, and Resistance, by Karma R. Chávez

Making Livable Worlds: Afro–Puerto Rican Women Building Environmental Justice, by Hilda Lloréns

Feminista Frequencies: Community Building through Radio in the Yakima Valley, by Monica De La Torre

Dancing Transnational Feminisms: Ananya Dance Theatre and the Art of Social Justice, edited by Ananya Chatterjea, Hui Wilcox, and Alessandra Williams